UNCTAD

THE LEAST DEVELOPED COUNTRIES REPORT 2018

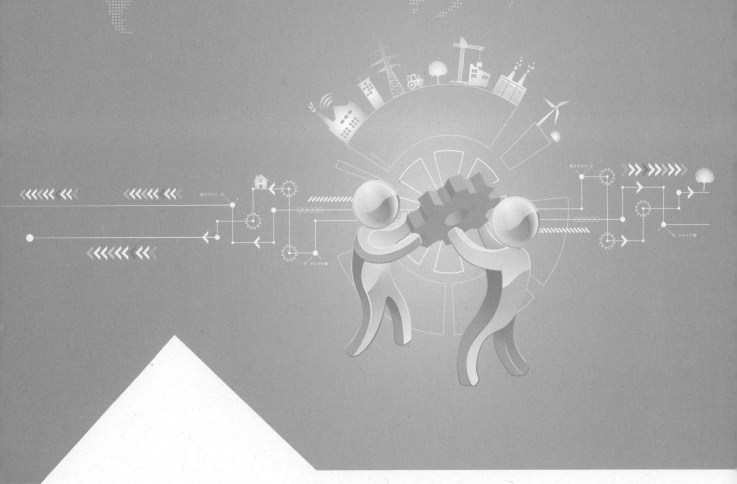

Entrepreneurship for structural transformation: Beyond business as usual

UNITED NATIONS
New York and Geneva, 2018

Requests to reproduce excerpts or to photocopy should be addressed to the Copyright Clearance Center at copyright.com.

All other queries on rights and licences, including subsidiary rights, should be addressed to:

United Nations Publications, 300 East 42nd Street,
New York, New York 10017,.
United States of America

Email: publications@un.org
Website: un.org/publications

The designations employed and the presentation of material on any map in this work do not imply the expression of any opinion whatsoever on the part of the United Nations concerning the legal status of any country, territory, city or area or of its authorities, or concerning the delimitation of its frontiers or boundaries.

United Nations publication issued by the United Nations Conference on Trade and Development.

UNCTAD/LDC/2018

ISBN: 978-92-1-112930-4

eISBN: 978-92-1-047247-0

ISSN: 0257-7550

Sales No. E.18.II.D.6

Acknowledgements

The Least Developed Countries Report 2018 was prepared by UNCTAD. Contributors to the report are: Rolf Traeger (team leader), Bineswaree Bolaky, Agnès Collardeau-Angleys, Pierre Encontre, Iacopo Monterosa, Tuba Busra Özsoy, Madasamyraja Rajalingam, Matfobhi Riba, Giovanni Valensisi and Stefanie West (the report team). The work was carried out under the overall supervision of Paul Akiwumi, Director, Division for Africa, Least Developed Countries and Special Programmes.

A meeting was held in Geneva on 16–17 May 2018 to conduct a peer review of specific chapters of the report and the report as a whole. It brought together specialists in the fields of entrepreneurship, development policies, enterprise development, international trade, social policies, industrial development and capacity-building. The participants were: Anders Aeroe (International Trade Centre), Feiçal Belaid (Graduate Institute for International and Development Studies), Vanina Farber (International Institute for Management Development), Abbi M. Kedir (University of Sheffield), Massimiliano Lamarca (International Labour Organization), Arthur Minsat (Development Centre, Organization for Economic Cooperation and Development), Ahmad Mukhtar (Food and Agriculture Organization of the United Nations), Benedict Musengele (Common Market for Eastern and Southern Africa), Donath Olomi (University of Dar-es-Salaam), Tapiwa Samanga (Southern African Development Community), Raymond Saner (Centre for Socioeconomic Development), Franck van Rompaey (United Nations Industrial Development Organization), Susanna Wolff (United Nations Office of the High Representative for the Least Developed Countries, Landlocked Developing Countries and Small Island Developing States), David Woodward (independent consultant), as well as the members of the report team and the following UNCTAD colleagues: Paul Akiwumi, Lisa Borgatti, Milasoa Cherel-Robson, Junior Roy Davis, Mussie Delelegn, Fulvia Farinelli, Stefanie Garry, Tamara Gregol de Farias, Christopher James, Aminata Loum, Arthur Mclean, Emily Meisel, Janvier Nkurunziza, Patrick Nwokedi Osakwe, Philippe Rudaz, Amelia Santos Paulino, Michaela Summerer, Antipas Touatam and Anida Yupari.

Ayman Eltarabishy (International Council for Small Business), Louis Jacques Filion (HEC Montreal), Donna Kelley (Babson College) and David Woodward (independent consultant) also provided substantive inputs and comments on the first draft of the report. Bruno Casella (UNCTAD) provided data on least developed country participation in global value chains based on the UNCTAD Eora database.

Feiçal Belaid, John Struthers and Dina Nziku prepared background papers for the report.

The UNCTAD Intergovernmental Support Service edited the text.

Nadège Hadjemian designed the cover. Nadège Hadjemian and Sonia Blachier designed the infographics.

Madasamyraja Rajalingam did the overall layout, graphics and desktop publishing.

Note

Material in this publication may be freely quoted or reprinted, but full acknowledgement is requested. A copy of the publication containing the quotation or reprint should be sent to the UNCTAD secretariat at:

Palais des Nations, CH-1211 Geneva 10, Switzerland.

The overview of this report can also be found on the Internet as a separate document, in all six official languages of the United Nations, at www.unctad.org/ldcr.

Main text

All websites referred to in the report were accessed in June 2018; databases were accessed in February 2018.

The term "dollars" ($) refers to United States dollars unless otherwise specified.

The term "billion" signifies 1,000 million.

Annual rates of growth and changes refer to compound rates.

Exports are valued "free on board" and imports, on a "cost, insurance, freight" basis, unless otherwise specified.

Use of a dash (–) between dates representing years, e.g. 1981–1990, signifies the full period involved, including the initial and final years. A slash (/) between two years, e.g. 1991/92, signifies a fiscal or crop year.

Throughout the report, the term "least developed country" refers to a country included in the United Nations list of least developed countries.

The terms "country" and "economy", as appropriate, also refer to territories or areas.

Tables

Two dots (..) indicate that the data are not available or are not separately reported.

One dot (.) indicates that the data are not applicable.

A dash (-) indicates that the amount is nil or negligible.

Details and percentages do not necessarily add up to totals, because of rounding.

Table of Contents

Note iv
Classifications viii
What are the least developed countries? ix
Abbreviations xii
Foreword xiii
Overview I

CHAPTER 1 Sustainable development, structural transformation and
entrepreneurship 1

    A. Introduction 3
    B. Sustainable development and structural transformation 3
    C. Entrepreneurship as a concept 8
    D. Entrepreneurship and structural transformation 11
    E. Determinants of entrepreneurship 13
    F. Conclusion 15

CHAPTER 2 Towards a nuanced appraisal of the entrepreneurial landscape
in the least developed countries 19

    A. Introduction 21
    B. The measurement of entrepreneurship 21
    C. Entrepreneurship in the least developed countries: Stylized facts 26
    D. Key sectors in the least developed countries: The informal sector and rural enterprise 38
    E. Firm heterogeneity and structural transformation 43
    F. Concluding remarks 49

CHAPTER 3 The local entrepreneurship dimension of global production systems .. 53

    A. Introduction 55
    B. Global value chains and entrepreneurship 55
    C. Participation of the least developed countries in global value chains 59
    D. Global value chains and beyond 69

CHAPTER 4 Entrepreneurship in the least developed countries:
Major constraints and current policy frameworks 79

    A. Introduction 81
    B. Constraints to the emergence and growth of firms 81
    C. Key obstacles to enterprise 86
    D. Current policy frameworks for entrepreneurship and structural transformation 98

CHAPTER 5 Policies for transformational entrepreneurship 107

    A. Introduction 109
    B. Policy principles 109
    C. Entrepreneurship policies 116
    D. Entrepreneurship within general economic policies 123
    E. Entrepreneurship and the developmental State 129
    F. Summary and conclusions 134

Annexes 137

References 143

Figures

1.1 Entrepreneurship: Purposes and agents 10

2.1 Number of available observations of total early-stage entrepreneurial activity, 2008–2017 24

2.2 Gross domestic product per person employed and common measures of entrepreneurship....................... 25

2.3 Self-employment as share of total employment in the least developed countries and other developing countries, period averages, 1990–2017 26

2.4 Self-employment by employment status, as share of total employment in the least developed countries, 2017 27

2.5 Early-stage and established entrepreneurship, latest available year.. 28

2.6 Perceptions of the adult population on entrepreneurship, latest available year.. 29

2.7 Motivational index and growth expectations of early entrepreneurs, latest available year 29

2.8 Size of shadow economy as share of gross domestic product, 2013–2015 31

2.9 Motivational index in selected least developed countries and by country group, latest available year............. 31

2.10 Sectoral composition of early-stage entrepreneurship and established businesses, selected least developed countries, latest available year 32

2.11 Importance of early-stage entrepreneurship relative to established businesses, selected least developed countries, latest available year... 33

2.12 Business discontinuation rates, latest available year.. 34

2.13 Reasons for business exit, selected least developed countries, latest available year.................................... 35

2.14 Early and established entrepreneurs by country group and age, latest available year.................................... 36

2.15 Gender-related gaps in total early-stage entrepreneurial activity, latest available year.................................. 37

2.16 Gender-related gaps in newly registered limited liability companies, selected least developed countries, 2016. 38

2.17 Composition of the informal sector by size of enterprise based on number of employees, selected least developed countries 39

2.18 Informal labour force composition by size of enterprise, selected least developed countries 39

2.19 Main reasons for not registering an informal business, selected least developed countries............................ 40

2.20 Share of firms in sample by number of permanent full-time employees 45

2.21 Employment share by type of establishment... 46

3.1 Entrepreneurial path to opportunity discovery and exploitation... 56

3.2 Stylized smile curve of upstream customization-led global value chains 57

3.3 Integration of least developed countries into global value chains, by country grouping, 2017 61

3.4 Towards greater value addition in developing country textile and clothing industries.................................... 65

4.1 Barriers to firm growth 81

4.2 Unemployment rates in the least developed countries by age, 2018 84

4.3 Small and medium-sized enterprise competitiveness by capacity pillar, selected least developed countries .. 87

4.4 Costs and procedures to start a business in the least developed countries, compared with the world average, 2015–2017 88

4.5 Sources of finance for day-to-day operations of informal firms, selected least developed countries.............. 89

4.6 Domestic credit to the private sector in the least developed countries as share of gross domestic product, 2004–2006 and 2014–2016 90

4.7 Internet use by country group, age and gender... 93

4.8 UNCTAD business-to-consumer electronic commerce readiness index score and rank, selected least developed countries, 2017 94

4.9 Women's entrepreneurship development assessment framework conditions and subconditions................... 97

4.10 Thematic coverage in development policies for microenterprises and small and medium-sized enterprises: Share of least developed countries with thematic element in policy.. 101

5.1 Official development assistance disbursements to the least developed countries, by sector, 2007 to 2016.. 124

5.2 Official development assistance disbursements to the least developed countries, 2016.............................. 124

Box figures

2.1 Schematic representation of the Global Entrepreneurship Monitor conceptual framework 23

3.1 Top five least developed country recipients of foreign direct investment by
(a) value, in billions of dollars, 2017 and (b) share, in percentage, of gross domestic product, 2016 60

4.1 Women, business and the law indicators: Average scores in the least developed countries 95

Boxes

2.1 Global Entrepreneurship Monitor conceptual framework and key terminology 23

2.2 Firm heterogeneity and structural transformation: Analytical methodology 44

4.1 Women, business and the law 95

4.2 Case studies of women's entrepreneurship in the least developed countries 96

5.1 Finland: A history of high-growth entrepreneurship policy 111

5.2 Republic of Korea: Revitalizing the economy through small and medium-sized enterprises 112

5.3 Chile: Harnessing immigration for entrepreneurship 113

5.4 India: In search of creative disturbers to foster a culture of entrepreneurship and innovation 114

5.5 Bangladesh and Uganda: Pharmaceuticals industry in the least developed countries 118

5.6 Rwanda: Finance for business development, innovation and research 122

5.7 UNCTAD eTrade for all initiative 127

5.8 Rwanda: Public–private partnerships in the information and communications technology sector 131

Tables

2.1 Pairwise Spearman's rank correlation across measures of entrepreneurship for 108 countries 24

2.2 Instrumental variable (two-stage least squares) regression results: Firm size and performance
in the least developed countries 47

2.3 Regression results: Firm characteristics and performance in the least developed countries 48

3.1 Types of economic upgrading in global value chains 57

4.1 Internal factors influencing growth in small firms 82

4.2 Indicators for small and medium-sized enterprise competitiveness surveys 86

4.3 Burkina Faso: Main pillars and objectives of national strategy for promotion of women's entrepreneurship 97

4.4 Mapping of government institutions in the least developed countries in charge of enterprise development .. 103

5.1 Framework of policy options for transformational entrepreneurship in the least developed countries 115

Box table

4.1 Women, business and the law indicators: Least developed countries with scores of less than 50
on a scale of 0 to 100 95

Annexes

1 Country and year coverage in Global Entrepreneurship Monitor data 138

2 Country and year coverage in World Bank Enterprise Surveys 139

3 Set of recommended actions in the *Entrepreneurship Policy Framework and Implementation Guidance* 140

Classifications

▶ LEAST DEVELOPED COUNTRIES

Unless otherwise specified, in this report, the least developed countries are classified according to a combination of geographical and structural criteria. The small island least developed countries that are geographically in Africa or Asia are thus grouped with Pacific islands to form the island least developed countries group, due to their structural similarities. Haiti and Madagascar, which are regarded as large island States, are grouped together with the African least developed countries.

The resulting groups are as follows:

African Least Developed Countries and Haiti:

Angola, Benin, Burkina Faso, Burundi, Central African Republic, Chad, Democratic Republic of the Congo, Djibouti, Eritrea, Ethiopia, Gambia, Guinea, Guinea-Bissau, Haiti, Lesotho, Liberia, Madagascar, Malawi, Mali, Mauritania, Mozambique, Niger, Rwanda, Senegal, Sierra Leone, Somalia, South Sudan, Sudan, Togo, Uganda, United Republic of Tanzania, Zambia.

Asian Least Developed Countries:

Afghanistan, Bangladesh, Bhutan, Cambodia, Lao People's Democratic Republic, Myanmar, Nepal, Yemen.

Island Least Developed Countries:

Comoros, Kiribati, Sao Tome and Principe, Solomon Islands, Timor-Leste, Tuvalu, Vanuatu.

▶ OTHER GROUPS OF COUNTRIES AND TERRITORIES

Developed countries:

Andorra, Australia, Austria, Belgium, Bermuda, Bulgaria, Canada, Croatia, Cyprus, Czechia, Denmark, Estonia, Finland, France, Germany, Greece, Greenland, Hungary, Iceland, Ireland, Israel, Italy, Japan, Latvia, Lithuania, Luxembourg, Malta, Netherlands, New Zealand, Norway, Poland, Portugal, Romania, San Marino, Slovakia, Slovenia, Spain, Sweden, Switzerland, United Kingdom of Great Britain and Northern Ireland, United States of America, Holy See, Faroe Islands, Gibraltar, Saint Pierre and Miquelon.

Other developing countries:

All developing countries (as classified by the United Nations) that are not least developed countries.

What are the least developed countries?

▶ 47 countries

Currently designated by the United Nations as "least developed countries" (LDCs).

There are 47 countries currently designated by the United Nations as least developed countries. They are Afghanistan, Angola, Bangladesh, Benin, Bhutan, Burkina Faso, Burundi, Cambodia, the Central African Republic, Chad, the Comoros, the Democratic Republic of the Congo, Djibouti, Eritrea, Ethiopia, the Gambia, Guinea, Guinea-Bissau, Haiti, Kiribati, the Lao People's Democratic Republic, Lesotho, Liberia, Madagascar, Malawi, Mali, Mauritania, Mozambique, Myanmar, Nepal, the Niger, Rwanda, Sao Tome and Principe, Senegal, Sierra Leone, Solomon Islands, Somalia, South Sudan, the Sudan, Timor-Leste, Togo, Tuvalu, Uganda, the United Republic of Tanzania, Vanuatu, Yemen and Zambia.

▶ Every 3 years

The list of least developed countries is reviewed every three years by the Committee for Development Policy, a group of independent experts that reports to the Economic and Social Council of the United Nations. In reporting to the Economic and Social Council, the Committee for Development Policy may recommend countries for addition to, or exclusion from (the so-called graduation), the list of least developed countries. The following three criteria were used by the Committee in the latest review of the list in March 2018:

(a) **A per capita income criterion,** based on a three-year average estimate of the gross national income per capita, with a threshold of $1,025 for identifying possible cases of addition to the list, and a threshold of $1,230 for possible cases of graduation from least developed country status;

(b) **A human assets criterion,** involving a composite index (the human assets index) based on indicators of nutrition (percentage of undernourished population); child mortality (under 5 years of age, per 1,000 live births); maternal mortality (per 100,000 live births); school enrolment (gross secondary enrolment ratio); and literacy (adult literacy ratio);

(c) **An economic vulnerability criterion,** involving a composite index (the economic vulnerability index) based on indicators of natural shocks (index of instability of agricultural production; share of victims of natural disasters); trade-related shocks (index of instability of exports of goods and services); physical exposure to shocks (share of population living in low-lying areas); economic exposure to shocks (share of agriculture, forestry and fisheries in gross domestic product; index of merchandise export concentration); smallness (population in logarithm); and remoteness (index of remoteness).

For all three criteria, different thresholds are used for identifying cases of addition to the list of least developed countries and cases of graduation from least developed country status. A country will qualify to be added to the list if it meets the addition thresholds on all three criteria and does not have a population greater than 75 million. Qualification for addition to the list will effectively lead to least developed country status only if the Government of the relevant country accepts this status.

A country will normally qualify for graduation from least developed country status if it has met graduation thresholds under at least two of the three criteria in at least two consecutive triennial reviews of the list. However, if the three-year average per capita gross national income of a least developed country has risen to a level at least double the graduation threshold (i.e. $2,460), and if this performance is considered sustainable, the country will be deemed eligible for graduation regardless of its score under the other two criteria. This rule is commonly referred to as the income-only graduation rule.

▶ 5 countries have graduated from LDC status:

Botswana in December 1994; Cabo Verde in December 2007; Maldives in January 2011; Samoa in January 2014; and Equatorial Guinea in June 2017.

In a resolution adopted in December 2015, the General Assembly endorsed the 2012 recommendation of the Committee for Development Policy to graduate **Vanuatu**, taking into consideration the setback which had been caused to the country by Tropical Cyclone Pam in March 2015. The General Assembly decided, exceptionally, to delay the graduation of Vanuatu from least developed country status to December 2020.

The Committee's 2015 recommendation to graduate **Angola** was endorsed by the General Assembly in February 2016, through a resolution seting February 2021 as the date for the graduation of Angola from least developed country status. This decision was an exceptional measure to take into account the high vulnerability of the commodity-dependent Angolan economy to price fluctuations.

In a June 2018 resolution, the Economic and Social Council recalled the Committee's 2012 recommendation to graduate **Tuvalu** from least developed country status and deferred to no later than 2021 consideration by the Economic and Social Council of the question of the country's graduation. In the same resolution, the Economic and Social Council also deferred to no later than 2021 its consideration of the graduation of **Kiribati** after the Committee's March 2018 review of the list of least developed countries recommended a reclassification of Kiribati out of least developed country status.

Also recommended for graduation in the 2018 review of the category were **Bhutan, Sao Tome and Principe** and **Solomon Islands**. The Economic and Social Council endorsed these three recommendations in July 2018. At the same time, two least developed countries that the Committee for Development Policy had found in March 2018, for the second time, to be technically eligible for graduation (**Nepal** and **Timor-Leste**) were not recommended for reclassification after the Committee accepted the plea made by these two States for deferred consideration, to 2021, of the question of graduation.

Lastly, in the 2018 review of the list of least developed countries, three Asian countries were found pre-eligible for graduation from least developed country status: **Bangladesh**, the **Lao People's Democratic Republic** and **Myanmar**. While pre-eligibility for reclassification of the Lao People's Democratic Republic is grounded in improved performance, above two of the three graduation thresholds as in most earlier graduation cases (per capita income and human assets), Bangladesh and Myanmar are the first historical cases of pre-qualification for graduation through a heightened performance under all three graduation criteria (per capita income, human assets and economic vulnerability).

After a recommendation to graduate a country has been endorsed by Economic and Social Council and the General Assembly, the graduating country benefits from a grace period (usually of three years) before graduation effectively takes place. This period, during which the country remains a least developed country, is designed to enable the graduating State and its development and trading partners to agree on a smooth transition strategy, so that the planned loss of least developed country status does not disrupt the country's socioeconomic progress. A smooth transition measure generally implies extending a concession to the graduated country, for a number of years after graduation, that the country had been entitled to by virtue of least developed country status.

Present graduation prospects and the 2011 Istanbul vision

The overall graduation landscape following the March 2018 review of the list of least developed countries by the Committee for Development Policy comprises:

a. Five cases of graduation: **Angola, Bhutan, Sao Tome and Principe, Solomon Islands** and **Vanuatu**, of which two have a known graduation date: Vanuatu (December 2020) and Angola (February 2021);

b. Two hypothetical graduation cases, subject to a decision by member States: **Kiribati** and **Tuvalu**;

c. Two cases in which the Committee for Development Policy deferred consideration of the question of graduation: **Nepal** and **Timor-Leste**;

d. Three cases of pre-eligibility for graduation (and likely full eligibility in 2021): **Bangladesh**, the **Lao People's Democratic Republic** and **Myanmar**.

This brings to 12 the number of least developed countries eligible or pre-eligible, as of 2018, for graduation from least developed country status. Adding these 12 qualifying cases to the two countries that have graduated since 2011 (**Samoa** and **Equatorial Guinea**), and taking into account the addition of **South Sudan** to the list of least developed countries in 2012, the overall graduation performance by 2018 amounts to a 29 per cent qualification ratio. This scenario will remain unchanged until 2020, as the next Committee for Development Policy review is scheduled for 2021. This graduation and qualification performance falls short of the 2011 vision of member States gathered in Istanbul of "enabling half the number of least developed countries to meet the criteria for graduation by 2020", as set out in paragraph 28 of the Programme of Action for the Least Developed Countries for the Decade 2011–2020.

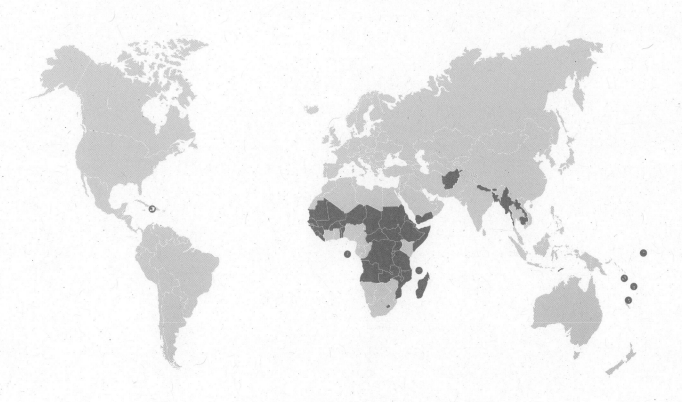

Abbreviations

ASEAN	Association of Southeast Asian Nations	**LDC**	least developed country
FAO	Food and Agriculture Organization of the United Nations	**OECD**	Organization for Economic Cooperation and Development
FDI	foreign direct investment	**SME**	small and medium-sized enterprise
GDP	gross domestic product	**UNIDO**	United Nations Industrial Development Organization
GEM	Global Entrepreneurship Monitor	**UNU-WIDER**	United Nations University World Institute for Development Economics Research
GVC	global value chain		
ICT	information and communications technology		
ILO	International Labour Organization		

Foreword

Nowhere else in the world is radical economic transformation more urgent than in the least developed countries, which have the challenge of accumulating productive capacities at an unprecedented speed, in the face of the rapid reorientation of global production and digital transformation, to achieve the Sustainable Development Goals by 2030.

At the centre of radical economic change is transformational entrepreneurship. The Least Developed Countries Report 2018: Entrepreneurship for Structural Transformation – Beyond Business as Usual demonstrates how transformational entrepreneurship generates many of the social and economic innovations that underpin sustainable development. Transformational entrepreneurs create new products and business models; they offer dignified employment; their success leads to broader improvements in the quality of life and even bolsters fiscal sustainability. Dynamic entrepreneurs also make a greater contribution to wealth accumulation and distribution.

In the least developed countries, however, underdevelopment and unfavourable forms of participation in global trade constrain the emergence of the dynamic, opportunity-seeking entrepreneurs needed for structural transformation. The dearth of dynamic local entrepreneurship endangers structural transformation and ultimately weakens national ownership and the potential impact of attaining the Sustainable Development Goals in the least developed countries.

The weakness of dynamic entrepreneurship has important implications in the least developed countries, where entrepreneurship policy is often mobilized as an alternative to unemployment and a remedy for structural inequalities. This type of policy is often an imperfect way of fostering high-impact and dynamic entrepreneurship, which requires a distinct and strategic approach and deliberate long-term nurturing that entail coordinated and coherent action and smart policies across a range of relevant policy areas.

The Least Developed Countries Report 2018 presents a compelling case for a structural transformation-centred approach to entrepreneurship policy in the least developed countries. The report underscores entrepreneurship policy based on a fundamental recognition of disparities in the contribution of different types of entrepreneurship to structural transformation and wealth creation. It establishes a more active and proactive stance for the State in steering the emergence of dynamic and transformational local entrepreneurship. Importantly, it calls upon the least developed countries not to overlook the pivotal and complementary role played by large enterprises, alongside medium-sized and smaller enterprises, with a view to the least developed countries formulating deliberate strategies to nurture entrepreneurship that has impact. By encouraging least developed country policymakers to avoid policies that might undervalue the benefits of entrepreneurship, this report makes an invaluable contribution to least developed country efforts to add value to their implementation of the 2030 Agenda for Sustainable Development.

Mukhisa Kituyi
Secretary-General of UNCTAD

Overview

Sustainable development, structural transformation and entrepreneurship

Sustainable development is enshrined as a global goal in the 2030 Agenda for Sustainable Development adopted by the international community in 2015 as an aspirational vision to shape the development strategies and policies of all countries, including the least developed countries (LDCs). Sustainable development implies a radical reconfiguration of patterns of production and consumption, and changes in the relationship between societies and the natural environment. It therefore requires the structural transformation of economies, especially in LDCs, which need to transition to high-productivity economic activities and sectors in order to tackle the traditional challenges of economic and social development in a new way that mainstreams environmental considerations.

The concept of sustainable development links three dimensions of sustainability — economic, social and environmental — and the 2030 Agenda emphasizes the unity of, and mutual support between, these dimensions. This three-dimensional view reflects the understanding that an exclusive focus on economic growth ignores and potentially hinders social development and environmental protection. It therefore calls for an integrated approach to development concerns, combining a growing and sustainable economy with environmental protection and the satisfaction of basic needs. Successive policy statements issued by Member States of the United Nations have emphasized the right and obligation of both developed and developing countries to pursue sustainable development strategies, while also acknowledging the policy space that this necessitates.

UNCTAD has long emphasized the importance of economic structural transformation to poverty eradication and long-term development in LDCs. Structural transformation refers to the transfer of production factors — particularly land, labour and capital — from activities and sectors with low productivity and value added to those with higher productivity and value added, which are typically different in location and organization, as well as technologically. This process allows an economy to continually generate new dynamic activities characterized by higher productivity and greater efficiency.

The 2030 Agenda is thus transformative, in so far as it requires a radical change in economic processes, in methods of production, consumption and transportation and in lifestyles. It also requires a transformation of the socioeconomic relationship within different societies, as well as with the natural ecosystem, to focus on the attainment of societal goals within environmentally sustainable boundaries.

In this context, LDCs need to undergo a process of structural transformation analogous to the historical transformations of developed countries and emerging market economies. However, they need to embark on this process while starting from a position of heightened structural vulnerabilities and in such a way as to avoid repeating the negative environmental consequences of the past. Such structural transformation has become a sine qua non for LDCs to fulfil the economic, social and environmental dimensions of sustainable development and achieve the Sustainable Development Goals.

Rural development in LDCs is an imperative, as agriculture continues to play a disproportionate role in LDC economies, absorbing two thirds of the labour force and generating some 22 per cent of economic output on average, compared with 8.5 per cent in other developing countries. This makes the transformation of rural economies central to the overall structural transformation of LDCs.

The expansion of productive capacities plays a pivotal role in sustainable development. According to UNCTAD, the notion of productive capacities encompasses the resources, entrepreneurial capabilities and production linkages that jointly determine a country's capacity to produce goods and services. Strengthening productive capacities is thus a key dimension of growth and structural transformation, which occurs through three interrelated processes, namely capital accumulation, technological progress and structural change. The development of productive capacities is thus inevitably influenced by the nature of the interaction between entrepreneurs, the State and markets.

Entrepreneurship is a diverse and multifaceted phenomenon that has been conceptualized in different ways. Behavioural definitions of entrepreneurship define an entrepreneur as a coordinator of production and an agent of change through innovation. Occupational definitions conceptualize entrepreneurship as the result of an individual's choice between wage employment and self-employment based on an evaluation of the returns offered by each. The latter conceptualization was formulated with the situation of developed countries in mind. However, self-employment in LDCs is less a matter of choice than a result of prevailing labour market conditions and a lack of alternatives. This underlies the distinction between entrepreneurship by necessity and by choice.

Most definitions of entrepreneurship share common elements, in particular innovation, opportunity seizing and opportunity creation, risk-taking, judgment in decision-making and the development of business organizations. Entrepreneurial activity occurs primarily in private firms or self-employment, but also in State-owned enterprises, cooperatives and non-governmental organizations. The most common organizational form in which entrepreneurial activity takes place is the firm, which encompasses a wide variety of types, including domestically owned and transnational companies, private firms and State-owned enterprises, and firms of different sizes and ages, operating in all sectors of economic activity.

Entrepreneurship, in particular through its innovative dimension, can make an important contribution to structural transformation in several ways. First, it is an important mechanism for shifting productive resources from economic activities with low value added and productivity to those with higher value added and productivity, whether in agriculture, industry or services. Second, it can stimulate investment and contribute to building a knowledge-driven economy, which plays a central role in economic growth. Third, even unviable innovations in production that introduce goods, services, production technologies or business models that are new to a particular setting may provide valuable information for future entrepreneurial decisions, including those of other entrepreneurs, in the form of cost discovery. All of these effects are particularly critical in LDCs that are in the initial stage of structural transformation. Entrepreneurship is thus a sine qua non of sustainable development.

Entrepreneurial activity also directly contributes to economic growth by stimulating job creation, improving skills and encouraging technological innovation, and can increase productivity by encouraging competition. Differences in the level of entrepreneurship or in types of entrepreneurship can thus have a significant effect on economic performance, and control for the traditional factors of production, namely land, labour and capital. Along with the benefit of increased incomes, economic growth is an important element of structural transformation. However, different types of entrepreneurs and firms vary in their contributions to structural transformation and economic growth. In particular, dynamic, opportunity-driven entrepreneurship may have significant positive effects in this regard, while survivalist entrepreneurs by necessity are typically less innovative, operate mostly in low productivity and low value added activities and produce traditional goods and services with established technologies. Their growth potential is therefore limited, and most related firms remain at a microenterprise stage. Such activities, although important to the survival of the entrepreneurs themselves, do not generate significant wider benefits. Survivalist entrepreneurs may become opportunity-driven entrepreneurs and have a more positive impact, yet such instances are rare.

The relative contributions to structural transformation and other developmental goals of different types of entrepreneurs and firms are an important consideration in policymaking. Resource allocation and vertical industrial policies directed towards particular sectors or economic activities should primarily target those firms with the greatest potential contribution to structural transformation. Equally, horizontal, economy-wide policies should be aimed at creating an environment conducive to the emergence of those types of entrepreneurship with the greatest potential to contribute to structural transformation.

The level and quality of entrepreneurship in a given country is influenced by both individual and social factors. A number of idiosyncratic factors influence an individual's propensity to engage in entrepreneurial activity, ranging from psychological, social and personality traits, to demographic characteristics such as age, gender and cognitive skills. The personality approach interprets entrepreneurial behaviours as reflecting behaviours such as a desire for success, a limited fear of failure, openness to experience, conscientiousness, extraversion, agreeableness, persistence in the face of failure and alertness to perceiving and acting on opportunities. Gender-based research has shown that the propensity of women to start a business may differ from that of men for cultural reasons or because of discrimination.

Entrepreneurship typically involves individuals yet occurs within an economic and social context that has a strong bearing on the types of entrepreneurs that arise and their chances of success. On the one hand, dynamic, innovative entrepreneurs can contribute to growth and structural transformation. On the other hand, the features of the broader environment, including the structure and dynamism of the local economy, can have a major impact on the kinds of enterprises than can be established and successfully operated. This relates in particular to the geographical location of entrepreneurial activity, specifically with regard to rural and urban areas in LDCs, as well as the level of development and structural characteristics of the national economy. Several structural features of LDC economies, including limited financial development, insufficient infrastructure, lack of institutional development, elevated risk levels and the disempowerment of women, tend to weaken entrepreneurship and enterprise development. Finally, limited urbanization and the disproportionate role of agriculture also have an important bearing on the nature of enterprises in LDCs.

Achieving a nuanced appraisal of the entrepreneurial landscape in the least developed countries

Entrepreneurship has increasingly become a focus of the development policy discourse and is presented, in the Programme of Action for the Least Developed Countries for the Decade 2011–2020 and the Addis Ababa Action Agenda of the Third International Conference on Financing for Development, as a key avenue to private sector development and employment generation, especially for women and youth. However, the analysis of entrepreneurship is fraught with complications and measurement problems, in particular in LDCs, impeding research on its role in economic development.

Widely used indicators of entrepreneurship include the extent of self-employment; the ownership, management or establishment of new businesses; and the number of new registrations of limited liability companies. However, aside from limited data coverage, these indicators are also strongly influenced by levels of development, limiting their usefulness as proxies for entrepreneurship. Moreover, the first two broad measures are negatively correlated with the third, narrower, measure. This results in high levels of entrepreneurship in LDCs according to the former, but low levels according to the latter.

Self-employment in LDCs is high, at 70 per cent of total employment compared with 50 per cent across other developing countries, and declining only slowly; around half the population is engaged either in early-stage entrepreneurial activity or in established businesses. However, since own-account workers and family workers comprise 97 per cent of self-employment, only a small fraction of the self-employed can be considered truly entrepreneurial.

Societal values towards business-related occupations in LDCs are remarkably favourable, yet there is an apparent disconnect between the considerable optimism of the general population and the more complex reality experienced by those who actually establish a business, and whose expectations of job creation are generally limited.

The most obvious distinction among enterprises in LDCs is between those in the formal and informal sectors. The prevalence of informal enterprises is difficult to measure; the scale of the shadow economy, at around 35 per cent of gross domestic product, provides a conservative indicator. The tenfold difference between broad indicators of entrepreneurship and the establishment of limited liability companies also highlights the predominance of informal enterprises.

A closely related, though by no means coextensive, distinction is between enterprises driven by opportunity and those driven by necessity. This is of particular importance because it is the former that primarily drive structural transformation. On average, there are 1.7 times as many early entrepreneurs in LDCs who describe themselves as opportunity-driven rather than necessity-driven, compared with 2.8 times as many in other developing countries; and the proportion of necessity-driven early entrepreneurs in LDCs ranges from 22 per cent in Ethiopia to 47 per cent in Malawi and Vanuatu, with the rest either opportunity-driven or having hybrid motivations. However, the subjective nature of self-reporting suggests that these figures are likely to understate the extent of necessity-driven entrepreneurship.

Innovation is limited among entrepreneurs in LDCs, and me-too businesses, based on imitations of existing activities, generally predominate. On average, only 15 per cent of early entrepreneurs in LDCs report the introduction of a new product or service, compared with 24 per cent in other developing countries, and entrepreneurial activity by employees is also more limited.

Entrepreneurial activity in LDCs occurs predominantly in sectors with low entry barriers and limited skill requirements, in particular consumer-oriented services such as those involving retail, motor vehicles, lodging, restaurants, personal services, health, education and social and recreational services. Involvement in more transformative activities, such as construction, manufacturing, transportation, communication, utilities, wholesaling and business-oriented services, is more limited. This suggests that the entrepreneurship potential in LDCs translates only to a limited extent into innovative businesses capable of playing a catalytic role in structural transformation.

Moreover, the entrepreneurial landscape in LDCs tends to be skewed towards early stages of entrepreneurship. In the majority of LDCs for which data are available, there are more than twice as many early entrepreneurs as established entrepreneurs, reflecting relatively higher rates of business discontinuation and lower survival rates. Some 14 per cent of adults in LDCs report having exited a business activity in the last year, compared with 6 per cent in other developing countries, and the principal reason for exit is low profitability.

Young adults aged 18 to 24 account for an average of 28 per cent of early entrepreneurs and 17 per cent of established entrepreneurs in LDCs, compared with 17 per cent and 7 per cent, respectively, in other developing countries, reflecting the youth bulge in LDC populations. Those aged 25 to 34 predominate among entrepreneurs across all country groups, yet LDCs are distinguished by a more rapid decline in the weight of older cohorts, in particular among early-stage entrepreneurs, giving rise to a lower average age.

LDCs also have particularly low levels of educational attainment among early entrepreneurs; only 12 per cent have a post-secondary education compared with 36 per cent in other developing countries. However, the relative youth of entrepreneurs in LDCs suggests that this proportion could increase rapidly as enrolment rates rise.

The gender distribution of early-stage entrepreneurial activity appears to be balanced in LDCs, with an average women-to-men ratio of 0.94, compared with 0.77 in other developing countries and 0.61 in developed countries and countries with economies in transition. However, this may reflect the disproportionate prevalence of survivalist forms of entrepreneurship among women in LDCs, as the women-to-men ratio among opportunity-driven entrepreneurs is similar across the three country groups. The gender distribution of registrations of limited liability companies is more unequal in LDCs than globally.

The informal sector in LDCs is dominated by microenterprises with fewer than five employees and small enterprises with between five and nine employees, which represent 74 per cent and 20 per cent of the total, respectively. The rest are medium-sized enterprises. Unpaid workers, generally family, make up 38 per cent of the employment in informal enterprises, and in most instances, the use of such labour declines sharply as size increases. Gender inequality is marked; 50 per cent of women employees are unpaid, compared with 33 per cent of men, while women have ownership over the largest part of their firms in only 30 per cent of the cases.

While most entrepreneurs by necessity are in the informal sector, some opportunity-driven entrepreneurs also choose to remain informal for strategic reasons based on the costs and benefits of formalization. The financial and non-financial costs of the registration process are a part of this calculation, yet other factors are also important, including a lack of information on the process and greater uncertainty about benefits rather than costs. Some enterprises may decide to remain in the informal sector to engage in cost discovery or ascertain the viability of a business model before incurring the fixed costs of registration. This may explain why formal enterprises that delay registration subsequently outperform those that registered during the start-up stage.

Rural enterprise is critical to structural transformation in LDCs, and differs significantly from urban enterprise. Most rural entrepreneurs combine agricultural production with non-farm enterprise, in a complex and multidimensional pattern of income diversification, directed both at mitigating risk and seasonality and at increasing income.

Non-farm rural income is increasing across sub-Saharan Africa, but tends to be concentrated in richer rural households and remains less important than agricultural income overall. As in urban areas, new rural enterprises tend to be concentrated in activities with low entry barriers, such as sales and trading, rather than in more transformative sectors. Consumption linkages with agriculture predominate in the initial stage of transformation, yet the supply of agricultural inputs and agroprocessing become more important as rural development progresses.

The rural enterprise situation in LDCs is strongly dominated by microenterprises, which account for 95 per cent of firms in some LDCs in Africa, and tends to be disproportionately located in areas closer to towns, where productivity is also generally higher. Proximity to urban markets is also an important determinant of enterprise success, as are enterprise size, land tenure and, to a lesser extent, the gender, educational level and prior income and/or wealth of entrepreneurs, as well as access to finance. There is a high turnover level and exit rate among rural enterprises, and seasonality is an important determinant of enterprise productivity and survival. Gender is not found to be a significant determinant of the likelihood of operating a non-farm enterprise, yet women-owned enterprises are on average less productive than men-owned enterprises, possibly reflecting broader constraints on women's time use.

Social capital, networking and trust play crucial roles in rural entrepreneurship, as either barriers or enablers. Networks such as farmers' associations, cooperatives and marketing bodies are often at the forefront of promoting rural development policies such as extension services, for example in agrobusiness, and access to rural credit.

An analysis conducted for The Least Developed Countries Report 2018: Entrepreneurship for Structural Transformation – Beyond Business as Usual assesses the effects of the characteristics of firms in the formal non-agricultural sector, excluding microenterprises, on their performance in employment and productivity growth. The dataset used confirms the dominance of small enterprises, yet the distribution of employment is more balanced; the median employment share is 20 per cent in small enterprises, 30 per cent in medium-sized enterprises and 47 per cent in large enterprises. Women account for 27 per cent of full-time employees, and the proportion declines slightly with enterprise size.

Overall, the analysis finds a significant positive relationship between firm size and labour productivity growth. Older firms experience significantly faster productivity growth, and both firm size and firm age have a significant negative effect on employment growth. This may reflect a tendency towards greater labour intensity among small firms and younger firms that have not yet attained a minimum scale of efficiency and therefore remain in a process of expansion.

An alternative specification confirms the effect of firm size on productivity growth, but suggests that it is largely driven by manufacturing firms, while the positive effect of firm age is only weakly significant. Small firms have a significantly higher rate of employment growth than medium-sized and large firms, and firm age again appears to significantly dampen employment growth. However, innovation is positively and significantly associated with productivity growth in manufacturing firms, and with employment growth in the full sample and both subsamples.

Access to finance consistently appears to boost employment creation by firms, while manager experience is associated with slightly lower employment growth, except for services firms. The presence of women in senior management is significantly associated with faster productivity growth, overall and in services alone; and exporting is associated with faster employment growth, overall and in manufacturing alone. The results also suggest faster productivity growth in enterprises that began as unregistered enterprises.

These results highlight the distinct roles played by firms with different characteristics in the structural transformation process. Smaller and younger firms are critical to employment creation, yet larger firms appear to be better placed to spur capital deepening and increased productivity. The sustainability of structural transformation thus hinges on a well-balanced ecosystem encompassing multiple types of firms, related in a dense network of production linkages. In this regard, enthusiasm about start-ups and microenterprises and small and medium-sized enterprises is understandable, yet it often appears to be overstated, in particular in the light of the low survival rates of such enterprises.

The local entrepreneurship dimension of major global trends

International trade is now widely seen as the primary source of developmental dynamism and industrial policy has largely been replaced by trade policy in developing countries. Whether and how the potential opportunities offered by global value chains (GVCs) can help to stimulate the entrepreneurship needed to drive structural transformation is a critical developmental question for LDCs.

GVCs are seen as having important advantages, allowing countries to specialize in particular functions or bundles of tasks rather than in specific industries. However, there has been surprisingly little research to validate the supposed advantages of GVCs in stimulating local entrepreneurship. The overwhelming emphasis of research is on employment gains, profit and learning opportunities for individual firms, as well as the benefits from foreign exchange earnings. Few conclusions can therefore be drawn about the potential benefits from GVCs for entrepreneurship, the sustainable expansion of industrial bases in LDCs or sustainable development, without considering the ownership of GVC beneficiary firms.

Assessing the effects of GVC participation on entrepreneurship for structural transformation requires an understanding of the nature and underpinnings of the process of economic upgrading that is widely associated with GVCs. The initial stages of upgrading, namely process and product upgrading, are typically the initial steps of structural transformation. However, the last two stages, namely functional and intersectoral upgrading, in most cases mark its accomplishment, and take place either through progression or leapfrogging. However, prospects for economic upgrading within GVCs are not straightforward. They are influenced by a complex and uncertain GVC environment and can be either hindered or facilitated by governance patterns and power relations within GVCs, which are overwhelmingly skewed in favour of lead firms. Entrepreneurs in LDCs are also severely constrained by the intense level of competition characteristic of the GVC segments most accessible to LDCs and by structural impediments in local business environments. Consequently, unlike those in more developed settings, entrepreneurs in LDCs may struggle to exploit GVC-related entrepreneurial opportunities or to adjust to changes in the GVC environment and therefore have to forego promising opportunities or be compelled to employ suboptimal competitive strategies.

The underdevelopment trap faced by LDCs is compounded by trade-related obstacles, which have contributed to the fact that the share of LDCs in global trade has remained below 1 per cent since 2008. Tariff escalation is an important barrier, both to the processing of agricultural products and to manufacturing, and tariff peaks continue to affect important sectors of GVC-related interest to LDCs, making preferential market access a critical factor in their integration into GVCs. This makes LDCs vulnerable to the tariff-hopping strategies of lead firms in GVCs, giving a high degree of footlooseness and uncertainty to GVC participation, in particular in light manufacturing sectors.

LDCs are predominantly a source of inputs for the exports of other countries in several sectors, largely reflecting their dependence on primary exports and increasing concentration in their export composition and export destinations. The participation of LDCs in GVCs is also marked by concentration in the production of traded goods that are particularly postponable, making them particularly vulnerable to global demand shocks.

The predominant mode of entry for LDCs into GVCs is through foreign direct investment, whereby the entrepreneurship element is chiefly foreign. This varies in importance between products, and is more concentrated in manufacturing than in agriculture-related GVCs, in which international trade remains important but GVCs tend to play a more limited role.

Agricultural sectors in LDCs are typically dominated by smallholdings and family farms, which are disproportionately affected by compliance costs linked to a variety of non-tariff measures, ranging from hygiene, health and traceability standards to ethical, labour and environmental criteria. However, LDCs are able to exploit niche markets in agriculture, especially through arm's-length trade.

Despite the importance of agriculture in LDCs, and their apparent comparative advantage in the sector, the participation of LDCs in such GVCs is generally more limited than in other sectors. Considerable growth in contract farming has helped to integrate some smallholders into GVCs, helping to alleviate some compliance constraints, though often relegating smallholders to positions with weak bargaining power. However, contract farming also facilitates the exercise of market power over producers by GVC lead firms and their intermediaries. There is evidence of new forms of foreign direct investment in agriculture and increasing concentration that will limit the scope for looser forms of association with local producers, which are generally more conducive to local entrepreneurship.

Agriculture is also likely to remain a strategic sector in LDCs, and strengthening the position of farmers and rural businesses remains a legitimate objective of rural development programmes in LDCs, as in other developing and developed countries.

In manufacturing, LDCs are increasingly integrated into production networks linked to GVCs related to clothing production, mostly in East Asia, and have benefited in terms of employment, in particular of women, and rapid export growth. However, despite improving employment prospects for women previously excluded from formal job markets, the feminization of the sector has often entrenched poor working conditions and a structural lack of gender equality, with gender-based pay gaps being exploited as a source of cost advantages.

Value addition in the textiles sector remains elusive in most LDCs and prospects for economic upgrading remain severely limited, although they are marginally greater where GVC investors operate nearshoring strategies, targeting neighbouring countries to supply their own regional markets. The integration of LDCs into production networks is heavily dominated by foreign ownership and the record of fostering local entrepreneurship is poor. In a few LDCs, arm's-length or other non-equity forms of foreign direct investment engagement, such as subcontracting, have been facilitated by the prior existence of a potential domestic supply chain. However, the readiness of entrepreneurs in LDCs to become original equipment manufacturers or original design players in the textiles industry is incipient and currently confined mainly to relatively unsophisticated sectors.

Global price competition is strong in the textiles industry, posing a serious constraint to LDCs in sustaining their positions in GVCs and depressing wages. Weaknesses in infrastructure and trade facilitation also hinder the competitiveness of LDCs and tend to favour larger firms and those that are already part of supplier networks, as do volume and flexibility requirements. Entrepreneurs in LDCs, who generally operate small enterprises, thus face often insurmountable barriers to engagement with clothing-related GVCs.

Despite the advantage of greater complexity and the potential for enhanced skills development in electronics-related GVCs, the participation of some LDCs in this sector exhibits similar characteristics to their participation in clothing-related GVCs.

LDCs are constrained in their abilities to attract GVCs with different degrees of potential for economic upgrading. They mostly participate in low-value segments of GVCs, in which potential benefits are dissipated by acute competition pressures and the scope of entrepreneurship opportunities is limited. The participation of LDCs has direct and visible short-term effects with regard to foreign direct investment presence, employment and export growth, yet longer term impacts on capacity-building and the sustainability of the local industrial base are less apparent. Moreover, policy instruments widely used to support GVC participation may divert attention from the higher priorities of building productive capacities and facilitating local entrepreneurship, disadvantage local investors and lead to local market structures that impede the flourishing of transformative entrepreneurship.

Increasing value retention from GVCs is essential to the domestic resource mobilization required, yet the potential conflict between lead firm strategies and policies enabling entrepreneurship and upgrading may exacerbate structural deficits in LDCs. At best, the purported potential of the GVC model to deliver rapid industrialization and flourishing entrepreneurship remains unproven. GVC participation may compound the risk of LDCs graduating from the LDC category without the structural transformation required to sustain developmental progress.

The opportunities and challenges of GVC participation highlight the importance of obtaining a balanced mix of enterprises of different scales, rather than placing excessive emphasis on microenterprises and small enterprises in LDCs. Larger firms are generally better placed to absorb the cost disadvantages faced by LDCs and can often serve as incubators for entrepreneurial talent and the transfer of tacit knowledge.

The issues surrounding the participation of LDCs in GVCs reinforce the importance of high-impact entrepreneurs with the ability to overcome the obstacles to upgrading faced by LDCs. Examples of individual entrepreneurs overcoming such obstacles exist in LDCs as well as in other developing countries and policymakers can leverage the demonstration effects of such ventures to unleash transformational entrepreneurship and build synergies between policy innovation and public investment. Social objectives such as poverty reduction and increased food security often imply a focus on the most disadvantaged, yet promoting entrepreneurship also requires attention to be paid to those best able to establish viable and thriving businesses.

A country's revealed comparative advantage may be a useful indicator and policymaking tool with regard to engagement with GVCs, yet the overriding objective in LDCs is to ensure the evolution of the revealed comparative advantage and the development of dynamic comparative advantage in line with the goals of sustainable development. Since the weakness of local entrepreneurship in LDCs creates barriers to capturing gains from GVC engagement, this implies a need to disrupt the revealed comparative advantage, to launch the process of structural transformation. LDCs may be better served by an eclectic industrial strategy that simultaneously targets low-skill and high-skill sectors, and by non-equity modes of GVC integration, which tend to have a higher probability of positive spillovers compared with other modes of GVC engagement with more restrictive governance structures.

Contemporary trade and production favour high-level skills and disruptive entrepreneurship. The global competition for highly skilled human capital is demonstrated by the establishment in several developing and developed countries of programmes to attract talented and high-impact entrepreneurs and innovators. Adapting strategies focused on migrants and emigrants to compete with such programmes is a high priority in LDCs. LDCs stand to gain from providing increasing opportunities and incentives for temporary or permanent highly skilled migrants and high-impact entrepreneurs to return from more developed destination countries. There are opportunities to learn from the programmes and experiences of other developing countries and developed countries. Well-designed and targeted programmes that seek to match skills, potential technology transfer and dynamic entrepreneurship to development needs are more likely to yield desired results.

Finally, services exports from LDCs are overwhelmingly concentrated in tourism. Strengthening linkages with agriculture and creative or cultural sectors, in particular, can be an effective strategy to promote entrepreneurship and structural transformation. Reorienting tourism development in LDCs from a tendency to be overly focused on satisfying export markets, as well as exploring new and innovative approaches to promoting local value added and fostering local entrepreneurial engagement, could generate multiplier effects in terms of investment, upgrading and beneficiation in all three sectors.

Entrepreneurship in the least developed countries: Major constraints and current policy frameworks

An important starting point for policies to promote structural transformation through entrepreneurship is to understand the major internal and external barriers to enterprise growth.

There is growing recognition that the most significant internal barriers are psychological factors, such as the commitment of entrepreneurs to growth. Other widely cited factors include management capability, funding levels, a shortage of orders, sales and/or marketing capacity and the products and/or services offered.

External barriers at the national level include the business climate, which can give rise to direct, indirect and hidden production costs for firms, inhibit their adoption of new technologies, deter investment, weaken competitiveness and reduce market size. The labour market can also be an important obstacle, as the absence of social safety nets or alternative income sources drives many people unable to secure wage employment into often informal self-employment activities, marked by low productivity and low survival rates. Access to markets, including export markets, has a direct effect on the productivity, profitability, growth and survival of firms. There is empirical evidence, in LDCs and elsewhere, that, other things being equal, exporting firms have higher productivity levels than non-exporters in the same industry.

Entry regulations represent a key element of the incentive structure affecting the creation and formalization of new enterprises and the emergence of start-ups capable of competing with incumbent firms and challenging their business models. Disproportionately high entry costs have long been identified as a potential hindrance to the establishment of firms in many developing countries and this remains the situation in many LDCs despite some signs of improvement. In 2015–2017, start-up costs in the median LDC were 40 per cent of per capita income, compared with a world average of 26 per cent. Moreover, costs to start a business exceeded yearly per capita income in seven of the 46 LDCs for which data is available. In some LDCs, women are required to undertake additional procedures to start a business.

Access to finance is a major constraint to entrepreneurship in LDCs. Informal firms, in particular, have limited access to finance from formal lenders. Internal funds are by far the predominant source of financing for day-to-day operations, typically followed by supplier credits and loans from relatives and friends. Financial actors, whether formal, such as banks and microfinance institutions, or informal, such as moneylenders, consistently play a limited role, and microfinance institutions appear to be significant in only a handful of LDCs. Limited access to finance may be a binding constraint to productivity and enterprise survival, in particular in rural areas, where credit availability and access are crucial to the success of both farm and non-farm enterprises.

Without access to modern, affordable, reliable and efficient modern energy, enterprises in LDCs can neither compete in global markets nor survive and expand in national markets, due to impaired productivity. Three out of four of firms in LDCs are affected by recurring electrical outages. In sub-Saharan Africa, electricity supply interruptions equate to around three months of lost production time per year, resulting in the loss of around 6 per cent of turnover, and about half of formal businesses use generators, giving rise to additional costs. Improved access to energy and water is a necessary condition for the development of agribusiness value chains, which could unleash entrepreneurial opportunities in rural areas. Limited energy access also accentuates the lack of gender equality arising from gender-based constraints, by limiting the participation of women in structural transformation and entrepreneurial activities.

Increased access to, and effective utilization of, technologies based on information and communications technology (ICT) can support both entrepreneurship and structural transformation in LDCs. For example, mobile telephones can be used to increase agricultural productivity and address specific challenges faced by farmers, such as a lack of information and limited market access. Despite recent impressive strides in mobile telephone penetration, however, LDCs remain far behind other countries with regard to the provision of ICT infrastructure, such as for Internet access. Only 17.5 per cent of the population in LDCs accessed the Internet in 2017, compared with 41.3 per cent in developing countries and 81 per cent in developed countries.

The gender gap in Internet use is wider in LDCs than in developing and developed countries and widened in 2013–2017. The digital gap between LDCs and developing countries is significantly narrower among young people aged 15 to 24. Such patterns of Internet use have potentially important implications for the use of ICT to boost entrepreneurship among women and youth and electronic commerce (e-commerce). E-commerce can provide a growing entrepreneurial and development opportunity in LDCs, if more producers and consumers in LDCs can link to e-commerce platforms and if policies for building entrepreneurial and productive capacities prove effective. Common barriers to e-commerce development in LDCs include the insufficient development of telecommunications services, deficits in energy and transport infrastructure, an underdeveloped financial technology industry, a lack of e-commerce skills development, financial constraints on e-commerce ventures and technology start-ups and a lack of or weakness in an overall national e-commerce strategy.

In LDCs, there are gender-based constraints to women's participation in economic activities, which arise in large part from gender-based discrimination in laws, customs and practices. Such constraints inhibit women's access to inputs and resources, which can reduce both their disposition to engage in entrepreneurial activities and their chances of entrepreneurial success. Unleashing the potential of women-owned enterprises requires an examination of not only where gender-based constraints exist but also their interplay and combined effects. For instance, the requirement in some countries for a woman to have her husband's consent to start a business not only exacerbates administrative burdens but also substantially reduces the proportion of women-owned enterprises. Women's work and entrepreneurial engagement remains restricted by law in many LDCs; 32 LDCs have laws preventing women from working in specific jobs and six LDCs require additional procedures for women to start a business. Reforming such laws and regulations could improve the performance of women-owned firms.

Relatively few national development strategies in LDCs identify structural economic transformation explicitly as a pillar, yet many encompass policies aimed at achieving aspects of such transformation. All of the national development strategies in the 44 LDCs for which data is available contain multiple references to the need to support entrepreneurship, mostly under the economic pillar, but also under the social pillar, and many include clearly defined policies for this purpose. Areas of intervention relate mainly to improving the business climate and access to finance and facilitating training and business advisory services. In at least one third of LDCs, small and medium-sized enterprises are viewed as potential engines of economic growth and sources of employment and income, to reduce poverty, yet fewer envisage support measures for large enterprises. Specific policy actions to promote entrepreneurship or enhance entrepreneurial culture are generally limited and sometimes vague. Notable gaps in development strategies include the elaboration of policies with regard to the clustering of enterprises and discussions on the interface between policies related to industry, trade, investment, regional integration and entrepreneurship.

The interface between entrepreneurship and structural transformation is generally articulated more clearly in national industrial policies than in development strategies, yet around half of LDCs have yet to formulate such a policy. Little attention is devoted to the determinants of entrepreneurship, but a wide range of approaches are envisaged, to place enterprises at the core of industrial development. All of the industrial policy frameworks in the 20 LDCs that have such a framework include a mix of vertical, horizontal and functional industrial policies, although the distinctions between them are often insufficiently clear, the discourse on the synergies between them is relatively weak and the types of enterprises to be promoted are insufficiently articulated.

The goals of entrepreneurship and enterprise development policies vary widely and are both economic and social in orientation. In addition, the periods covered by national development strategies, enterprise development policies and national industrial policies are often inconsistent. About half of all LDCs also have yet to formulate an entrepreneurship development policy and the remainder have a development policy for microenterprises and small and medium-sized enterprises or a charter for small and medium-sized enterprises. Burkina Faso, the Gambia and the United Republic of Tanzania have formulated full national entrepreneurship strategies.

Most LDCs have a blanket approach to supporting entrepreneurship, and do not distinguish between different types of enterprises for policy purposes. The primary focus of policy interventions is to improve access to finance and provide a business-enabling environment by improving legal, regulatory, institutional and policy frameworks.

There is a need for entrepreneurship policies to extend beyond providing a business-enabling environment, to enable the greater prioritization of structural transformation in the strategic development plans and visions of LDCs and for a stronger alignment between development plans, industrial policies and entrepreneurship development policies towards achieving structural transformation. Entrepreneurship development policies in LDCs should include a monitoring and evaluation framework that assesses results against performance indicators and allows for lessons learned from successes and failures to be integrated into policies. Public support must also be steady throughout the different stages of the life cycle of an enterprise, recognizing that sustaining and scaling up businesses are as important as starting them. Policy priorities should also vary over the course of structural transformation, with some forms of support declining in importance as the private sector gains strength while other forms become more important as the needs of enterprises evolve.

Policies for transformational entrepreneurship

Harnessing entrepreneurship for structural transformation requires policies to support and sustain the dynamic and innovative enterprises that are central to structural transformation rather than to promote enterprise creation simply for its own sake. This requires effective enterprise development policies, institutions and reward structures to influence the trajectory of firms over time, support their sustainability and maximize their contribution to structural transformation and sustainable development.

The wider context of enterprise policies is critical. Entrepreneurship policies need to be an integral part of a wider set of strategies and policies for structural transformation and sustainable development, making coordination, coherence and a whole-of-government approach essential. Collaboration, consultation and dialogue between the public and private sectors is also important, and requires strengthening the capabilities of both the public and private sectors in line with development objectives. Internationally, developmental regionalism, official development assistance and South–South cooperation also have important roles.

Development plans, industrial policies and enterprise development policies in LDCs need to be more strongly aligned towards the goal of structural transformation. This requires clearly distinguished and effectively articulated entrepreneurship and enterprise development policies, tailored to national circumstances and stages of transformation; vertical, horizontal and functional industrial policies; and supportive policies in many different sectors, with effective coordination to ensure coherence. Enterprise development policies in LDCs should include a monitoring and evaluation framework, supported by an alignment between the time frames of different policies.

The experiences of countries with successful records of structural transformation demonstrate the potential impact of government-led initiatives and the benefits of broad-based, diverse entrepreneurship development programmes based on a holistic approach underpinned by public–private sector dialogue and collaboration. Lessons learned also include recognition of the importance of the following factors: achieving complementarity between programmes and between entrepreneurship development programmes and trade policies; combining continuity in the face of domestic political changes with flexibility in response to any flaws in programme design; and ensuring independence, transparency and accountability to avoid capture by vested interests.

There is also a need for a clear differentiation between types of enterprises, by size, nature and motivation, to tailor policy incentives according to their respective roles in structural transformation. Important policy objectives include absorbing survivalist entrepreneurs into more productive economic activities, through employment creation by more dynamic and transformative enterprises, and prioritizing support to more dynamic and innovative opportunity-driven enterprises. Formalization should be promoted and facilitated. The primary aim is not to eradicate the informal sector, but to maximize the contribution of enterprises currently in the informal sector to structural transformation. A gradualist approach, informed by the specific conditions in an economy, may be appropriate, focused on improving the understanding, ease and desirability of formalization and addressing the constraints faced by informal enterprises in achieving the necessary levels of productivity.

Entrepreneurship policies are often preoccupied with enterprise creation and with microenterprises and small enterprises, yet the expansion of large enterprises also requires support, given their critical role in increasing productivity, shifting production patterns, creating employment and fostering entrepreneurial skills and innovation capabilities among employees. Linkages between microenterprises, small and medium-sized enterprises and large enterprises should also be promoted, to foster national and regional value chains and open up opportunities for upgrading and growth in microenterprises and small and medium-sized enterprises.

Support to enterprises should be tailored to their specific needs and reflect the different stages of their typical life cycle, whether starting, sustaining and scaling up businesses or managing failure. Support should be sufficiently sustained to allow enterprises to grow and withstand market cycles and fluctuations, with clear performance-related criteria for the eventual removal of support, as well as for entitlement. The UNCTAD Entrepreneurship Policy Framework provides the basis for an effective entrepreneurship strategy to promote the creation of start-up businesses and promoting the expansion of dynamic enterprises requires policies to address the many obstacles faced by firms in LDCs.

The end of the life cycle of an enterprise can be as informative as the start to the rest of the economy. Successful entrepreneurship development strategies can maximize learning from enterprise failure by promoting informational spillovers and supporting a process of entrepreneurial discovery. Rather than denying the possibility of failure, entrepreneurship development programmes should therefore include an exit strategy for those enterprises that fail, to minimize the costs and maximize the benefits.

State-owned enterprises also have a role in boosting entrepreneurship for structural transformation in LDCs, including by increasing access to public services, notably energy and water supply, ICT services and transportation; providing public and merit goods; generating public funds; limiting private and/or foreign control of the economy; sustaining priority sectors; launching new industries; and controlling the decline of sunset industries. The role of State-owned enterprises is particularly important where the domestic private sector is weak and there is little interest from foreign investors, circumstances that are commonly found in LDCs. However, the conditions for their effectiveness are less typical in LDCs, highlighting the need for governance frameworks for State-owned enterprises underpinned by performance and learning feedback mechanisms, monitoring and evaluation frameworks and sunset clauses or exit plans.

Special measures for women and youth in development policies for microenterprises and small and medium-sized enterprises may be beneficial, but should be aimed primarily at addressing the particular obstacles faced by women and young entrepreneurs in accessing the inputs and resources required for successful entrepreneurship. Constraints to women's entrepreneurship may be a specific obstacle to rural transformation.

In this context, the extent to which a developmental State assumes its entrepreneurial functions is particularly pertinent in LDCs, where the private sector is weakened by a lack of institutional support and by information and coordination failures. The importance of innovation for the structural transformation process calls for a State that is entrepreneurial in its approach and marked by ambition, willingness and ability to lead the development process. This also encompasses making mission-oriented public investments that create and shape markets and providing long-term capital to sectors overlooked by private investors, in order to gradually crowd them in.

Public-sector capabilities are limited in many LDCs, yet they can gradually be acquired and one of the functions of a developmental State is specifically to spur such acquisition. Among such capabilities is the fostering of synergies and exploitation of complementarities with the private sector. A pragmatic, strategic, incremental and evolutionary approach is therefore needed, increasing public sector capabilities in parallel with progressively increasing engagement in spurring structural transformation through locally appropriate institutional reforms and by building on centres of excellence, promoting policy learning and nurturing coalitions for change.

In this context, the entrepreneurial role of the State includes improvements to regulatory regimes, including reviews and impact analysis, and extends further, to encompass efforts to address the constraints faced by entrepreneurs, through public investment in infrastructure, measures to improve access to finance, the nurturing of business clusters, the promotion of technological capabilities among firms, the enabling of firms to exploit opportunities for digitalization and the promotion of entrepreneurial skills development within education systems.

Public investment in infrastructure is particularly important in LDCs, especially in transport and trade facilitation, ICT and energy supply. The scale of investment required for transformational energy access requires exploiting the synergies between the public and private sectors.

National development banks can play an important role in financing structural transformation. They can support a developmental State by providing financing to public–private ventures and State-owned enterprises, financing infrastructure development and providing small and medium-sized enterprises in priority sectors with preferential credit or credit guarantees. However, effective regulatory and governance frameworks are important to their success, learning from past experiences.

The State can also play a useful role as a co-provider with the private sector of venture capital to entrepreneurs for research and development and innovative activities in designated sectors and by providing guarantees against risks in the early stages of innovative activity. Public support can also be targeted towards entrepreneurship, microenterprises and small and medium-sized enterprises and large enterprises through State-owned specialized agencies, funded by cost-sharing between the domestic and international private sectors and the State. In LDCs with substantial natural resource rents, well-managed sovereign wealth funds can help to attract additional long-term private investments in strategic sectors.

Special economic zones and industrial parks can offer a means of relieving the most binding constraints to firm productivity by holistically addressing multiple soft and hard infrastructure constraints within a defined area. If tailored to the binding constraints faced by producers and geared to the promotion of continuing innovation and the emergence of business clusters, such tools can generate positive spillover effects, in particular in countries with large infrastructural gaps. Such prospects hinge, however, on the gradual establishment of a dense network of linkages between businesses and between businesses and supportive institutions, in terms of both upstream and downstream activities and know-how and knowledge diffusion.

The technological capabilities that firms need to survive and thrive can be promoted through fiscal and other incentives for firm-level innovation, government procurement policies, training, public research centres to support innovation in particular sectors and public innovation awards. Accelerator programmes, business incubators, science parks and technology research hubs are widely used to kick-start high-growth entrepreneurship. Coherence and coordination between industrial policies and policies for science, technology and innovation are also critical, and policies for intellectual property rights should ensure that patent rights reward risk-bearing inventors and innovators while clearly defining conditions for patents to be transferred, to encourage further innovative activity.

Bridging the widening digital gap between developed and developing countries is essential for LDCs, to avoid further marginalization in the global economy. This requires significant additional public and private investment. Supporting digitalization, by helping enterprises to harness ICT and engage in the global digital and knowledge-based economy, also merits much greater policy support. The State has a leading role in this process, as a co-investor and through public procurement policies. E-readiness policies should be established to enable domestic firms to access and exploit e-commerce markets.

Finally, entrepreneurship education policies should be established that include soft skills, such as persistence, networking and self-confidence, and hard skills, such as business planning, financial literacy and managerial skills. Entrepreneurial skills development could also benefit from a shift in emphasis from education based solely on memorization and rote learning towards education based on experiential learning, problem solving, team building, risk taking, critical thinking and student involvement in community activities. Such changes increase the need for expanded education budgets.

PRODUCTIVE
RESOURCES

ENTREPRENEURIAL
CAPABILITIES

PRODUCTION
LINKAGES

ENTREPRENEURSHIP

ENTREPRENEURSHIP SPURS
DEVELOPMENT OF
PRODUCTIVE CAPACITIES

STRUCTURAL
TRANSFORMATION

DYNAMIC FIRMS HAVE HIGHER IMPACT
ON STRUCTURAL TRANSFORMATION

Sustainable development, structural transformation and entrepreneurship

CHAPTER 1

Sustainable development, structural transformation and entrepreneurship

A. Introduction	**3**
B. Sustainable development and structural transformation	**3**
1. Sustainable development	3
2. Structural transformation as a concept	4
3. Sustainable development and structural transformation	6
4. Transforming least developed country rural economies	7
5. Productive capacities	7
C. Entrepreneurship as a concept	**8**
1. Definitions	8
2. Agents of entrepreneurship	9
3. Entrepreneurship and innovation	11
D. Entrepreneurship and structural transformation	**11**
1. Entrepreneurship's impact on structural transformation and growth	11
2. Transformational entrepreneurship	13
E. Determinants of entrepreneurship	**13**
1. The influence of economic and social structures	13
2. Individual-level determinants	15
F. Conclusion	**15**
Notes	**17**

A. Introduction

The focus on entrepreneurship of the present edition of *The Least Developed Countries Report* is grounded in the series' vision of sustainable development through development of productive capacities and structural transformation of the economy. Innovation as an entrepreneurial activity is an essential element of structural transformation that implies shifting production factors from traditional economic activities towards those with higher value added and higher productivity. Entrepreneurship is thus indispensable for sustainable development. This is true of developed countries and other developing countries, but even more so of LDCs, where much more radical economic transformation is required.

The global objective of sustainable development, as enshrined in the 2030 Agenda for Sustainable Development adopted by the international community in 2015, provides direction for the development strategies and policies of developed and developing countries, including LDCs. Sustainable development implies a radical reconfiguration of production and consumption patterns and changes in the relationship between societies and the natural environment. It therefore requires the structural transformation of economies, especially in LDCs, where the objective of sustainable development requires a new way of tackling the traditional challenge of structural economic transformation for economic and social development, while mainstreaming environmental considerations and sustainability.

Chapter 1 presents the rationale for this report and the conceptual framework underpinning subsequent chapters. Sustainable development is defined and its relationship with structural transformation, outlined, in section B, while alternative concepts of entrepreneurship and the sense in which the term is used in the report are discussed in section C. The contribution of entrepreneurship to sustainable development in section D brings together these two concepts, and the individual and contextual determinants of entrepreneurship are introduced in section E. The chapter concludes with section F, which introduces the remaining chapters of the report.

B. Sustainable development and structural transformation

The international community has committed itself to the pursuit of sustainable development, enshrining this commitment in the 2030 Agenda for Sustainable Development. A multitude of actors are currently establishing strategies and policies to follow this path,

> **Entrepreneurship is indispensable for sustainable development**

including states, sub-national authorities, international organizations, non-governmental organizations and the private sector. The LDCs are striving to embark on a path towards sustainable development by pursuing both the Sustainable Development Goals established by the 2030 Agenda and the development goals included in the Programme of Action for the Least Developed Countries for the Decade 2011–2020 (Istanbul Programme of Action) adopted in 2011 at the Fourth United Nations Conference on the Least Developed Countries. In order to understand what this strategic orientation means and why it necessitates structural transformation and entrepreneurship, this section recalls the concept of sustainable development and its relationship with structural transformation.

1. Sustainable development

The classic formulation of sustainable development as a concept comes from the 1987 United Nations report of the World Commission on Environment and Development, also known as the Brundtland report, entitled "Our common future":

> Sustainable development is development that meets the needs of the present without compromising the ability of future generations to meet their own needs. It contains within it two key concepts:
>
> - the concept of "needs", in particular the essential needs of the world's poor, to which overriding priority should be given; and
> - the idea of limitations imposed by the state of technology and social organization on the environment's ability to meet present and future needs.

This definition reflects that, to improve conditions in the developing world, a growing and sustainable economy should be integrated with environmental protection and satisfying basic needs. Implicit is a process of change that ensures harmony between the exploitation of resources, direction of investments, orientation of technological development and institutional changes, so that all enhance current and future potential to meet human needs and aspirations. Ultimately, there is an understanding that focusing exclusively on economic growth ignores and impedes social development and environmental protection.

United Nations Member States have emphasized the obligation of States to pursue sustainable development

---

Over time, the definition of sustainable development became more holistic, linking the three aspects of sustainable development: economic development, social inclusion and environmental sustainability. This three-fold view of sustainable development was emphasized in "The future we want", the outcome document of the 2012 United Nations Conference on Sustainable Development (Rio+20 Conference). Of note, this broadened concept applies not only to developing countries, but also to developed countries.

The outline below is a useful way of understanding the need for the environmental, economic and social aspects of sustainable development to be embedded simultaneously in systems (Purvis and Granger, 2004):

- Environmental sustainability requires the maintenance of a constant and lasting resource base, prevention of the depletion of non-renewable resources (e.g. fossil fuels) and preservation of biodiversity.

- Economic sustainability requires management of the production of goods and services at a constant rate without causing inequalities among organizational entities.

- Social sustainability requires the attainment of social justice in the allocation of goods (e.g. food) and services (e.g. education and health), gender empathy and governmental cooperation.

The Rio+20 Conference mandated the formulation of a set of Sustainable Development Goals to guide the development agenda beyond the 2015 time frame of the Millennium Development Goals. This process resulted in the 17 Sustainable Development Goals and 169 targets adopted under the 2030 Agenda for Sustainable Development.

In the outcome document of the United Nations summit for the adoption of the post-2015 development agenda, Transforming our world: the 2030 Agenda for Sustainable Development (paragraph 13), the unity of, and mutual support among the economic, social and environmental dimensions of sustainable development is emphasized: "Sustainable development recognizes that eradicating poverty in all its forms and dimensions, combating inequality within and among countries, preserving the planet, creating sustained, inclusive and sustainable economic growth and fostering social inclusion are linked to each other and are interdependent."

The 2030 Agenda furthermore evenly distributes the Goals and targets across these dimensions. More importantly, it stresses their complementarity and mutual support and, in turn, that of the Goals and targets, which are considered integrated and indivisible in light of the "deep interconnections and many cross-cutting elements across the new Goals and targets" (paragraph 17). Goal 7, for example — to ensure access to affordable, reliable, sustainable and modern energy for all — is a pre-condition for the achievement of several health, education and economic development goals, as UNCTAD has highlighted (2017a).

Notwithstanding the interdependence of the three dimensions of sustainable development, there can also be trade-offs between different components of the Agenda. For example, there may be tensions between employment generation and rising productivity, industrialization in land-scarce countries may reduce the availability of arable land or lead to deforestation or loss of biodiversity and the construction of physical infrastructure can lead to the population displacement from project areas. Such trade-offs need to be addressed through mechanisms such as appropriate technology, environmentally efficient infrastructure, regulation for the adoption of clean technologies and strengthened labour market institutions (Basnett and Bhattacharya, 2015).

Successive policy statements issued by United Nations Member States have emphasized the right and obligation of States to pursue sustainable development strategies. In the 2030 Agenda, Member States not only explicitly recognize "that each country has primary responsibility for its own economic and social development" (paragraph 41), but also acknowledge the policy space required: "We will respect national policy space for sustained, inclusive and sustainable economic growth, in particular for developing States, while remaining consistent with relevant international rules and commitments" (paragraph 21).

2. Structural transformation as a concept

UNCTAD (2006a; 2014a) has long emphasized the importance of economic structural transformation for poverty eradication and long-term development in the LDCs. In recent years, attention to structural transformation among domestic and international development policymakers has risen to a level not seen since the 1960s (te Velde, 2013a), largely because "the failure of quantitative growth to trigger economic and social development [has] shifted attention to the quality of the growth process, to structural change and to catching up" (Nübler, 2011).

Efforts to implement the 2030 Agenda have intensified that attention.

Traditionally, structural change in economics has referred mainly to "changing weights of the elements which compose an aggregate" (Landesmann, 1988), particularly output, employment, trade and demand (Landesmann et al., 2003). While "[t]he most common use of structure in development and in economic history refers to the relative importance of sectors in the economy in terms of production and factor use" (Syrquin, 1988), structural change has been defined as "change in the long-term composition and distribution of economic activities" (United Nations Industrial Development Organization (UNIDO), 2013a). Such structural change arises from the transfer of production factors (especially labour, capital and land) between economic activities and sectors, leading to corresponding changes in the composition of output, employment and, typically, trade. These themes have been clearly present in development research and policy at least since the 1960s.

The characterization above highlights changes in the composition of economic aggregates, such as output, employment or demand, but is relatively neutral. It does not indicate in which direction the transfer of resources leads the economy, nor especially whether the economy is evolving towards socially preferable forms of organization and structuring. Therefore, some authors have put forward a normative concept, indicating that "a normative perspective of structural change often emphasizes desirability in the direction of change. For example, Ocampo (2005), Ocampo and Vos (2008) and [the United Nations, Department of Economic and Social Affairs] (2006) define structural change as the ability of an economy to continually generate new dynamic activities characterized by higher productivity and increasing returns to scale" (UNIDO, 2013a).

Such favourable structural transformation (sometimes also referred to as structural change) results from the transfer of production factors — especially labour, capital and land — away from activities and sectors with low productivity and value added, to those with higher productivity and value added and greater efficiency, which are typically different in location and organization, as well as technologically (Rodrik, 2013). It results from two distinct processes: intra-sectoral transfer of resources, mainly through the adoption of superior technologies (e.g. from subsistence farming to higher value crops) and intersectoral transfer of resources (e.g. from agriculture to manufacturing) (UNCTAD, 2014a). It may thus also be characterized

Favourable structural transformation results from transferring resources to activities with higher productivity

as "improvements in economic structure, through diversification, increased capability to produce higher technology products and services, higher productivity, greater international competitiveness and the expansion of formal sector employment" (African Centre for Economic Transformation, 2014).

A distinction between any type of change in the composition of economic activities and sectors, on one side, and the type of transformation which is desirable from a development perspective, on the other, is important as it cannot be taken for granted that structural change will lead the economy to a new configuration favourable to sustainable development. LDCs have typically experienced a transfer of labour from low-productivity agricultural activities to low-productivity urban services, sustained over the medium term. While labour productivity in such services is marginally higher than in agriculture, this does not amount to structural transformation and has been characterized, in the context of African LDCs, as "static gains, dynamic losses" (de Vries et al., 2015). Successful structural transformation processes, for example, in developed countries and other developing countries, such as China and Viet Nam, have instead entailed the transfer of rural labour to manufacturing activities with much higher productivity (UNCTAD, 2014a). Other examples of structural transformation not evolving in the socially desirable direction in LDCs are the premature deindustrialization observed since the 1980s and the "re-primarization", which has taken place at different points of time, including most recently during the period of high international commodity prices (2003–2011).

In broader terms, structural transformation is not restricted to the economic sphere, but also has broader social aspects. Structural transformation thus typically involves four main features (Timmer, 2007):

- A declining share of agriculture in economic output and employment.
- A rising share of industry and modern services.
- Migration from rural to urban areas.
- A demographic transition, entailing a temporary acceleration of population growth to reach a new equilibrium level.

Transformation requires attacking the root causes of problems and inequities

3. Sustainable development and structural transformation

In the preamble of Transforming our world: the 2030 Agenda for Sustainable Development, Member States highlight the outcome document's transformational nature, stating that they "are determined to take the bold and transformative steps which are urgently needed to shift the world on to a sustainable and resilient path".

This has far-reaching consequences. The United Nations Research Institute for Social Development (2016) consequently notes that "transformation requires attacking the root causes that generate and reproduce economic, social, political and environmental problems and inequities, not merely their symptoms".

Realization of sustainable development in its three dimensions thus requires a radical change in economic processes and production methods and in consumption, transportation and lifestyles. It encompasses transforming the relationship between societies and the natural environment, to focus on the attainment of societal goals within environmental boundaries. Achieving the Sustainable Development Goals also necessitates changing social relations and the distribution of resources within and among countries in line with the objectives of inclusiveness, leaving no one behind and reducing economic, social and gender inequality. This requires profound institutional and policy changes. The consequent economic, social and institutional changes apply to all countries, irrespective of their level of development.

In LDCs, these changes go beyond the historical imperative of structural transformation for economic and social development, as discussed in this section. They require economic and social transformations consistent with environmental boundaries. LDCs also need to undergo a process of structural transformation to more modern, more efficient forms of production and consumption, with higher value added, analogous to the historical transformations of developed countries and emerging market economies. Yet they need to achieve this in a way that avoids repeating the negative environmental consequences of these processes in other countries.

UNCTAD has long called for LDCs to adopt economic development strategies based on the development and upgrading of productive capacities and diversification of their economic activities, leading to structural transformation of their economies that is rich in employment growth (UNCTAD, 2006a; UNCTAD, 2013a; UNCTAD, 2014a). The 2030 Agenda reinforces the need for such strategies, as structural transformation is essential for LDCs to achieve the Sustainable Development Goals across sustainable development's economic, social and environmental dimensions. Several Sustainable Development Goals (e.g. Goals 2, 8, 9 and 11) refer directly to specific features of structural transformation, and others (e.g. Goals 3, 4, 5, 7 and 17) are relevant to the means of achieving it. Goals 10 and 16 are likely to result from a successful structural transformation process that moves in a desirable direction, while Goals 6, 12, 13, 14 and 15 contribute to environmental sustainability. Finally, the only economically sustainable way to eradicate poverty (Goal 1) is to generate sufficient jobs for the workforce with earnings above the poverty line, matched by productivity — that is, poverty-oriented structural transformation (UNCTAD, 2015a). Without this approach to structural transformation, the economic, social and environmental aspects of sustainable development cannot be ensured.

As noted above, structural transformation has typically been associated with a demographic transition. Most LDCs remain in the initial phases of both these processes, and both are, at best, proceeding slowly. The result has been a combination of rapid population growth and predominantly young populations that have added, and will continue to add, almost 11 million to the labour force annually between 2010 and 2050, requiring employment creation on an equivalent scale (UNCTAD, 2013a).

LDCs thus face the double challenge of accelerating both structural transformation in a desirable direction and job creation. This means redirecting productive resources to higher value added activities and increasing productivity within sectors much more rapidly than in the past, while ensuring that this structural transformation is employment-intensive. This requires addressing the tension between increasing labour productivity (reducing labour use relative to output) with employment creation (increasing overall labour use), both of which will need to accelerate considerably from historical rates to eradicate poverty (Goal 1) and generate enough jobs that are higher in productivity and better paying to employ rapidly growing labour forces (UNCTAD, 2013a).

4. Transforming least developed country rural economies

As noted above, another major feature of structural transformation is a decline in agriculture's share of output and employment. For most LDCs, this process also remains at an initial stage. Agriculture continues to play a disproportionate role in LDC economies, generating on average some 22 per cent of economic output, compared with 8.5 per cent in other developing countries and 1.3 per cent in developed countries. Its role in employment is greater still. Agriculture absorbs two thirds of the LDC labour force, similar to the rural share of the population, whereas this is less than 7 per cent in most developed countries. Even by 2030, more than half of the population in LDCs (56.5 per cent) is projected to continue living in rural areas, making the transformation of rural economies central to the overall structural transformation of LDCs and highlighting "the rural development imperative" (UNCTAD, 2015a).

Rural transformation occurs in part by stimulating changes in demand associated with economic growth and urbanization, which promotes the production of more diverse and higher-value agricultural produce and other goods. Agriculture must become more productive to contribute effectively to structural transformation, rather than grow only through increased labour and land use or higher commodity prices, as appears to have been the case in the recent past (UNCTAD, 2015a; International Fund for Agricultural Development, 2016; Wiggins, 2016). This implies seeing agriculture primarily as a business, not only as a livelihood, and improving its links with market opportunities, and supply and global value chains, and strengthening agricultural enterprises' ability to exploit such opportunities. Agricultural development and the entrepreneurship on which it depends, built on a foundation of increasing agricultural productivity, are crucial to structural transformation, especially in LDCs.

Within rural areas, there is also an important distinction between areas close to urban areas and markets, and with good transport and logistical connections to them, and more remote and marginal areas, which are often dominated by small-scale ("minifundia") operations (Wiggins, 2016). Farming and non-farming activities in the former areas can more readily commercialize their operations through direct purchase of their produce by wholesalers and are also often better equipped to scale up their activities and diversify into non-farm entrepreneurship, whether in industry or services.

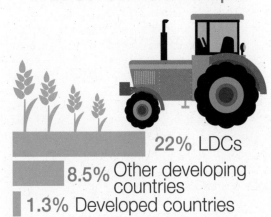

Agriculture continues to play a disproportionate role in LDCs' economic output

22% LDCs

8.5% Other developing countries

1.3% Developed countries

Increasing rural wages can play a crucial role, as both cause and consequence of the transformation of rural economies. Accelerating rural–urban migration can give rise to labour shortages in rural areas, increasing wages (though this has been a more prevalent pattern in Asia than in Africa or Latin America in recent years). When such labour shortages arise, they can contribute to reducing rural poverty by setting a floor for rural incomes, shifting rural consumption towards higher-value agricultural and non-farm products (Wiggins, 2016). This also increases labour costs in agriculture, encouraging greater use of mechanization and technology, which can also increase value addition. Combined, these two forces can thus transfer comparative advantages from the farming sector to the non-farming sector, contributing to structural transformation.

Diversification from agriculture into non-farm entrepreneurship contributed to a yearly overall improvement in rural labour productivity of 4.1 per cent, between 2001 and 2012, across a number of LDCs (Diao et al., 2017). In addition to expansion of the non-agricultural sector, such diversification can also improve agricultural labour productivity, as labour moves from agriculture to non-agricultural enterprises.

5. Productive capacities

Productive capacities play a pivotal role in sustainable development. This is increasingly recognized in the policy discourse and in international frameworks, such as the 2030 Agenda and the Istanbul Programme of Action for LDCs, where productive capacities feature as a priority.

Interaction between entrepreneurs and the State influences productive capacities

The concept of productive capacities reflects the intellectual contributions of different strands of development research, from early development economists to evolutionary and structuralist thinking.

UNCTAD (2006a) defines productive capacities as "the productive resources, entrepreneurial capabilities and production linkages which together determine the capacity of a country to produce goods and services and enable it to grow and develop". The three main components are outlined below:

- **Productive resources.** Includes natural resources, human resources, and financial and physical capital.

- **Entrepreneurial capabilities.** The core competencies and technical capabilities that allow enterprises to mobilize resources effectively for production, innovate and upgrade products and their quality, including both technological capabilities and managerial capacities.

- **Production linkages.** Includes backward and forward linkages and the circulation of ideas and explicit and/or tacit knowledge among firms operating along the supply chain.

Strengthening domestic productive capacities is one key to structural transformation, which occurs through capital accumulation, technological progress and structural transformation (as defined in section B.2). The interplay of these three processes can allow expansion of the production possibility frontier, emergence of new goods and services and higher productivity activities, and development of a denser network of production linkages.

Strengthening productive capacities is of particular importance in LDCs, which are typically characterized by a weak domestic private sector, heavy reliance on primary commodity exports and undiversified economic structures (UNCTAD, 2014a; UNCTAD, 2016a). By underpinning economic growth, enhancing the scope for domestic value addition and setting in motion economic diversification, development of LDC productive capacities can provide a sustainable means of improving welfare, generating productive employment and reducing aid dependence (UNCTAD, 2006; UNCTAD, 2018a).

The link between sustainable development, structural transformation and productive capacities is recognized in paragraph 27 of the 2030 Agenda for Sustainable Development:

We will strengthen the productive capacities of least developed countries in all sectors, including through structural transformation. We will adopt policies which increase productive capacities, productivity and productive employment; financial inclusion; sustainable agriculture, pastoralist and fisheries development; sustainable industrial development; universal access to affordable, reliable, sustainable and modern energy services; sustainable transport systems; and quality and resilient infrastructure.

While the primary focus of productive capacities is on supply-side constraints, utilization of productive capacities is also important, to incentivize investment in their expansion. This is contingent on demand-side factors, both domestically and globally. A sustained increase in productive capacities thus hinges on a process of cumulative causation, driven by mutually reinforcing increases in demand and supply. Domestically, such a virtuous circle occurs primarily through the expansion of productive employment opportunities fuelling growth in domestic demand, which, in turn, drives a further supply-side response via Keynesian multipliers (UNCTAD, 2014a). At the global level, it relies essentially on the animation of a profit–investment–export nexus, whereby profitability in the tradable sector attracts additional investment, further boosting exports flows and dynamically easing balance of payments constraints (UNCTAD, 2006; UNCTAD, 2016b).

The nature of interaction between entrepreneurs and the State thus inevitably influences development of productive capacities. Investment decisions by entrepreneurs — in addition to directly affecting the acquisition of entrepreneurial capabilities and know-how, innovation and establishment of a viable network of production linkages — also affect the accumulation of productive resources and animate the profit–investment nexus. As discussed in the next section, this makes the nature of entrepreneurship in LDCs central to their prospects for structural transformation.

C. Entrepreneurship as a concept

1. Definitions

Entrepreneurship is a diverse and multifaceted phenomenon. As Casson et al. (2008) have said, "there is hardly any aspect of economic and social behaviour which is not affected by entrepreneurship". Consequently, conceptualizations of entrepreneurship differ, with definitions grouped into three categories: behavioural, occupational and synthesis (Naudé, 2013).

Behavioural definitions of entrepreneurship define the entrepreneur as the coordinator of production and agent of change, which is achieved through innovation (see section C.3). Definitions in this category typically derive from the seminal definition of Schumpeter (1934; 1942).

Occupational definitions conceptualize entrepreneurship as the result of an individual's choice between waged employment and self-employment (Lucas, 1978; Murphy et al., 1991). The choice of becoming an entrepreneur is thus viewed as the result of an evaluation of the returns generated by self-employment (profits plus non-pecuniary benefits), relative to the wages and other benefits available from waged employment. This distinction typically refers to opportunity-driven entrepreneurs, rather than necessity-driven entrepreneurs (a distinction explained in section C.2).

Synthesis definitions of entrepreneurship have been proposed by Gries and Naudé (2011), Naudé (2013) and Szirmai et al. (2011). According to Szirmai et al., entrepreneurial activity "consists of the creation, recognition, and utilization of positive opportunities within existing firms (or through creation of new firms) in such a way that involves 'innovation' — or the provision of 'new combinations'".

While most of the definitions of entrepreneurship presented above (and others) share common elements, the emphasis differs. The diversity of the concept is conveyed by listing the most frequently occurring elements:

- Innovation. This element is described in section C.3 below.
- Opportunity-seizing or -creating. With this emphasis, the entrepreneur is defined as a person who facilitates adjustment to change by recognizing and seizing opportunities for profitable arbitrage arising from imperfect information in markets and proposing and undertaking transactions on this basis (Kirzner, 1973; Casson, 2003). Such information asymmetries typically arise in disequilibrium situations in markets, which are pervasive in developing countries, especially LDCs.
- Risks. Entrepreneurs take risks because they face uninsurable uncertainties when managing production (Kanbur, 1979), especially when they introduce innovation.
- Judgement. Entrepreneurs exercise judgement in decision-making about the combination and allocation of resources and the use of knowledge elements (Casson et al., 2008), taking difficult and

complex decisions for which other people are unwilling to take responsibility.
- Development of business organizations. This element emphasizes that most entrepreneurs either establish firms (start-ups) or carry out their activities (allocating resources, raising finance, taking decisions, etc.) within existing firms.

Different types of actors and organizations can undertake entrepreneurial activities

2. Agents of entrepreneurship

As the broad and multiple concepts of entrepreneurship mentioned above would suggest, different types of actors and organizations can undertake entrepreneurial activities. Figure 1.1 provides an indicative classification of entrepreneurial agents, according to the goal of the entrepreneurial undertaking, whether profits or survival. The goal of profits is the most commonly associated with entrepreneurial activity and is typically carried out by individual entrepreneurs, acting alone or, more commonly, within firms which they either establish themselves (start-ups) or already exist (often called intrapreneurship). These firms can vary by size (microenterprises, small, medium-sized and large), type of ownership (domestic, international or mixed; private, public or mixed) and degree of formalization (informal, formal), and their activities can take place in any sector of economic activity (agriculture, industry, services) and in different geographical areas (rural, urban).

At the other end of the spectrum are not-for-profit entrepreneurs. They typically pursue social and collective goals such as mutual support, collective action, protection of the environment and broader social good. They include cooperatives, non-governmental organizations and public administration (Mazzucato, 2013; Hughes, 1966). These agents do not always act entrepreneurially, but whether or not they do so depends on the modes of action and particular objectives their managers pursue.

Finally, some potentially entrepreneurial agents have a mix of purposes, which can range between profit-seeking and purely social goals, pursuing different levels of mixes from broad socially desirable goals to some form of profit. These agents include social entrepreneurs and State-owned enterprises (figure 1.1).

Figure 1.1

Entrepreneurship: Purposes and agents

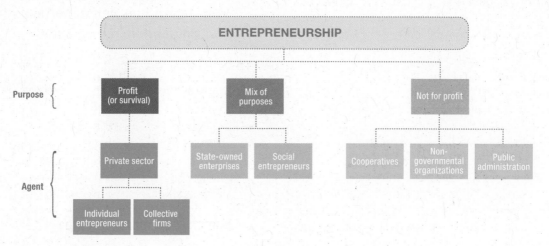

Source: UNCTAD secretariat.

The entrepreneurial landscape in LDCs presented in chapters 2 and 3 focuses mainly on private sector entrepreneurship. The policy analysis and recommendations in chapter 5, while concentrating on this segment, also refer to other types of entrepreneurial agents.

Individual entrepreneurs also vary widely and are often categorized according to their abilities (typically represented by educational attainment), gender, age (particularly distinguishing youth entrepreneurship), location (rural and urban) and sector of operation. Making a distinction between whether an entrepreneur's motivation is opportunity-driven or necessity-driven is particularly important, especially in LDCs. Opportunity-driven entrepreneurs are those who choose to become entrepreneurs because they identify a business opportunity, while necessity-driven entrepreneurs are those who are obliged to become entrepreneurs due to a lack of alternatives, especially the option of wage employment as a source of income.

These different types of motivation for entrepreneurship have important consequences, not only for business performance, but also for the broader economic and social impact of enterprises. Typically, opportunity-driven entrepreneurs have better business performance (higher profits, stronger growth), a higher educational level, higher non-cognitive skills (e.g. conscientiousness, perseverance and team work) and better management practices than necessity-driven entrepreneurs (Calderon et al., 2016). By contrast, necessity-driven entrepreneurs tend to have lower cognitive and non-cognitive skills, concentrate on low-productivity activities and

have poor growth prospects. The goal of survival — rather than profits — is more prevalent among the self-employed and small enterprises in developing countries, especially LDCs (see chapter 2). Crucially, innovation (as defined in section C.3) is more likely to be introduced by opportunity-driven entrepreneurs than by necessity-driven entrepreneurs. Therefore, the former are more likely to be agents of structural transformation than the latter (section D).

A further distinction between different types of entrepreneurs can be made by looking at the economic impact of entrepreneurial activity. While the usual assumption is that entrepreneurial activity leads to socially desirable outcomes (section D.1), this is not always the case. The most important driver of private entrepreneurial activity is profits, and the types of activities most likely to generate profits depend on the structure of returns and on institutions (the "rules of the game"). These are the activities most likely to draw entrepreneurial talent. The socially desirable situation is that in which entrepreneurship is geared towards the adoption and diffusion of innovation and technology, employment generation, creation of new economic activity, expansion of jobs and economic growth, a situation which Baumol (1990) terms "productive entrepreneurship". However, an economy's rewards structure may be such that it draws entrepreneurial talents to unproductive uses (e.g. rent-seeking) or even destructive ones (e.g. criminal activities, depredation). Therefore, a fundamental role for policy is to set an incentive structure that results in higher returns for productive activities and therefore draws entrepreneurial talent to them (chapter 5).

Another distinction made is between high-impact entrepreneurs and routine entrepreneurs. High-impact entrepreneurs are a Schumpeterian type that identify inventions and implement them in the productive process (i.e. that innovate) and whose firms generate technological progress and jobs and expand strongly (Acs, 2008). A routine entrepreneur, by contrast, refers to "activities involved in coordinating and carrying on a well-established, [on]going concern in which the parts of the production function in use (and likely alternatives to current use) are well known and which operates in well-established and clearly defined markets" (Leibenstein, 1968).

Entrepreneurs and their creations — firms — can also be distinguished in terms of their level of success, a distinction related in part to the various categories detailed above. The issue of survival and success is especially relevant among start-ups. These firms typically have higher failure rates than more mature firms, but also faster growth rates among survivors (Cressy, 2006).

3. Entrepreneurship and innovation

Innovation is central to the definition of transformational entrepreneurship adopted in this report. The classic definition of innovation is that of Schumpeter (1934): newness in products, production processes, sources of inputs or raw materials, markets and business or organizational models. These types of innovation are production-centred, allowing for no role for consumers (Metcalfe, 2006). They entail producers' use of knowledge that is not currently used by firms in their production of goods or services (Audretsch and Keilbach, 2006). The incorporation of these types of innovation into production processes can be concomitant to the creation or expansion of new firms, which may eventually push incumbent firms out of markets in a process Schumpeter termed "creative destruction". Innovative entrepreneurs are thus the agents of a continuous process of self-transformation, in which each entrepreneur changes in response to volatility generated by other entrepreneurs (Metcalfe, 2006).

There is a widespread tendency to assume that innovation is always positive and, therefore, socially desirable. This is in fact most often the case. However, there are times when innovation has socially deleterious effects. It can benefit the few at the expense of the many. In the financial sector, for instance, this includes situations that allow actors to realize large gains in the short term, while at a later stage creating even greater costs for society as a whole. In manufacturing, examples include innovations involving planned obsolescence and

> **In LDCs innovation introduced by entrepreneurs is crucial for structural transformation**

innovations leading to unsustainable consumption growth and environmental degradation. Rather than leading to Schumpeterian "creative destruction", such situations have been qualified as the opposite, "destructive creation" (Soete, 2013). Such possible adverse outcomes point to the importance of policy to put in place incentives for stimulating socially constructive innovations, while hindering adverse types of innovation (chapter 5).

Innovation of the socially desirable type is important at all levels of development, although its nature and consequences differ between the earlier and later stages of the development process. In LDCs, while low levels of physical and human capital make factor accumulation essential to development, the central role of innovation in structural transformation means that innovation is also critical. However, unlike developed countries (where the changes introduced by innovation are generally "new to the world", pushing the technological frontier outwards), innovation in LDCs typically entails the introduction of items and processes that already exist elsewhere but are new to the local market and thus far from a worldwide technological frontier (UNCTAD, 2007). Innovation is thus as important to economies where growth is driven by factor accumulation as those where it is driven by knowledge accumulation.

D. Entrepreneurship and structural transformation

1. Entrepreneurship's impact on structural transformation and growth

Entrepreneurial activity, and particularly innovation (as defined in section C.3), can make a crucial contribution to structural transformation, in several ways. First, it is an important mechanism for shifting productive resources from economic activities with low value addition and productivity, to those with higher value addition and productivity, whether in agriculture, industry or services. Innovative entrepreneurial activity can thus provide a direct contribution to economic structural transformation. It can be the means of adopting new and better performing technology and/or its diffusion. In both cases, the likely result will be improvements in productivity.

Entrepreneurship's contribution to economic growth:

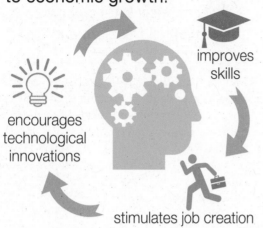

encourages technological innovations

improves skills

stimulates job creation

Second, entrepreneurship can stimulate investment and contribute to building a knowledge-driven economy, which plays a central role in economic growth (Aghion and Howitt, 2005). Third, even unviable innovations in production (introducing goods, services, production technologies or business models new to a particular setting) provide valuable information for future entrepreneurial decisions, including those of other entrepreneurs, in the form of "cost discovery" (Hausmann and Rodrik, 2003). These effects are especially critical in LDCs that are in the initial stage of structural transformation.

Entrepreneurial activity also contributes to economic growth by stimulating job creation, improving skills and encouraging technological innovation, and can increase efficiency and productivity by encouraging competition (Audretsch and Fritsch, 2002; Audretsch and Keilbach, 2004; Wong et al., 2005; Naudé, 2011). Differences in entrepreneurship have a significant effect on economic performance, controlling for traditional production factors (land, labour and capital) (Casson et al., 2006). In addition to its benefits for increasing incomes, economic growth is, in turn, an important element of structural transformation.

The different types of entrepreneurs and firms, however, vary in their contributions to structural transformation and economic growth. In particular, while dynamic, opportunity-driven entrepreneurship may have significant positive effects in these respects, survivalist "entrepreneurs by necessity" are typically not innovative, operating mostly in low-productivity and low value added activities, and producing traditional goods and services with established technologies. Their growth potential is very limited, and most remain microenterprises. While important to the survival of the entrepreneurs themselves and their families, they mostly do not generate significant

wider benefits. While survivalist entrepreneurs may become opportunity-driven entrepreneurs and have a more positive impact, such cases are very rare, especially in LDCs.

Firms that introduce radical socially desirable innovation (considering the national or local context) and which also have a high growth potential make the most direct and significant contribution to structural transformation (Wong et al., 2005). This does not imply that only these firms are important for structural transformation. Other, less performant and possibly smaller firms are also important, to the extent that they establish business linkages (both backward and forward) with the former. Business linkages are part of the very definition of productive capacities and hence development of these linkages is part of development of productive capacities. This view of the enterprise sector highlights the importance of variety in LDC enterprises, especially in terms of size. A healthy enterprise sector that leads to structural transformation comprises firms of all sizes.

The relative contributions to structural transformation (and other development goals) of entrepreneurs and firms of different types are an important consideration in policymaking (chapter 5). Resource allocation and vertical industrial policies (those directed towards particular sectors or economic activities) should target primarily firms with the greatest potential to contribute to structural transformation.

The relationship between the wider economic and social environment and entrepreneurship is two-pronged. This means that the economic and social context influences the intensity of entrepreneurial activity, but also the types, growth prospects and innovativeness of enterprises that can develop under a given context. The influence of the types, growth prospects and innovativeness of enterprises is examined in section E.1.

In sum, given the fundamental role of entrepreneurship activity in bringing about structural transformation, transformational entrepreneurship (defined hereafter) is fundamental to achieving sustainable development and the Sustainable Development Goals in the LDCs. The 2030 Agenda for Sustainable Development acknowledges the role to be played by different types of entities and organizations, which have a potential for entrepreneurial functions in the pursuit of the Sustainable Development Goals: "We acknowledge the role of the diverse private sector, ranging from microenterprises to cooperatives to multinationals, and that of civil society organizations and philanthropic organizations in the implementation of the new Agenda" (paragraph 41).

2. Transformational entrepreneurship

This chapter has so far focused on the concepts of sustainable development, structural transformation, productive capacities, innovation and entrepreneurship and how they are linked to each other. The discussion has also shown that structural transformation, innovation and entrepreneurship, while generally considered positively and contributors to sustainable development, can occasionally have adverse results, depending on how these processes evolve in a specific country and over a specific period of time.

Some forms of entrepreneurship (or innovation), while not necessarily negative in themselves, may simply not be conducive to growth and structural transformation (Brixiova, 2010). This is the case, generally, for most survivalist entrepreneurship, which is pervasive in LDCs (chapter 2).

At the same time, the discussion has shown that innovation, entrepreneurship and structural transformation that move in a socially desirable direction are necessary elements of sustainable development, especially in the case of LDCs. Thus, this report puts forward the concept of "transformational entrepreneurship". This consists of the creation, recognition and utilization of positive opportunities within existing organizations (or through the creation of new organizations) in such a way that "innovation" is involved – or the provision of "new combinations", which ultimately contribute to the structural economic transformation of a country. It is this conception of transformational entrepreneurship that is therefore a fundamental condition of sustainable development in the LDCs.

The forms of entrepreneurship most likely to be transformational are opportunity-driven, high-impact (as defined above) and innovative and have high growth potential. Policymakers of LDCs striving to achieve structural transformation of the economy are advised to concentrate scarce resources (financial, institutional, administrative, political, etc.) on transformational entrepreneurship, as it has the strongest transformational impact, rather than spreading resources among a large number of firms with limited growth and innovation potential (chapter 5).

The concept of transformational entrepreneurship also foresees the possibility of transformational contribution by non-firms, that is, organizations such as cooperatives, non-governmental organizations and public institutions which can also undertake entrepreneurial activities (figure 1.1). This report, however, focuses mainly on commercial innovation

Transformational entrepreneurship is a condition for sustainable development in LDCs

and entrepreneurship as it is the most pervasive form of entrepreneurship and as this is the type of entrepreneurship which is primarily emphasized in the existing international policy discourse and debate.

By contrast, the concept of transformational entrepreneurship excludes the cases of socially undesirable innovation, entrepreneurship and structural change mentioned earlier (e.g. destructive creation, unproductive entrepreneurship and "re-primarization").

E. Determinants of entrepreneurship

As seen in the previous section, different types of entrepreneurship and firms have contrasting impacts on the economy through their contributions to growth and structural transformation. The relevant issue is then what determines both the intensity of entrepreneurial activity in a given economy and the types of enterprises and entrepreneurs that arise within it. The question matters as the determinants of a type of entrepreneurship and firm will, in turn, ultimately determine the patterns of structural change the economy will undergo.

Research on this issue has typically focused on two lines of explanation. The first line of research focuses on the ecosystem in which the entrepreneur is active, i.e. the attributes of the economy, society or country in which the entrepreneur operates (e.g. economic structure, institutions and cultural values). The second line of research emphasizes factors that influence a person's propensity to engage in an entrepreneurial activity and typically highlights the importance of personal traits of entrepreneurs, especially individual attributes such as personality, demographic factors, cognitive skills and genetic factors. All of these features can influence an entrepreneur's chances of success. Therefore, the level and quality of entrepreneurship in a given country is influenced by both socioeconomic and individual factors.

1. The influence of economic and social structures

Even though entrepreneurship typically involves one or more individuals, it always takes place in a given economic and social context. Therefore, the environment in which entrepreneurs evolve has a

Structural features of LDC economies tend to slow entrepreneurship

strong bearing on the type of entrepreneurs which can arise and on their chances of success. "Successful entrepreneurship is as much a cooperative endeavour, mediated by social networks, as a purely individualistic and competitive ones" (Casson et al., 2006). Entrepreneurship is strongly affected by the overall environment in which it takes place, including the economic structure, institutional framework and sociocultural environment in which it is realized.

Economic structure. While the activities of dynamic, innovative (and typically opportunity-driven) entrepreneurs can contribute to both structural transformation and economic growth (as discussed in section D), the structure of the national and local economy also has a major impact on the types of enterprises than can be established and operated. This refers particularly to the geographical zone where entrepreneurial activity takes place and the national economy's level of development. A particularly important aspect of the local dimension is the distinction between rural and urban areas, as discussed in chapter 2.

The level of development and structural characteristics of the economy where entrepreneurial activities evolve condition the types of entrepreneurship that can emerge, the patterns of enterprise growth and, thus, their economic and social impacts. Several structural features of LDC economies, including limited financial development, insufficient infrastructure, limited institutional development, elevated risks and disempowerment of women, tend to slow entrepreneurship and enterprise development. Limited urbanization and the disproportionate role of agriculture also have an important bearing on the nature of enterprises in LDCs.

The relationship of entrepreneurship to a country's level of economic development (measured by gross domestic product (GDP) per capita) tends to be U-shaped, according to some research findings (Wennekers et al., 2010; Acs et al., 2008; Gollin, 2008), with a higher prevalence of entrepreneurial activity at both the lower and higher levels of income. However, this reflects the entirely different structural characteristics of economies at opposite ends of the income scale (chapter 2). The majority of empirical evidence confirms that entrepreneurship in low-income countries (including LDCs) tends to be largely necessity-based, while entrepreneurship in higher-

income countries is primarily opportunity-based. This is reflected in a desire among many self-employed people in low-income countries to move to waged employment with a higher level of security, while the opposite tends to be the case in high-income countries (La Porta and Shleifer, 2014; Acs et al., 2008).

Institutional framework. The institutional framework also has a strong impact on the type of entrepreneurship that arises, and thus on its broader societal impact, including its contribution to structural transformation. A well-functioning national system of innovation (Lundvall, 1992; Nelson, 1993) that fosters domestic absorptive capacity (UNCTAD, 2014b) is of particular importance to transformative entrepreneurship.

According to Casson et al. (2006), the institutions most likely to foster entrepreneurship are those of a liberal market economy: private property, freedom of movement and of association with partners, confidentiality of specific business information, protection of intellectual property rights, enforcement of property rights by court systems, currency stability, democratic government and openness to immigration. These conditions typically prevail in developed countries, but they are, however, quite different from the institutional and economic conditions prevailing in LDCs. Moreover, it is highly unlikely that simply transposing these institutions from a developed country context to LDCs would have the desired result of fostering transformational entrepreneurship. Simple institutional transfer to radically different national contexts does not achieve the expected results (UNCTAD, 2009). It is therefore important that LDC policymakers focus on some critical institutions that can foster transformational entrepreneurship (chapter 5). This includes especially the national regulatory framework on firm entry and exit, the financial system, infrastructure and the energy system (UNCTAD, 2017).

Attitudes towards entrepreneurship. Societies differ in multiple ways, which has consequences for attitudes towards entrepreneurship. Social features with a bearing on the intensity of entrepreneurship, and its variations across countries, include (Cacciotti and Hayton, 2017):

- Power distance: acceptance of differences in power and wealth (Hofstede and Bond, 1988).

- Uncertainty avoidance: tolerance or intolerance of uncertainty and insecurity.

- Institutional collectivism: encouragement and reward of collective distribution of resources and collective action.

- In-group collectivism: expression of pride, loyalty and cohesiveness in organizations and families.

- Gender egalitarianism: balance in society's valuation of achievement, cooperation, ambition, nurturing and assertiveness.

- Future orientation: includes valuation of persistence and perseverance or of tradition and fulfilment of social obligations.

- Performance orientation: encouragement and reward of performance improvement and excellence.

- Human orientation: encouragement and reward of fairness and kindness to others.

2. Individual-level determinants

Factors that influence an individual's propensity to engage in entrepreneurial activity include demographics such as age, gender and cognitive skills, as well as psychological, social, ethnic and personality traits. The economic role played by women has major developmental impacts (Duflo, 2012). It is well known that the women's contribution to development is often hampered by social norms and rules which prevent their economic and social empowerment and therefore diminish their contribution to the development process. This is especially true in LDCs and even more so in rural areas, where women are often prevented from realizing their full potential contribution to economic growth and development by social norms and customs, in spite of their strong participation in the rural workforce (UNCTAD, 2015a).

The prevailing institutions, rules and norms of a society also tend to impact on women's entrepreneurial activities and on the prospects for expansion and growth of women-led enterprises. Gender-based research sheds light on how a given factor affects women and men differently, and that they exhibit different patterns of entrepreneurial behaviour. Typically, women take account of considerations related to marriage, child-bearing or social norms in entrepreneurial decisions more than men do, while entrepreneurial activity by women is affected by gender-based differences in preferences, traits or personality (e.g. perceptions of opportunity, preferences for self-employment, risk aversion and self-confidence) (Garcia-Cabrera and Garcia-Soto, 2008; Minniti and Naudé, 2010). Women's propensity to start a business may differ from that of men's for cultural reasons or due to discrimination (Neumark and McLennan, 1995).

The personality approach interprets entrepreneurial behaviours as reflecting traits such as desire for success, limited fear of failure, openness to

The economic role played by women has major developmental impacts

experience, conscientiousness, extraversion, agreeableness, persistence in the face of failure and alertness to perceive and act on opportunities. Behaviour is central to entrepreneurship and new venture creation, though a cohesive theory of entrepreneurial behaviour has yet to emerge (Teague and Gartner, 2017).

Another relevant body of literature analyses entrepreneurial behaviours from a psychological perspective. There are two schools of thought (Shaver and Davis, 2017). The personality approach describes entrepreneurial behaviours as characterized by specific traits. Some researchers depict the successful entrepreneur as someone with either an extreme desire for success or a very low fear of failure (Atkinson, 1958). Others see "driven" entrepreneurial behaviours as being favoured by a high propensity for risk (Palich and Bagby, 1995). It has also been suggested (Costa and McCrae, 1992) that entrepreneurial attitudes can be described by the following factors: openness to experience, conscientiousness, extraversion, agreeableness and neuroticism. The first factor refers to curiosity and innovation, the second stresses the importance of efficiency and the third highlights entrepreneurs' social skills. Agreeableness and neuroticism pertain to the idea of friendliness and an analytical nature, coupled with a confident attitude.

In a separate line of research, the social cognition approach considers instead how entrepreneurs might "think differently". A prominent example is the attribution process theory. It is usual for people to continue doing something in which they are successful and avoid failure. However, entrepreneurs are more persistent than implied by such behavioural norms in starting or continuing an entrepreneurial project in the face of difficulties. One interpretation is that this reflects that business failure is considered less shameful than failures of other kinds (Shaver and Davis, 2017).

F. Conclusion

This chapter has shown the critical contribution that entrepreneurship can and should make to LDCs' progress towards sustainable development, which provides the rationale for devoting this report to the topic of entrepreneurship. Building on the conceptual framework presented in this chapter, chapter 2 presents a summary of the empirical evidence on the state of and context for entrepreneurship in LDCs and analyses the main determinants of enterprise and productivity growth in these countries. Chapter 3 discusses the relationship between entrepreneurship and the nature of LDCs' integration into the international economy, especially through global value chains. Chapter 4 provides a picture of the constraints on entrepreneurship and enterprise growth in LDCs and takes stock of the existing policy and institutional environment of enterprise development in LDCs. Chapter 5 concludes by providing a detailed discussion of policy alternatives which LDC Governments can use to strengthen entrepreneurship and entrepreneurship's contribution to structural transformation and sustainable development.

Notes

1   In this report, "other developing countries" refers to all developing countries, as defined by the United Nations, that are not LDCs.

2   This report's definition of transformational entrepreneurship is based on the synthesis definition by Szirmai et al. (2011) quoted in section C.1.

3   This includes, inter alia, so-called gazelle companies, which are high-growth companies that have raised their revenues by at least 20 per cent annually for four years or more, starting from a revenue base of at least $100,000.

SELF-EMPLOYMENT IS
THE MAIN FORM OF "ENTREPRENEURSHIP" IN LDCs

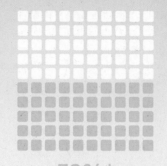

70%*
LDCs

50%*
Other developing countries

14%*
Developed countries

*Percentage of total employment

DIFFERENT CONTRIBUTIONS
TO STRUCTURAL TRANSFORMATION

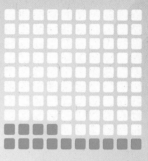

Smaller and younger firms

+ More employment growth

− Lower survival rates

Larger firms

+ Higher productivity growth
More stable and secure jobs

− Lower employment growth

DISTRIBUTION OF FORMAL FIRMS IN LDCs
REVEALS A "MISSING MIDDLE"

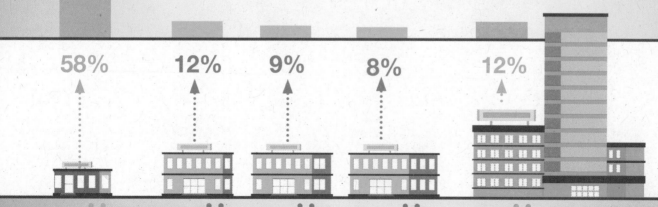

58%	12%	9%	8%	12%
5–20	20–30	30–50	50–100	100+

Number of employees

CHAPTER

2

Towards a nuanced appraisal
of the entrepreneurial landscape
in the least developed countries

CHAPTER 2

Towards a nuanced appraisal of the entrepreneurial landscape in the least developed countries

A. Introduction — **21**

B. The measurement of entrepreneurship — **21**

C. Entrepreneurship in the least developed countries: Stylized facts — **26**

1. The prevalence of entrepreneurial activities in the least developed countries — 26
2. Traits of entrepreneurship in the least developed countries — 30
3. Who are entrepreneurs in the least developed countries? — 35

D. Key sectors in the least developed countries: The informal sector and rural enterprise — **38**

1. The informal sector — 38
2. Rural non-farm enterprises — 41

E. Firm heterogeneity and structural transformation — **43**

1. Data — 44
2. Empirical results — 46

F. Concluding remarks — **49**

Notes — **50**

A. Introduction

Entrepreneurship has increasingly become an area of focus in the development policy discourse, and is presented by various agreements, from the Istanbul Programme of Action to the Addis Ababa Action Agenda, as a key avenue to private sector development and employment generation, especially for women and youth. However, consensus has not yet been reached on the definition or the measurement of entrepreneurship and the nature of its relationship with the development process, despite the insights of theoretical contributions on the role of entrepreneurs in investment and innovation (see chapter 1).

Such general issues are arguably more problematic in LDCs, with regard to which theoretical definitions of entrepreneurship are blurred, given structural features such as predominantly agricultural labour forces; a preponderance of small-scale informal enterprises, which are more difficult to monitor; and limited economic diversification. A nuanced mapping of the multifaceted entrepreneurial landscape in LDCs is therefore critical to harnessing entrepreneurship effectively for structural transformation and aligning enterprise policies with broader development strategies.

This chapter presents some stylized facts on the state of entrepreneurship and enterprise development in LDCs, making the case for adding nuance and texture to the current understanding and noting the need for better articulation of the implications for structural transformation. To contain the problem of data limitation, two complementary steps are taken. First, occupational data, principally from labour and population surveys, is used to characterize the profiles, attributes and aspirations of individual entrepreneurs, largely based on commonly used dichotomies such as formality and informality and opportunity and necessity; and to consider the life cycle of enterprises from start-up to business discontinuation. Second, more formal evidence is presented, based on two key determinants of firm performance, mainly from World Bank Enterprise Surveys. The surveys focus on formal non-agricultural enterprises, thus excluding a major part of the economy, yet the richness of the data allows for a more rigorous assessment of the contributions of different types of firms to structural transformation.

The chapter is structured as follows. Section B outlines key challenges in the measurement of entrepreneurship and related data limitations, underscoring the extent to which they constrain the debate on the role of entrepreneurship in economic development. Section C triangulates different

The analysis of entrepreneurship is fraught with theoritical complications and measurement problems

methodological approaches and data sources to highlight the particular characteristics of LDCs in terms of the prevalence of entrepreneurial activities; the key features of entrepreneurship, that is formality versus informality and opportunity versus necessity; and the profile of entrepreneurs. Section D presents a closer look at two areas of particular importance in LDCs, namely the informal sector and rural non-farm enterprises. Section E provides a more formal analysis of the drivers of firm performance in LDCs, highlighting the need for a nuanced approach to enterprise development to harness the contribution of the private sector to structural transformation in a context of firm heterogeneity. Section F provides a summary and highlights policy considerations.

B. The measurement of entrepreneurship

The analysis of entrepreneurship is fraught with complications and measurement problems, particularly in developing countries and LDCs, impeding research on its role in economic development (Ahmad and Hoffman, 2007; Hessels and Naudé, 2017; Naudé, 2013; Ahmad and Seymour, 2008; Struthers and Nziku, 2018). The concept of entrepreneurship has been the subject of prolonged and intense theoretical debate at the intersection of economic theory and business strategy, with different strands of the literature proposing competing definitions based on occupational, institutional and functional perspectives (Klein, 2008; Naudé, 2013).

The interpretation of evidence on entrepreneurship therefore requires caution, as these approaches are different in nature. The occupational perspective focuses on the determinants of an individual entrepreneur's choice to start a business. It therefore treats the individual as the unit of analysis and sheds light on the influence of psychological, educational and socioeconomic attributes on the choice between entrepreneurship and wage employment, given the risk-adjusted expected returns to each. The institutional perspective emphasizes instead the establishment of enterprises and related dynamics, assessing variables such as start-up rates and the prevalence of high-growth firms. Finally, the functional (Schumpeterian) perspective focuses on a more elusive aspect, namely the role of entrepreneurs

Entrepreneurship manifests in the economy in different forms and with distinct economic effects. Hence a nuanced mapping is critical

in identifying potential opportunities and investing capital to reap the associated profits, thereby catalysing the process of creative destruction (Klein, 2008; Schumpeter, 1934).

These conceptual differences are mirrored in the measurement of entrepreneurship, leading to the development of competing metrics that directly or indirectly segment entrepreneurial activities in various ways, for example into formal and informal businesses and those motivated by necessity and those motivated by opportunity (Desai, 2011). Consequently, available indicators measure everything from personal attributes of entrepreneurs such as gender to outcomes of the entrepreneurial process such as start-up rates (Hoffmann et al., 2006). A careful contextualization, interpretation and comparison of the various indicators is therefore critical.

A growing strand of the literature documents how entrepreneurship manifests in the economy in different forms and with distinct economic effects (Ahmad and Hoffman, 2007; Baumol, 1990; Hessels and Naudé, 2017; Vivarelli, 2016). However, the various categories of entrepreneur delineated are not mutually exclusive, and co-exist in varying proportions in each country. Since no one measure captures all forms of entrepreneurship, the thorough mapping of the entrepreneurial landscape and the identification of policy strategies and priorities necessarily rely on an array of complementary indicators (Ahmad and Hoffman, 2007; UNCTAD, 2012a). The complementarity of the occupational and institutional perspectives, in particular, is critical to ensuring consistency and alignment between entrepreneurship strategies and broader private-sector development policies (UNCTAD, 2012a).

Indicators vary in how appropriate they are for different contexts and types of analysis, and each has its advantages and disadvantages and is subject to different caveats. In LDCs, for example, the prevalence of informal activities and self-employment may make occupational metrics focusing on the individual more pertinent than those based on formal business registration (Desai, 2011). However, many occupational indicators, notably those based on labour force surveys, do not allow for assessments

of key dimensions of entrepreneurship such as employment generation, innovation and growth potential (Margolis, 2014).[1] Different indicators are also required to analyse the determinants of enterprise formalization and to identify firms with high growth potential.[2]

Among the most widely used measures of entrepreneurship are the following (Desai, 2011; Naudé, 2013; Struthers and Nziku, 2018):

- The share of self-employment in total employment, computed by ILO.

- Total early-stage entrepreneurial activity, assessed by GEM, and defined as the share of the adult population in the process of starting a business or that owns and/or manages a new business (box 2.1).

- The density of new businesses, compiled by the World Bank on the basis of information from national business registries, and defined as new registrations of limited liability companies per 1,000 people of working age (15–64 years).[3]

An important practical problem in mapping the status of entrepreneurship in developing countries, in particular in LDCs, is the lack of reliable and internationally comparable data, in contrast with the availability of well-structured and regularly updated sets of indicators for OECD member countries (Ahmad and Hoffman, 2007). For example, total early-stage entrepreneurial activity data for 2008–2017 are available for only 11 of the 47 LDCs and, on average, there are only two yearly observations from this decade, compared with five for other developing countries and seven for developed and transition economies (figure 2.1). The World Bank Enterprise Surveys cover 41 of the 47 LDCs, and often have little or no longitudinal dimension. Each measure is also subject to various methodological caveats, including how representative the samples surveyed are and the imputation of missing data, as well as more detailed statistical qualifications (Margolis, 2014; Timm, 2018).

Interpretation of the three measures as proxies for the prevalence of entrepreneurial activity also requires caution, as they capture such activity to some extent, yet also partly reflect inter-State differences in levels of development. Self-employment and total early-stage entrepreneurial activity are likely to reflect, at least in part, the disproportionate importance in developing countries of activities that are notionally entrepreneurial but lack the critical element of creative destruction underscored by Schumpeter (1934). As with the definition of self-employment, the GEM definition of entrepreneurship is deliberately broad and therefore likely to include small-scale and informal

Box 2.1 Global Entrepreneurship Monitor conceptual framework and key terminology

The conceptual approach and terminology used by GEM in its data collection differ somewhat from those used in this report. The adult population surveys of GEM adopt an occupational perspective of entrepreneurship, broadly defined as "any attempt at new business or new venture creation, such as self-employment, a new business organization or the expansion of an existing business, by an individual, a team of individuals or an established business" (see https://www.gemconsortium.org/wiki/1149). This definition includes business activities of a notionally entrepreneurial character that lack the element of innovation, which is at the core of both structural transformation and the Schumpeterian view of the entrepreneur. The relationships between the entrepreneurial process and the GEM operational definitions are outlined in box figure 2.1.

Box figure 2.1

Schematic representation of the Global Entrepreneurship Monitor conceptual framework

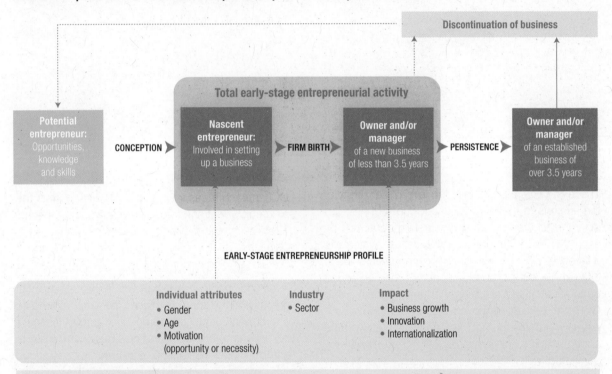

Total early-stage entrepreneurial activity, the most well-known index of GEM, measures the percentage of adults (18–64 years) that are either in the process of starting a business ("nascent entrepreneurs") or have started a business within the last 3.5 years ("baby entrepreneurs"). GEM also provides information on the ownership of established businesses, that is, those in operation for over 3.5 years; and business discontinuation. In addition, GEM collects information on entrepreneur motivation, asking the following question: "Are you involved in this start-up to take advantage of a business opportunity or because you have no better choices of work?" (see https://www.gemconsortium.org/wiki/1177). This allows entrepreneurs driven by necessity to be distinguished from those driven by opportunity.

Source: UNCTAD secretariat, based on GEM, 2018.

activities of a survivalist nature, ranging from family businesses to seasonal rural non-farming activities. Conversely, the reliance of the new business density indicator on data on the formal registration of limited liability companies makes the measurement prone to an underestimation of entrepreneurship in developing countries, in which such a legal structure is relatively uncommon.

The need for caution is demonstrated by using the pairwise Spearman's rank correlation for 108 country-level observations across the three indicators (table 2.1). There is a highly significant positive correlation between the share of those self-employed and total early-stage entrepreneurial activity, and a negative correlation between each of these and new business density, which is statistically significant with regard to total early-stage entrepreneurial activity. This reflects the distinction between new business density and total early-stage entrepreneurial activity, which provides a broader view of entrepreneurship that implies neither registration nor legal frameworks such as limited liability companies.

Figure 2.1

Number of available observations of total early-stage entrepreneurial activity, 2008–2017

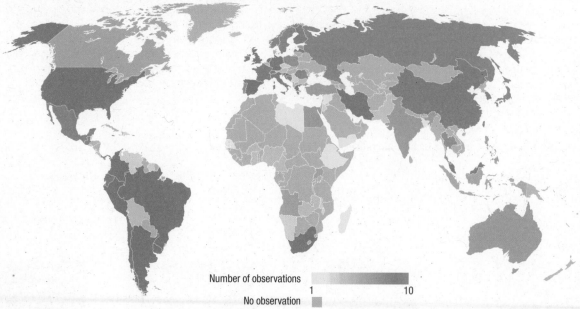

Number of observations

1   10

No observation

Source: UNCTAD secretariat calculations, based on data from GEM database.

These findings highlight the high level of sensitivity of the analysis to the indicator used, due to the widely different facets of entrepreneurship captured by each. Moreover, the results partly reflect systematic differences in the nature of entrepreneurship at different levels of development, as demonstrated by the relationship between the three measures and GDP per person employed (figure 2.2).[4] Both self-employment (figure 2.2. (a)) and total early-stage entrepreneurial activity (figure 2.2 (b)) are negatively correlated with GDP per person employed overall, exhibiting a pattern broadly consistent with the alleged U-shaped relationship postulated in the literature (Naudé, 2013; Quatraro and Vivarelli, 2015; Wennekers and Thurik, 1999). New business density (figure 2.2 (c)), by contrast, appears to increase with GDP per person employed, at least for plausible values of the latter.[5] This suggests that the effects of entrepreneurship, broadly defined, differ between contexts, in part reflecting its particular manifestations at different levels of development. This view is reinforced by the marked clustering of

LDCs in each measure in figure 2.2, with double the self-employment and total early-stage entrepreneurial activity as in other developing countries, yet with new business density at only one quarter of the average in other developing countries.

These findings are consistent with previous empirical findings that the spread between the subcomponents of total early-stage entrepreneurial activity (nascent and baby entrepreneurs) and new business density is related to local institutional and business conditions after controlling for levels of economic development, which also play a significant role (Acs et al., 2008; Desai, 2011).

The apparently contradictory message in figure 2.2 epitomizes the "micro–macro paradox" noted by Hessels and Naudé (2017) on the role of entrepreneurship in development. Macroeconomic theories offer reasons to expect that at least some traits of entrepreneurship are conducive to economic growth, yet caution is required in identifying a microeconomically relevant measure that can provide

Table 2.1

Pairwise Spearman's rank correlation across measures of entrepreneurship for 108 countries

	Share of self-employment (percentage of total employment)	Total early-stage entrepreneurial activity	New business density
Share of self-employment (percentage of total employment)	1		
Total early-stage entrepreneurial activity	0.513**	1	
New business density	-0.529***	-0.175	1

Source: UNCTAD secretariat calculations, based on data from ILOstat; GEM and World Bank Doing Business databases.
Notes: Country-level observations refer to the latest year for which contemporaneous variables are available; *, ** and *** indicate a 10, 5 and 1 per cent significance level, respectively.

Figure 2.2

Gross domestic product per person employed and common measures of entrepreneurship

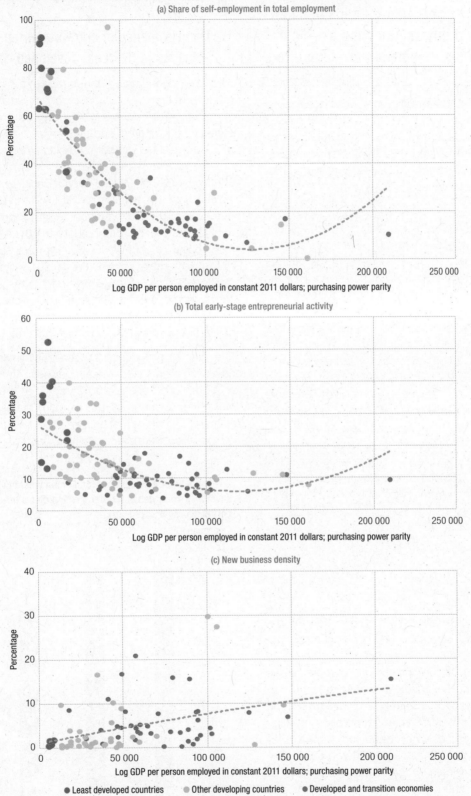

Source: UNCTAD secretariat calculations, based on data from ILOstat, GEM and World Bank Doing Business databases.

Note: Country-level observations considered include the latest year for which at least two entrepreneurship measures are available; the specification of the fitted lines is assumed to be quadratic, consistent with the postulated U-shaped relationship between entrepreneurship and GDP per capita.

> **Entrepreneurship mapping in LDCs requires a careful triangulation of scant sources of information, and a critical assessment of complementary indicators**

information on the mechanisms postulated rather than reflecting other spurious effects. Since the level of development itself may have a strong bearing on the manifestations of entrepreneurship, different metrics, as well as different econometric specifications, may lead to different results.[6]

Mapping entrepreneurship status in LDCs is thus particularly challenging and this limits the scope for evidence-based discussion of entrepreneurship strategies and policy measures. It is further complicated by the elusive nature of many of the most common forms of entrepreneurial activities in LDCs — notably small-scale establishments, informal businesses and seasonal rural non-farming activities — from a statistical perspective (African Development Bank et al., 2017; International Monetary Fund, 2018; UNCTAD, 2014a; UNCTAD, 2015a). Mapping therefore requires a careful triangulation of scant sources of information, from the few available data sets to qualitative case studies, and a critical assessment of complementary indicators. This highlights the importance of improving statistical capacities in LDCs and enhancing the quality of local data collection systems, to enable policymakers to make better-informed decisions.

C. Entrepreneurship in the least developed countries: Stylized facts

This section attempts to characterize the entrepreneurial landscape in LDCs, taking into account the limitations identified in section B. As the data-related issues preclude a comprehensive assessment of the status of entrepreneurship in LDCs, the objective is rather to contextualize the remainder of the analysis in this report by highlighting commonalities and variations among LDCs and comparing them with other country groups. The discussion considers, in particular, the prevalence and types of entrepreneurial activity in LDCs and the characteristics of entrepreneurs. The evidence reviewed is merely suggestive, and none of the available indicators corresponds exactly to the working definition of entrepreneurship discussed in chapter 1. However, it is possible to glean some

insights and identify some stylized facts about several dimensions of entrepreneurship that are critical to structural transformation.

1. The prevalence of entrepreneurial activities in the least developed countries

It is well documented that wage employment is relatively limited in LDC labour markets, while various forms of self-employment, including as employers, own-account workers and family workers, are visibly more prevalent, notably in rural areas and in the urban informal sector (Margolis, 2014; UNCTAD, 2014a; UNCTAD, 2015a; World Bank, 2012). The incidence of self-employment in LDCs is high, even by developing country standards, at 70 per cent of total employment, compared with 50 per cent in other developing countries, with an estimated 268 million self-employed workers in 2017 (figure 2.3). The prevalence of self-employment has declined somewhat over time in almost all LDCs,[7] but relatively slowly, suggesting that it will remain a critical feature of labour markets in LDCs in the long term.

The greater prevalence of self-employment is by no means an unequivocal indication of a lively entrepreneurial scene, however. The breakdown of self-employment by employment status reveals a more serious situation, in particular from the perspective of structural transformation (figure 2.4).

Figure 2.3

Self-employment as share of total employment in the least developed countries and other developing countries, period averages, 1990–2017

(Percentage)

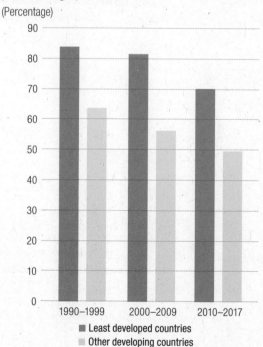

■ Least developed countries
▢ Other developing countries

Source: UNCTAD secretariat calculations, based on data from ILOstat database.

Figure 2.4

Self-employment by employment status, as share of total employment in the least developed countries, 2017

(Percentage)

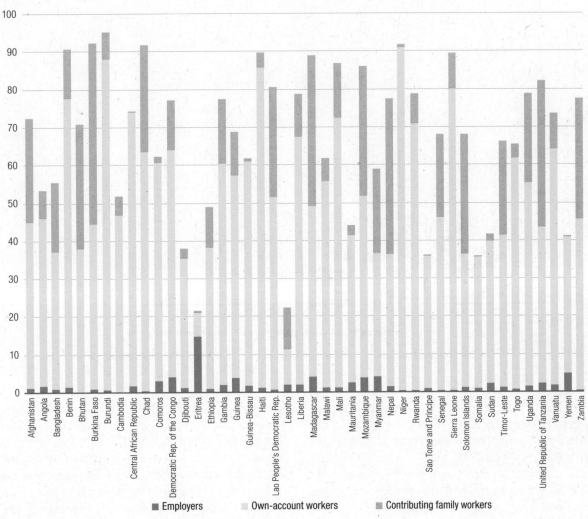

■ Employers   Own-account workers   ■ Contributing family workers

Source: UNCTAD secretariat calculations, based on data from ILOstat database.

There is considerable variability among individual economies, yet the overwhelming majority of self-employed workers in LDCs can more accurately be defined as own-account workers; in 2017, this category accounted for nearly 70 per cent of self-employment in LDCs (185 million people). Contributing family workers, typically predominant in agriculture, accounted for 28 per cent (76 million people) and the remaining 3 per cent (close to 8 million people) were employers.[8] Therefore, while self-employment is ubiquitous in LDCs, only a fraction of the self-employed may be considered truly entrepreneurial or engaged in progressive forms of entrepreneurship. Existing empirical studies broadly put this proportion at around one third for developing countries as a whole (Gindling and Newhouse, 2012; Grimm et al., 2012; Margolis, 2014).

The adult population surveys of GEM also indicate a significant prevalence in LDCs of both early-stage and established entrepreneurs, broadly defined (figure 2.5; see annex 1 for country and year coverage in GEM data used in figures 2.5–2.7 and 2.9–2.15).[9] The unweighted average in the 11 LDCs for which data are available suggests that close to half of the adult population is, on average, engaged in entrepreneurial activity in some form; 29 per cent are engaged in total early-stage entrepreneurial activity and 18 per cent, in established businesses, compared with 16 and 8 per cent, respectively, in other developing countries, and 9 and 7 per cent in developed and transition economies. Adults in LDCs are twice as likely as those in other developing countries to be engaged in entrepreneurial activities, broadly defined. The pervasiveness of business-related occupations

Figure 2.5

Early-stage and established entrepreneurship, latest available year

(Percentage)

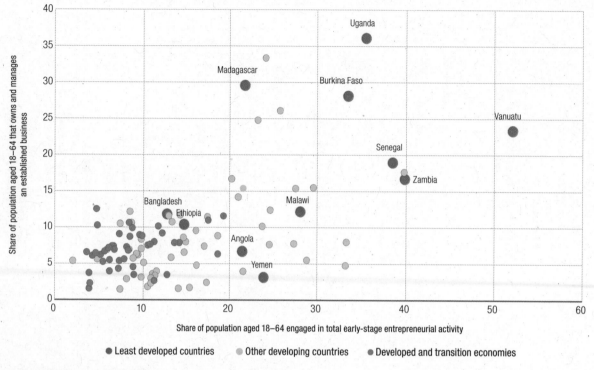

Source: UNCTAD secretariat calculations, based on data from GEM database.

in LDCs is accompanied by favourable societal values towards entrepreneurship; an unweighted average of 86 per cent of adults state that successful entrepreneurs receive high status and 76 per cent, that starting a business is a good career choice; these are more favourable views than in other developing countries and developed economies (GEM, 2017; GEM, 2018). Entrepreneurial intentions also appear more optimistic in LDCs than elsewhere; 44 per cent of adults not already involved in entrepreneurial activities report an intention to start a business within three years.

GEM data also show an apparent disconnect between generalized perceptions about the business world in LDCs and the more complex reality experienced by those who cross the "entrepreneurial Rubicon" from considering establishing a business to doing so (Delanoë-Gueguen and Fayolle, 2018). In eight of the 11 LDCs for which data are available, a substantial majority of adults consider that there are good opportunities to start a business, and in 10 of the 11 LDCs, that they possess the necessary skills to do so (figure 2.6). These views appear optimistic, both in absolute terms and by international standards.[10] Risk aversion in LDCs, as proxied by the GEM "fear of failure" variable, is not significantly different than in other country groups.[11]

Based on their motivational index and growth expectations, early entrepreneurs in LDCs appear less optimistic (figure 2.7). Aside from the greater prevalence of necessity-driven rather than opportunity-driven motivations, as discussed in section C.2, the proportion of early entrepreneurs with high job-growth expectations is particularly low in LDCs: on average, 9 per cent expect to create six or more jobs within five years, compared with 21 per cent in both other developing countries and developed and transition economies.

Data from perception-based surveys should be treated with caution and GEM recognizes issues with regard to its reliability, especially in cross-country comparisons at different points in time (Timm, 2018). There is also the issue of reference dependence, to the extent that the level and nature of economic activity itself influences perceptions; it is plausible that the ubiquity of small-scale businesses with low margins and low barriers to entry give rise to exaggerated perceptions of the extent and accessibility of business opportunities.

Overall, therefore, the entrepreneurship landscape in LDCs is mixed, as presented in this section. Between half and two thirds of the labour force in LDCs is typically engaged in notionally

Figure 2.6

Perceptions of the adult population on entrepreneurship, latest available year

(Percentage)

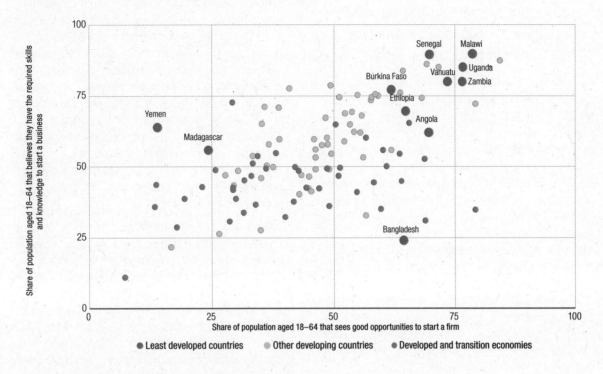

Source: UNCTAD secretariat calculations, based on data from GEM database.

Figure 2.7

Motivational index and growth expectations of early entrepreneurs, latest available year

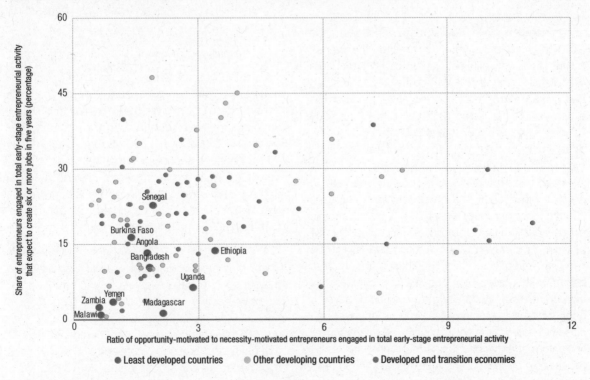

Source: UNCTAD secretariat calculations, based on data from GEM database.

Note: The motivational index, as defined by GEM, represents the ratio of opportunity-motivated to necessity-motivated entrepreneurs engaged in total early-stage entrepreneurial activity. .

Between half and two thirds of the labour force in LDCs is engaged in notionally entrepreneurial activities, but their contribution to structural transformation is limited

---

entrepreneurial activities, depending on the indicator used, suggesting considerable entrepreneurial potential. However, the contribution to structural transformation is more limited, as a disproportionate share of such activities is confined to small-scale and often informal survivalist businesses. This shortcoming is further underlined by the low level of job creation anticipated by entrepreneurs themselves. Redressing this situation requires disentangling the various types of entrepreneurial activities and leveraging those that present the greatest innovative potential. This is particularly important because structural transformation in LDCs is likely to require a consolidation of the entrepreneurial landscape through job creation by more productive and innovative enterprises, to absorb the survivalist self-employed into wage employment.

2. Traits of entrepreneurship in the least developed countries

There is growing consensus that the role of entrepreneurship in development cannot be fully understood without unravelling the varied contributions of different types of entrepreneurs (Hessels and Naudé, 2017; Margolis, 2014; Quatraro and Vivarelli, 2015). In this context, entrepreneurship is typically characterized according to dichotomies such as formal and informal enterprises and opportunity-driven and necessity-driven entrepreneurs. Such conceptual distinctions are highly pertinent in LDCs, in which such divides are particularly marked. In practice, however, distinguishing between enterprises for analytical purposes according to administrative or essentially subjective criteria, such as those based on motivation, is problematic and transitions between categories are by no means uncommon. Informal enterprises may become formalized, while entrepreneurs by necessity may, over time, develop opportunity-driven enterprises. In addition, although closely related, the distinctions between formal and informal and opportunity-driven and necessity-driven are by no means coextensive (Amin and Islam, 2015; Desai, 2011). However, a comparison of different entrepreneurship metrics, if appropriately contextualized and interpreted, can provide important insights into the nature of entrepreneurship in LDCs.

a. Formality and informality

The most obvious distinction is that between formal and informal enterprises. The lack of systematic and comprehensive data hinders a formal assessment, yet the pervasiveness of informal entrepreneurship can be indirectly gauged from the size of the informal economy in LDCs. A recent study of 158 countries suggests that the shadow economy (defined as all economic activities hidden from official authorities for monetary, regulatory or institutional reasons) accounts for, on average, approximately 35 per cent of GDP in LDCs, compared with 27.7 per cent worldwide (figure 2.8). However, the typically smaller size of informal enterprises compared with their formal counterparts suggests that they represent a considerably larger proportion of businesses.

The prevalence of informal and small-scale firms in LDCs is further demonstrated by the deviation between metrics of entrepreneurship derived from an occupational approach and new business density as measured by new registrations of limited liability companies. In contrast with the diffusion of business-related occupations, new business density in LDCs remains significantly low by international standards, notwithstanding some signs of dynamism.[12] Measures of entrepreneurship based on nascent and baby entrepreneurs are typically nearly 10 times as great as measures based on new business density, implying that the overwhelming majority of new businesses do not fall into the latter category (Acs et al., 2008; Desai, 2011).

b. Opportunity and necessity

The distinction between opportunity-driven and necessity-driven entrepreneurs is of particular importance in LDCs, given the key role of the former in structural transformation (African Development Bank et al., 2017; Brixiova, 2010; Struthers and Nziku, 2018). Although strongly connected, the dichotomies between formal and informal and opportunity-driven and necessity-driven are by no means equivalent, in that many opportunity-driven enterprises may choose to remain below the radar in the informal sector (Amin and Islam, 2015; see section D).

There is some variation between LDCs, yet overall they appear to have a particularly low motivational index, reflecting a relatively high proportion of necessity-driven entrepreneurs. On average, there are 1.7 times as many early entrepreneurs in LDCs that describe themselves as opportunity-driven rather than necessity-driven, compared with 2.8 times as many in other developing countries and 3.6 times as many in developed and transition economies (figure 2.9). At the national level, the proportion of necessity-driven early entrepreneurs in LDCs ranges from 22

Figure 2.8

Size of shadow economy as share of gross domestic product, 2013–2015

(Percentage)

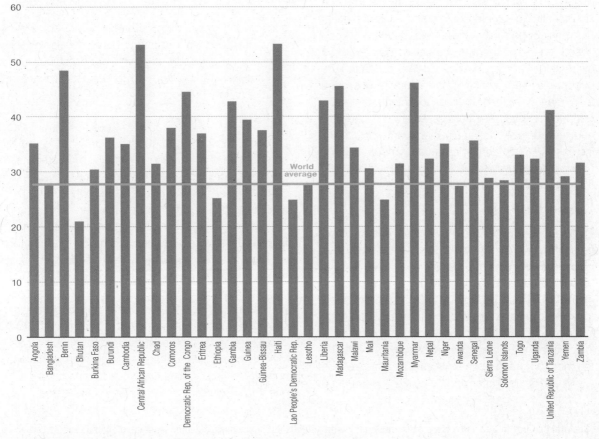

Source: UNCTAD secretariat calculations, based on data from International Monetary Fund, 2018.

Figure 2.9

Motivational index in selected least developed countries and by country group, latest available year

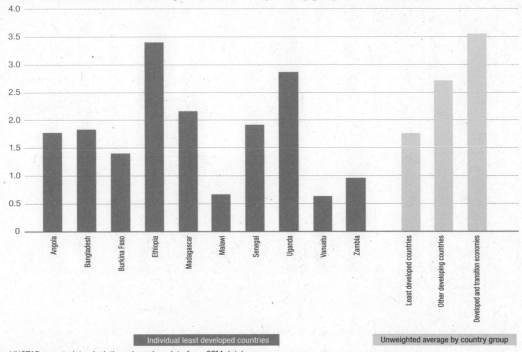

Source: UNCTAD secretariat calculations, based on data from GEM database.

Note: The motivational index, as defined by GEM, represents the ratio of opportunity-motivated to necessity-motivated entrepreneurs engaged in total early-stage entrepreneurial activity.

per cent in Ethiopia to 47 per cent in Malawi and Vanuatu.

Some caution is required in interpreting these figures due to the limited size of the sample and, more significantly, the subjective nature of the distinction between opportunity-driven and necessity-driven, based on respondent perceptions (box 2.1). For example, a woman selling corn or coffee on the street or a man waiting for a motorbike passenger at a market may be taking advantage of market opportunities, yet their businesses are not innovative and are unlikely to entail significant productivity increases. Such enterprises are more akin to underemployment as characterized by Lewis (1954) than to transformational businesses.

c. Innovation

The incidence of innovation among early entrepreneurs presents a broadly similar picture to that of motivation, regardless of reference dependence and possibly biased perceptions about how innovative products might be. Case studies in African LDCs show, for example, that "me-too businesses", based on imitations of existing activities, are predominant at lower levels of development and typically constitute the most common route for survivalist entrepreneurs (GEM, 2015; Herrington and Kelley, 2013; Wyngaard,

2015). On average, only 15 per cent of early entrepreneurs in LDCs report the introduction of a new product or service that few other businesses offer, substantially less than the 24 per cent in other developing countries and the 28 per cent in developed and transition economies.[13] Entrepreneurial employee activities, such as, among others, developing or launching new goods or services and setting up a new business unit, also tend to be less frequent in LDCs than in other country groups.

d. Sectoral composition

Limited innovation is reflected in the sectoral composition of activities in LDCs, which is dominated by those with low entry barriers and limited skill requirements.[14] In the nine LDCs for which data are available, the majority of activities are consumer-oriented services (such as personal services, social and recreational services and services in retail, motor vehicles, lodging, restaurants, health and education), which, on average, account for 63 per cent of early entrepreneurs and 57 per cent of established businesses (figure 2.10). Conversely, the backbone of structural transformation, that is, activities that GEM categorizes as falling under the transformative sector (namely construction, manufacturing, transportation, communications, utilities and wholesale) and business-oriented services (namely finance, insurance, real

Figure 2.10

Sectoral composition of early-stage entrepreneurship and established businesses, selected least developed countries, latest available year

(Percentage)

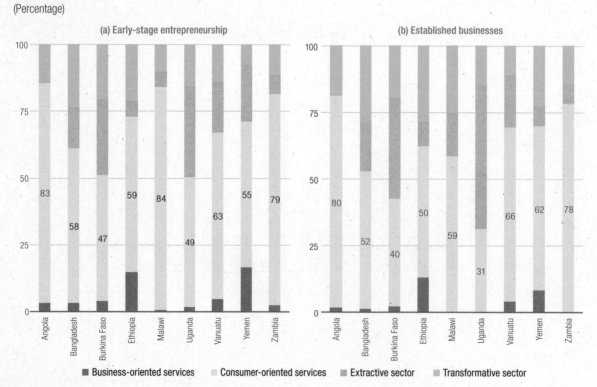

Source: UNCTAD secretariat calculations, based on data from GEM database.
Note: Figures refer to GEM database full national data sets.

estate and all business services) play a much more subdued role. Only 15 per cent of early entrepreneurs and 20 per cent of established businesses operate in the transformative sector and only 6 and 3 per cent, respectively, in business-oriented services. The extractive sector (namely agriculture, forestry, fishing and all mining activities) appears to be significant only in Burkina Faso, Uganda and Yemen and, to a lesser extent, in Bangladesh and Vanuatu.

This contrasts sharply with the situation in other developing countries and developed economies, in which the transformative sector and business-oriented services play a much more prominent role. In other developing countries, the transformative sector accounts for, on average, 23 per cent of early entrepreneurs (a level achieved solely by Bangladesh among LDCs) and business-oriented services account for 10 per cent. The contrast with developed and transition economies is even more sharp; on average, 25 per cent of early entrepreneurs in these economies operate in the transformative sector and 27 per cent, in business-oriented services.

> ## Me-too-businesses constitute the most common route for survivalist entrepreneurs in sectors with low entry barriers and low margins

These findings largely reflect the modest progress towards economic diversification made to date in LDCs and the concentration of non-agricultural employment creation in low-productivity services, which lead to little or no increase in labour productivity (UNCTAD, 2015a; UNCTAD, 2016a). There have been some signs of productivity-enhancing structural transformation since the mid-2000s (McMillan et al., 2014; McMillan et al., 2017). However, the evidence presented here suggests that entrepreneurship potential translates to a limited extent into innovative businesses capable of playing a catalytic role in structural transformation, catch-up growth and economic diversification in LDCs. This raises

Figure 2.11

Importance of early-stage entrepreneurship relative to established businesses, selected least developed countries, latest available year

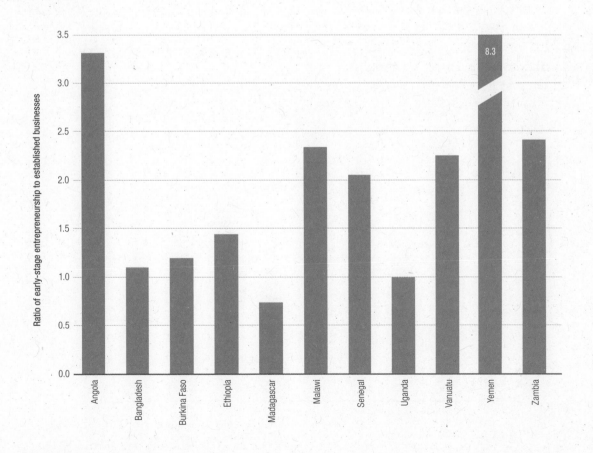

Source: UNCTAD secretariat calculations, based on data from GEM database.
Note: Figures refer to GEM database full national data sets.

first five years (Johnson, 2005; Quatraro and Vivarelli, 2015). Moreover, survival rates are ceteris paribus lower among firms with smaller start-up sizes and, in particular, low-margin businesses, whose success largely depends on their ability to fill a strategic niche or acquire the capability to engage in international trade (Agarwal and Audretsch, 2001; Page and Söderbom, 2015; Wagner, 2013).

Data on firm discontinuation appear to reinforce such concerns, particularly in countries in Africa (Herrington and Kelley, 2013). In most LDCs for which data are available, with some variation, there are high discontinuation rates (figure 2.12).[15] On average, 14 per cent of the adult population in LDCs report having exited a business in the past year, compared with 6 per cent in other developing countries and 3 per cent in developed and transition economies. In most cases of exit, the business itself was discontinued (figure 2.12 vertical axis), suggesting that limited sustainability is a major driver.

This is further underlined by the main reasons for exit. Personal reasons and incidents play an important role, yet the most important economic driver of exit by far is low profitability. On average among LDCs, 29 per cent of those who discontinued a business did so because it was unprofitable, and this is the most important factor in five of the nine LDCs for which data are available (namely Bangladesh, Burkina Faso, Malawi,

Notwithstanding high entrepreneurship potential, LDCs are characterized by low survival rates and less transformative firms

questions regarding the definition and measurement of entrepreneurship and the contribution of current patterns of entrepreneurship in LDCs to structural transformation.

e. Life cycle

The entrepreneurial landscape in many LDCs tends to be skewed towards early stages of entrepreneurship, although with considerable variation between countries (figure 2.11). In six of the 11 LDCs for which data are available (namely Angola, Malawi, Senegal, Vanuatu, Yemen and Zambia), there are more than twice as many early entrepreneurs as established entrepreneurs. Large numbers of start-ups and young businesses may in principle signify a vibrant and competitive environment, yet coupled with relatively limited numbers of established businesses, they may also indicate poor firm survival and high levels of discontinuation. Available econometric evidence suggests that survival rates are quite low; more than 50 per cent of new firms exit the market within the

Figure 2.12

Business discontinuation rates, latest available year

(Percentage)

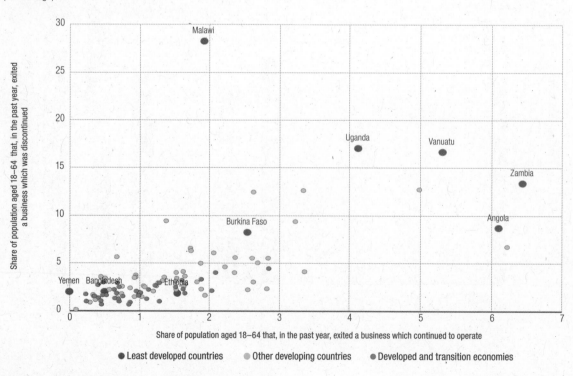

Source: UNCTAD secretariat calculations, based on data from GEM database.
Note: Figures refer to GEM database full national data sets.

Figure 2.13

Reasons for business exit, selected least developed countries, latest available year

(Percentage)

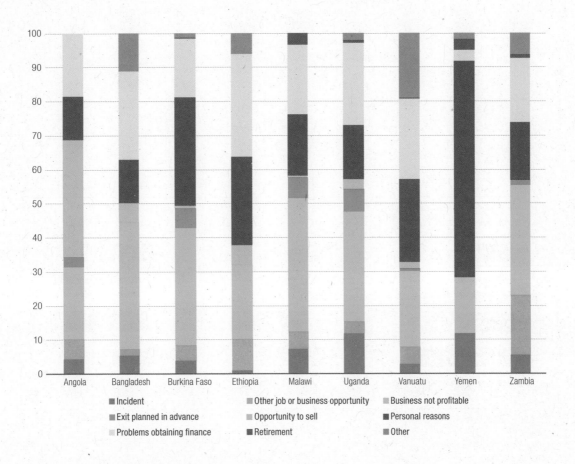

■ Incident   ■ Other job or business opportunity   ■ Business not profitable

■ Exit planned in advance   ■ Opportunity to sell   ■ Personal reasons

■ Problems obtaining finance   ■ Retirement   ■ Other

Source: UNCTAD secretariat calculations, based on data from GEM database.
Note: Figures refer to GEM database full national data sets.

Uganda and Zambia), including some that may be assumed to be the most entrepreneurial (figure 2.13). In some countries, notably Ethiopia and Zambia, a significant number of people also discontinued their businesses because of better opportunities, highlighting the limited appeal of many businesses as an occupation. Business discontinuation in LDCs is rarely planned in advance or motivated by retirement, and positive reasons to exit, such as an opportunity to sell the business, appear to be significant only in Angola. Financial constraints are a significant challenge in entrepreneurship in most LDCs, yet they are less relevant in explaining business exit than low profitability.

3. Who are entrepreneurs in the least developed countries?

As well as shedding light on patterns of entrepreneurship and the related challenges, the demographic profile of entrepreneurs, for example in terms of age, educational attainment and gender, can help inform policymaking, in particular with regard to goals such as poverty reduction, employment creation and women's empowerment.

a. Age

Population dynamics and labour market trends make employment generation critical in LDCs, especially for the 11 million youth entering the labour market each year (UNCTAD, 2013a). This youth bulge is also conspicuous in the demographic characteristics of entrepreneurs. In the nine LDCs for which data are available, young adults (18–24 years) account for an unweighted average of 28 per cent of early entrepreneurs, around double the shares in other developing countries and developed and transition economies, at 17 and 13 per cent, respectively (figure 2.14). This share is greatest in LDCs characterized by faster demographic growth and young population structures, such as Yemen (40 per cent), Uganda (38 per cent) and Zambia (29 per cent). The difference

Figure 2.14

Early and established entrepreneurs by country group and age, latest available year

(Percentage)

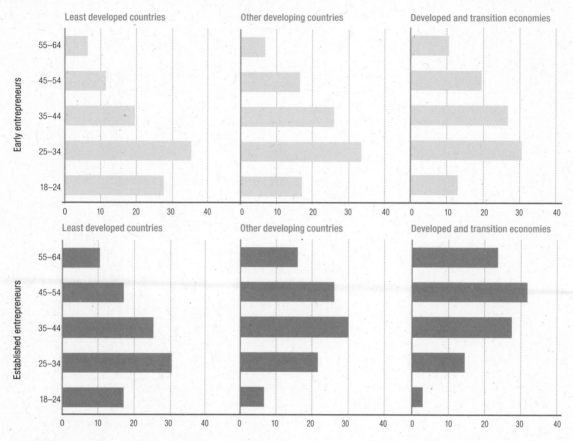

Source: UNCTAD secretariat calculations, based on data from GEM database.
Note: Figures are unweighted averages.

compared with other country groups is greater with regard to established entrepreneurs; on average, young adults account for 17 per cent of the total in LDCs (and more than 30 per cent in Yemen and Zambia), compared with 7 per cent in other developing countries and 3 per cent in developed and transition economies. This may not be surprising given the high levels of youth unemployment prevalent in many LDCs, yet the poorer economic outcomes and odds of survival of businesses established to escape unemployment (Quatraro and Vivarelli, 2015) make this pattern a matter of concern from the perspective of structural transformation.

In terms of overall age distribution, those of 25–34 years of age predominate among early entrepreneurs in all country groups. However, LDCs are distinguished by a more rapid decline in the weight of older cohorts (35–44, 45–54 and 55–64 years) among both early entrepreneurs and, to a lesser extent, established entrepreneurs. Those of 18–34 years of age constitute the majority of early entrepreneurs in LDCs and more than two thirds of early entrepreneurs

in some countries, such as Ethiopia, Malawi and Uganda. By contrast, the weight of older cohorts in the distribution of early entrepreneurs declines more gradually in other developing countries and a fortiori in developed and transition economies, in which those of 35–44 years of age are the second largest group. The distinctive age profile in LDCs implies a substantially lower median age of entrepreneurs, in particular established entrepreneurs, than elsewhere.

b. Education

Entrepreneurship in LDCs is also characterized by a low level of educational attainment among entrepreneurs by international standards, consistent with patterns in the population as a whole. On average, only 12 per cent of early entrepreneurs have a post-secondary education in LDCs, compared with 36 per cent in other developing countries and 50 per cent in developed and transition economies. However, these averages hide considerable inter-State variations, with proportions above 20 per cent in Angola and Ethiopia and below 5 per cent in Burkina Faso, Malawi and Yemen.

Educational attainment is often considered a proxy for human capital, yet it does not necessarily reflect either the quality of education or business-related skills, which rarely feature in curricula in LDCs. Studies have often found that technical and managerial skills are one of the main constraints to entrepreneurship in LDCs (African Development Bank et al., 2017; Herrington and Kelley, 2013; UNCTAD, 2012a).

These distinctive features of the entrepreneurial landscape in LDCs have an important bearing on the scope for different and possibly more transformational forms of entrepreneurship, including through technological upgrading and the uptake of ICT. The young age structure of entrepreneurs, coupled with increasing enrolment ratios in LDCs, suggests that the average educational attainment of entrepreneurs in LDCs could increase relatively rapidly over time. However, as well as increasing managerial capacities, and thereby the appeal of a business career, higher levels of education can be expected to increase options for wage employment. In the majority of developing countries, the latter effect outweighs the former, so that educational attainment appears to reduce the probability of self-employment (Van der Sluis et al., 2005). This might strengthen the consolidation of the entrepreneurial landscape, especially if the level

While **women participate** nearly **as much as men** in early-stage entrepreneurship,

they are **5 times** less likely **to own** a company

of education is positively correlated with opportunity-driven entrepreneurship, as for example in South Africa (Herrington and Kelley, 2013).

c. Gender

Early-stage entrepreneurial activity appears to be relatively more balanced between women and men in LDCs than in other countries, including a number of developed countries, signified by their greater

Figure 2.15

Gender-related gaps in total early-stage entrepreneurial activity, latest available year

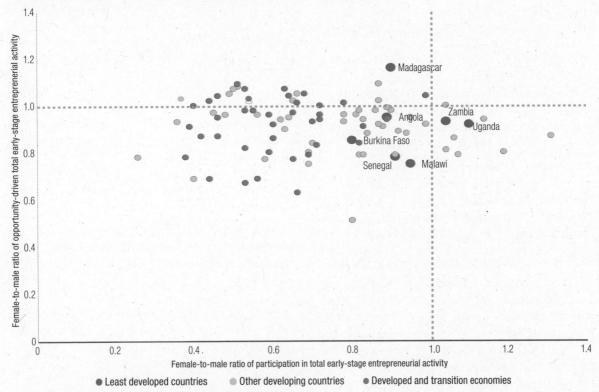

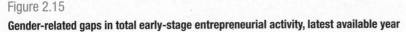

● Least developed countries　● Other developing countries　● Developed and transition economies

Source: UNCTAD secretariat calculations, based on data from GEM database.

Note: Vertical dashed line represents gender equality in participation in total early-stage entrepreneurial activity and horizontal dashed line represents gender equality in the weight of opportunity-driven early entrepreneurs.

Figure 2.16

Gender-related gaps in newly registered limited liability companies, selected least developed countries, 2016

(Percentage)

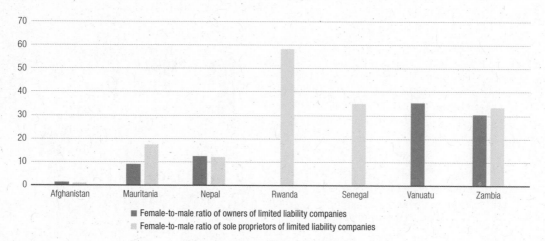

■ Female-to-male ratio of owners of limited liability companies
■ Female-to-male ratio of sole proprietors of limited liability companies

Source: UNCTAD secretariat calculations, based on data from World Bank Doing Business database.
Note: Data are unavailable with regard to owners of limited liability companies in Rwanda and Senegal and sole proprietors of limited liability companies in Vanuatu.

proximity to the vertical dashed line in figure 2.15. The average female-to-male ratio of participation in total early-stage entrepreneurial activity is 0.94 for LDCs, compared with 0.77 for other developing countries and 0.61 for developed and transition economies.

This apparently positive picture, however, largely reflects the disproportionate prevalence of survivalist forms of entrepreneurship among women in LDCs, whereas a lack of gender equality is more pronounced in more transformational forms of entrepreneurship.[16] The fact that most LDCs are below the horizontal line in figure 2.15 shows that women are relatively underrepresented among opportunity-driven early entrepreneurs, although not substantially more so than in other developing countries or in developed and transition economies; the female-to-male ratio averages 0.9 in all three country groups.

Gender-disaggregated data on registrations of newly registered limited liability companies, although not complete, indicate still wider gender-related gaps with regard to the participation of women in such companies (figure 2.16). Socioeconomic and idiosyncratic cultural factors play an important role, yet there is a considerable level of gender inequality in LDCs in this regard, even by already high international standards. In the seven LDCs for which data are available, women are five times less likely than men to be owners of newly registered limited liability companies and four times less likely to be sole proprietors. This reflects the extent to which factors such as unequal access to wealth, inheritance and finance constrain women's opportunities for more sophisticated forms of entrepreneurship.

D. Key sectors in the least developed countries: The informal sector and rural enterprise

1. The informal sector

The informal sector in LDCs is dominated by microenterprises and, to a lesser extent, small enterprises. The World Bank Enterprise Surveys of the informal sector find that, in the eight LDCs for which underlying questionnaires are directly comparable,[17] 74 per cent of informal enterprises are microenterprises with fewer than five employees; 20 per cent are small firms with five to nine employees; 6 per cent are small–medium, medium-sized and medium–large firms together; and there are no large firms. With regard to the weight of microenterprises in the total, Angola has the most diverse balance (30 per cent) and Madagascar has the least (97 per cent) (figure 2.17).

Informal enterprises make heavy use of unpaid workers, frequently including family members, who account for an overall average of 38 per cent of the employees; the proportion ranges from 11 per cent in Angola to 75 per cent in Madagascar. Within the pooled sample of informal enterprises from the Enterprise Surveys, there is a statistically significant negative correlation (-0.21) between the share of unpaid workers and the size of informal enterprises; the share declines steadily, from 43 per cent in microenterprises to 1 per cent in medium–large enterprises (figure 2.18). However, the incidence

Figure 2.17

Composition of the informal sector by size of enterprise based on number of employees, selected least developed countries

(Percentage)

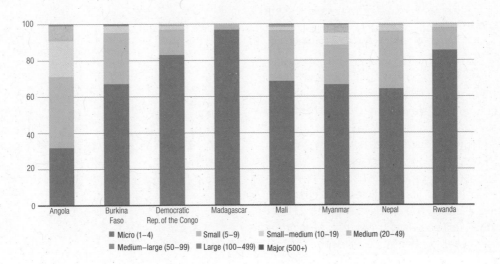

Source: UNCTAD secretariat calculations, based on data from World Bank Enterprise Surveys.

of unpaid labour among distinct size categories is relatively similar in some LDCs, such as in Burkina Faso and Mali, and erratic in others, such as in Rwanda.

Figure 2.18

Informal labour force composition by size of enterprise, selected least developed countries

(Percentage)

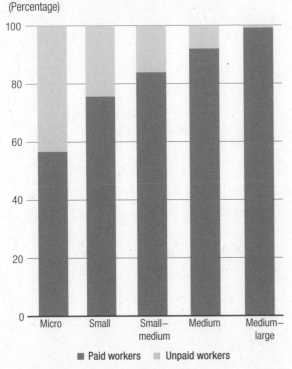

Source: UNCTAD secretariat calculations, based on data from World Bank Enterprise Surveys.

The data from the World Bank Enterprise Surveys of the informal sector also highlight a significant lack of gender equality in unpaid labour and ownership within the sector. In the pooled sample for eight LDCs, 50 per cent of women employed in informal enterprises are unpaid, compared with 33 per cent of men, and only 30 per cent of firms feature a woman as their main owner.

Most necessity-driven entrepreneurs are likely to be in the informal sector, as noted in section C.2, yet so are some opportunity-driven entrepreneurs. Whether an enterprise is in the formal or informal sector is essentially the result of a decision, or at least a tacit decision, on the part of the entrepreneur, based on the costs and benefits of formalization. This is related, in part, to the time and financial costs of the formalization process, as well as to the financial and non-financial costs and benefits of a formal rather than an informal enterprise, for example in terms of taxation, regulation and access to finance. Understanding the nature of this process is important, to both disentangle the potential contribution of the enterprise sector to structural transformation and enhance the formulation of enterprise policies.

Data from the World Bank Enterprise Surveys suggest that 50–90 per cent of informal entrepreneurs in LDCs would like to register their businesses, with some variation between countries and sectors.[18] The conventional wisdom is that business registration is discouraged by administrative costs, higher tax rates, corruption and fear of inspections (Djankov et al., 2002; International Monetary Fund, 2018; UNCTAD, 2012a) and this is broadly confirmed by the reasons given for non-registration in LDCs (figure 2.19). The greater unwillingness to register in contexts in which unpaid labour is more prevalent suggests that the burden of social security contributions is also a significant factor. However, decision-making on formalization is by no means straightforward. Accessibility of information about registration is also an important and unnecessary obstacle in some cases, notably in Angola, Mali and Nepal. Moreover, while costs may be certain and readily quantifiable, benefits are more elusive and are contingent on firm performance following registration, especially when enterprises rely on unpaid labour or have little expectation of legal protection or access to credit. In Afghanistan, Burkina Faso and Nepal and to a lesser extent in Mali, a substantial proportion of informal entrepreneurs see no potential benefits to registering their businesses.

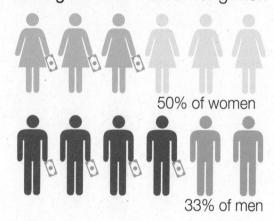

Unpaid work in the informal sector – is more common among women than among men

50% of women

33% of men

Figure 2.19

Main reasons for not registering an informal business, selected least developed countries

(Percentage)

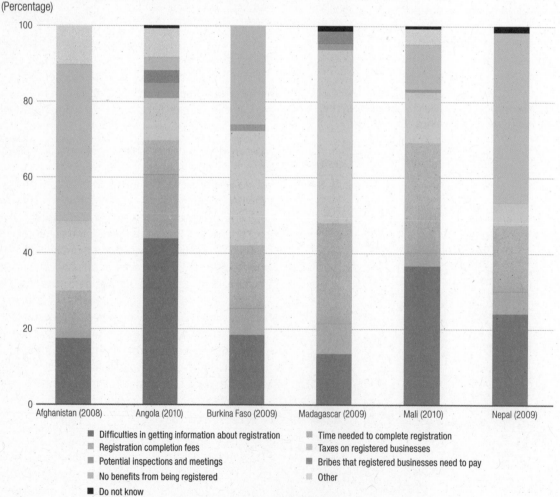

Source: UNCTAD secretariat calculations, based on data from World Bank Enterprise Surveys.

Note: Evidence is only presented for those LDCs for which the format of the relevant questions is directly comparable and not those for which the corresponding question has a wholly different wording or a different range of response options.

There is also some evidence that the incentive structures created by entry regulations may affect the size of informal establishments and post-registration firm performance (Amin and Islam, 2015; Williams et al., 2017). For some enterprises, at least, informality may be the result of a deliberate strategic decision on the "optimal degree of participation in formal institutions" (Maloney, 2004). The predominance of microenterprises and small enterprises within the informal sector may therefore stem partly from deliberate decisions by relatively productive firms to remain small as a means of limiting evasion costs, that is, the costs of remaining unregistered and not being detected by authorities.

For young firms, informality may represent a deliberate, and possibly transitory, choice to engage in cost discovery without incurring the fixed costs associated with registration, as a means of reducing the costs associated with the liabilities of newness and ensuring the viability of their business models before registration. This could help explain why formal enterprises that delayed registration subsequently outperform those that registered in the start-up phase (Williams et al., 2017).

2. Rural non-farm enterprises

Transformation of the rural economy plays a central role in structural transformation in LDCs and, as in the broader economy, enterprise is central to this process (see chapter 1). The nature of enterprise in rural areas differs significantly, however, from enterprise in urban areas. Empirical studies show that in rural areas, household decisions to engage in non-farming activities and diversify income sources are multidimensional, reflecting a combination of risk mitigation, seasonality of agricultural labour demand and potential areas of specialization within households, that is, they stem from the interplay of push and pull factors (Davis et al., 2017; Nagler and Naudé, 2017).

A distinctive feature of rural entrepreneurship is the possibility, for most entrepreneurs, of alternating between agricultural production and non-farm entrepreneurship. The seasonality and uncertainty of agricultural income is an important driver, as such entrepreneurship is motivated partly by the need to smooth income over time and reduce risk and uncertainty in the absence of adequate insurance and credit markets, along with limited opportunities for wage employment (Tamvada, 2010). Some studies indicate that high levels of risk in agriculture in Africa are a strong push factor in encouraging entrepreneurship. Food shortages in the preceding 12 months have been found to be a driver of rural

> **A distinctive feature of rural entrepreneurship is the possibility of alternating between agricultural production and non-farm entrepreneurship**

entrepreneurship (Nagler and Naudé, 2017) and there is evidence of income diversification by farming households in response to the risk of harvest failure or unanticipated shocks. The family firm that emerges from non-farm entrepreneurship can effectively provide informal insurance (Dercon, 2009; Liedholm and Kilby, 1989).

Linkages between agriculture and non-farm entrepreneurial activities are an important pull factor, giving rise to a potential virtuous circle of agricultural non-farm entrepreneurship development, driven by rising demand for agricultural inputs, agroprocessing and consumer goods (Mellor and Lele, 1973) and providing resources and incentives for increased investment in both sectors. Equally, the insurance provided by non-farm entrepreneurship allows farmers to undertake riskier and more profitable activities.

The interconnection of non-farm entrepreneurship activities and the complex pattern of income diversification at the individual and household levels, together with the lack of data and wide variations between countries in the definitions of rural and urban areas, make systematic analysis of rural entrepreneurship problematic (UNCTAD, 2015a). However, some general observations are possible on the basis of local and national studies, as noted in this subsection.

a. Prevalence

Rural entrepreneurship and engagement in non-farm entrepreneurship appear widespread in LDCs. Non-farm rural income, however, tends to be concentrated in richer rural households, who also have greater shares in non-agricultural wage employment, whereas less well-off households derive income mainly from crops, livestock and agricultural wage labour (Davis et al., 2017).

Considering the level of development of domestic economies, rural households in Africa are no less engaged in non-farm entrepreneurship than in other regions, with a greater focus on non-farm household enterprises than non-agricultural wage employment. In six LDCs in Africa, namely Ethiopia, Malawi, the

Rural households closer to towns are more likely to be engaged in non-farm entrepreneurship

Niger, Nigeria, Uganda and the United Republic of Tanzania, no less than 42 per cent of rural households have enterprises in the non-farm sector (Davis et al., 2017). There is, however, a high turnover and exit rate among rural enterprises, with many firms operating for only part of the year, and non-farm entrepreneurship survival is strongly affected by seasonality (Nagler and Naudé, 2017).

Despite the high prevalence of non-farm activities, non-farm entrepreneurship generally remains less important than agriculture as an income source. Overall, 92 per cent of rural households in Africa are involved in agriculture, which represents 69 per cent of total income for the average rural household in the region (Davis et al., 2017). Non-farm entrepreneurship, conversely, generates barely 15 per cent of overall rural household income in Africa, compared with, for example, 39 per cent in Brazil, 50 per cent in Chile and Colombia, 46 per cent in China, 59 per cent in Costa Rica, 55 per cent in Mexico and 51 per cent in Peru (Escobal, 2001; De Janvry and Sadoulet, 2001; Lanjouw and Lanjouw, 2001; Shi et al., 2007). In Ethiopia, 27 per cent of all households obtain half or more of their total income from non-farm entrepreneurship and 5 per cent of these receive all their income from that source (Nagler and Naudé, 2017). In urban areas, the share of income derived from self-employment is typically higher, for example, 22 per cent in Malawi, 48 per cent in the Niger, 33 per cent in Uganda and 43 per cent in the United Republic of Tanzania (Nagler and Naudé, 2017).

b. Size and sector

The majority of rural non-farm entrepreneurship is composed of microenterprises and small enterprises, and 95 per cent employ fewer than five workers in some African LDCs (Nagler and Naudé, 2017). A study of four districts in Ethiopia found that farm experience had a positive impact on non-farm entrepreneurship and that households with larger landholdings were less likely to engage in such entrepreneurship, while those with less than 1.43 hectares tended to rely more on non-farm income (Alemu and Adesina, 2017). In larger families, to the extent that labour exceeds the needs for a fixed supply of farmland, some family members may be pushed into entrepreneurship. Equally, however, the availability of labour and capital might be a pull factor stimulating entrepreneurship

(Reardon, 1997; Reardon et al., 2007; Reardon et al., 2009).

New enterprises in rural areas in African LDCs tend to be established in sectors with low entry barriers, such as sales and trading activities, and there is a lack of investment in higher value added activities such as transport, education and other professional services (Nagler and Naudé, 2017). In the early stages of rural transformation, consumption linkages with the farm sector tend to predominate, leading to an initial concentration of non-farm entrepreneurship in services and cottage industries. However, as transformation progresses and incomes rise, other types of linkages become more important, namely backward production linkages from agricultural inputs and forward linkages to agroprocessing activities.

c. Location

Geography and location are important determinants of the agglomeration effects of farm and non-farm enterprises, even where soil conditions and climate are identical (Davis et al. 2017). In LDCs in Africa, distances to large population centres play a major role in determining the success of rural enterprises (Nagler and Naudé, 2017). For example, in the Amhara region of Ethiopia, households located in rural towns are 21–24 per cent more likely than others to participate in non-farm entrepreneurship, and the figures are similar for households located closer to food markets (Rijkers et al., 2010). In addition, rural households closer to towns are more likely to be engaged in non-farm entrepreneurship, as their location allows for easier access to credit and telecommunications facilities (Alemu and Adesina, 2017).

In African and Asian LDCs, the proportion of non-farm wage employment is typically inversely related to household distance from urban areas (Fafchamps and Shilpi, 2003; Owoo and Naudé, 2017). In Nepal, however, there is a non-linear pattern in the location of rural enterprises; for example, in the high-value horticultural sector, wage employment tends to be clustered in rural areas that are close to cities but not close enough to be dominated by unskilled urban wage labour (Fafchamps and Shilpi, 2003).

d. Productivity and profitability

Labour productivity is also influenced by location, and is generally lower in rural rather than urban enterprises and in those further from large, usually urban, populations (Nagler and Naudé, 2017). In manufacturing enterprises in Ethiopia, for example, the output-to-labour ratio is 0.43 in remote rural areas, compared with 0.95 in rural towns and 2.30 in urban areas (Rijkers et al., 2010). Labour productivity is also lower in enterprises that operate only during certain times of the year, a pattern common in rural areas (Nagler and Naudé, 2017). Notably, the development of non-farm entrepreneurship tends to have a positive effect on agricultural productivity. The opportunity for non-farm entrepreneurship income also enhances average agricultural proceeds by providing resources for input purchases and increasing financial security, which allows farmers to adopt activities with higher risks but higher returns (Liedholm and Kilby, 1989).

The success of rural non-farm entrepreneurship varies between sectors and is strongly associated with proximity to markets, in particular urban markets; enterprise size; land tenure; and, to a lesser extent, with the gender and education levels of entrepreneurs. Many studies have shown that the availability of credit and access to finance are major determinants of the success of rural enterprises in LDCs (Baye, 2013; Singh and Belwal, 2008; Gajigo, 2014; Osondu, 2014). Similarly, literacy has been found to have a significant positive effect on the success of rural enterprises in African LDCs (Nagler and Naudé, 2017). For example, in the Amhara region of Ethiopia, those with greater access to electricity, the ability to use land as collateral and divorcées are more likely to run a non-farm entrepreneurship, and an inverse U-shaped relationship has been found between the likelihood of engaging in non-farming activities and the age and educational attainment of the household head (Rijkers and Söderbom, 2013). Prior income and wealth indicators, such as the number of rooms in a residence, have a positive impact on the success rate of rural enterprises in African LDCs (Nagler and Naudé, 2017).

Response to excessive risk may lead entrepreneurs to take on activities with potentially lower returns but lower volatility. A choice often made is to reduce investment in fixed capital such as equipment in favour of holding more liquid assets, including cash (Rijkers et al., 2010). In addition, short-term responses to shocks can have long-term negative effects on the livelihoods of individuals and households in rural communities (Dercon and Krishnan, 2000).

e. Gender

In African LDCs, labour productivity tends to be lower in rural non-farm enterprises headed by women rather than men, yet the entrepreneur's gender does not have an impact on the success rate of the rural enterprise (Nagler and Naudé, 2017). For example, in Ethiopia, men's participation is greater than women's in both farm and non-farm activities, but a significant role for women has a positive impact on non-farm entrepreneurship and, in the Amhara region,

women are more likely than men to run a non-farm entrepreneurship (Alemu and Adesina, 2017; Rijkers et al., 2010). Effective institutions, good governance and the availability of appropriate networks are particularly important for success among women entrepreneurs.

f. Social capital

Social capital, networking and trust play crucial roles in rural entrepreneurship, as either barriers or enablers. Networks such as farmers' associations, cooperatives and marketing bodies are often at the forefront of promoting rural development policies such as access to rural credit and extension services, for example in agrobusiness (Struthers and Nziku, 2018; Witt, 2004). For example, in four districts in Ethiopia, rural households that are active members of various farmers' networks and cooperatives participate more in non-farm entrepreneurship, as do rural households located nearer farmer's training centres (Alemu and Adesina, 2017).

E. Firm heterogeneity and structural transformation

There is a well-established literature assessing, through various approaches, the effects of the microeconomic characteristics of firms and of broader institutional and macroeconomic variables on firm performance (African Development Bank et al., 2017; Andreoni and Chang, 2016; Audretsch, 1995; Baumol, 1990; Djankov et al., 2002; Harrison et al., 2014; Naudé, 2013; Nkurunziza, 2010; Quatraro and Vivarelli, 2015). The latter include, inter alia, the wider business climate with regard to infrastructure provision, access to credit, protection of property rights, level of corruption, administrative conditions, trade facilitation provisions and other regulatory issues. For example, controlling for key differences in geography, infrastructure, access to finance and political and institutional factors, firms in Africa perform better than those in other regions at similar income levels (Harrison et al., 2014). Such factors are important determinants of the post-entry performance of new firms, yet are fraught with market failures, from information asymmetries to externalities. The poor quality of hard and soft infrastructure, as well as limited access to credit, can be binding constraints to enterprise performance.

Assessing the role of firm characteristics as determinants of firm performance is important with a view to informing enterprise policy. This section analyses formal non-agricultural enterprises in LDCs using firm-level data from the World Bank Enterprise

Box 2.2. **Firm heterogeneity and structural transformation: Analytical methodology**

The analysis considers the effects of firm characteristics on labour productivity growth and employment growth. Following the World Bank methodology, labour productivity growth is measured as the annual percentage change in labour productivity between the last fiscal year and two years previously, whereby labour productivity is measured as the value of sales, adjusted for inflation, divided by the number of permanent full-time employees, consistent with the relevant literature (see Amin and Islam, 2015; Ayyagari et al., 2011; Harrison et al., 2014). Employment growth is the annual percentage change in full-time permanent employees over the same period. A log transformation of the labour productivity growth and employment growth variables is used to stabilize variance. To resolve negative values, a constant (α) is added to the data prior to log transformation, such that $\min(Y + \alpha) = 1$. Two variants of the following specification are tested:

$$Y_{i,k,j,z,(t-1,t-3)} = \beta_0 + \beta_1 \text{ Size} + \beta_2 \text{ Age} + \delta_{i,k,j,z} + \beta_3 \text{ Region FE} + \beta_4 \text{ Country FE} + \varepsilon_{i,k,j,z}$$

where

$Y_{i,k,j,z,(t-1,t-3)}$ represents the performance indicator (the log transformation of labour productivity growth or employment growth) of firm i in country k, region j and industry z. $t-3$ is the beginning of the period for which growth rates are computed and firm size and age are measured. Firm size is measured in two complementary ways. In the first set of regressions it is measured as a continuous variable (the log of the number of permanent full-time employees); in the second set of regressions it is captured by dummy variables representing small, medium-sized and large firms, with 5–19, 20–99 and 100 or more permanent full-time employees, respectively. Firm age is consistently measured as a continuous variable expressing the number of years since the firm began operations, irrespective of registration status. Robustness checks, in which firm age is instead captured by a dummy variable for start-ups, are reported separately in Valensisi et al. (2018).

$\delta_{i,k,j,z}$ represents a set of additional control variables introduced in the second set of regressions, which include additional firm characteristics such as self-declared innovative behaviour, ownership structure, access to finance, gender and years of experience of the top manager, export status and whether or not the firm registered at start-up.

Region fixed effects and country fixed effects are included in all regressions to control for location-specific factors, such as differences in hard and soft infrastructure, consistent with the relevant literature.

β_0, the constant term, and $\varepsilon_{i,k,j,z}$, the error term, are included in all regressions.

In order to address potential endogeneity concerns, an instrumental variable approach (two-stage least squares) is adopted in the first set of regressions, whereby the number of employees at start-up is used as an instrument for firm size at $t-3$.

Source: UNCTAD secretariat.

Surveys for 39 LDCs. The data are described in section E.1, the methodology is set out in box 2.2 and the results are presented in section E.2. The following two key determinants of firm performance are assessed in order to shed light on how firm characteristics shape performance and, accordingly, their role in structural transformation:

- Labour productivity growth, which broadly encompasses the combined effect of capital deepening and increasing total factor productivity within each firm, as an indicator of the importance of high-growth firms in technological upgrading.

- Employment growth, as an indicator of the role of labour reallocation from low-productivity activities such as smallholding farming and petty trade to higher productivity businesses in the manufacturing and high-value services sectors.

1. Data

The analysis in this section uses pooled firm-level data from the World Bank Enterprise Surveys database

for 39 LDCs, covering the non-agricultural private economy, and thereby excluding fully government-owned firms. To ensure cross-country comparability, only surveys conducted according to the standard global methodology of the World Bank are included,[19] and only the most recent survey is used for countries surveyed more than once (see annex 2 for country and year coverage in World Bank Enterprise Survey data).[20] The surveys use a stratified random sampling approach, with three criteria of stratification, namely sector of activity, geographical location and firm size, whereby small firms have 5–19 employees, medium-sized firms have 20–99 employees and large firms have 100 or more employees. This provides an overall sample of 15,298 establishments prior to data cleaning, of which 44 per cent are in the manufacturing sector and 56 per cent are in services.

There are three caveats with regard to use of this data set. First, since only formal establishments with five or more employees are targeted by the surveys, the results presented in this section do not take into account the roles of microenterprises and informal enterprises.[21] Second, since the data relate only to surviving firms, the analysis cannot capture the effects of firm liquidation or the associated employment reduction. Third, the unit of analysis of the surveys is the establishment and not the firm, and this makes the measurement of the size of multi-establishment firms problematic, although it also allows for changes in the actual number of jobs to be captured more accurately by excluding apparent changes arising from mergers and acquisitions. However, 78 per cent of the establishments in the pooled sample are stand-alone establishments and the main results in this analysis are robust only with regard to this subsample of firms. Notwithstanding these limitations, the data set provides a representative picture of non-agricultural private firms in LDCs.

The data set shows that the balance of firms in LDCs, even among formal enterprises with at least five employees, is heavily skewed towards smaller establishments (figure 2.20). Firms with 5–10 employees account for some 35 per cent of the total, but the weight declines steeply as the number of employees increases. Large firms, with 100 or more employees, account for some 10 per cent, and the proportion of medium-sized firms,

The balance of firms in LDCs is heavily skewed towards smaller establishments and displays a "missing middle"

with 20–99 employees, is low, showing the validity of long-standing concerns over a "missing middle" and highlighting the dualistic structure of the enterprise landscape in LDCs, whereby a few large players coexist with a plethora of small competitors and suppliers. This corroborates detailed censuses of manufacturing firms in LDCs, such as Myanmar and the United Republic of Tanzania, which show a polarization between a multitude of small enterprises and a few large enterprises, whereby the latter often have a disproportionate level of market power (Andreoni, 2017; United Nations University-World Institute for Development Economics Research (UNU-WIDER) et al., 2018). This uneven structure indicates the weakness of the private sector in LDCs and poses significant challenges to the emergence of a dense network of production linkages, as discussed in previous editions of this report. In addition, it hampers domestic value addition, as domestic small and medium-sized enterprises (SMEs) are often unable to

Figure 2.20

Share of firms in sample by number of permanent full-time employees

(Percentage)

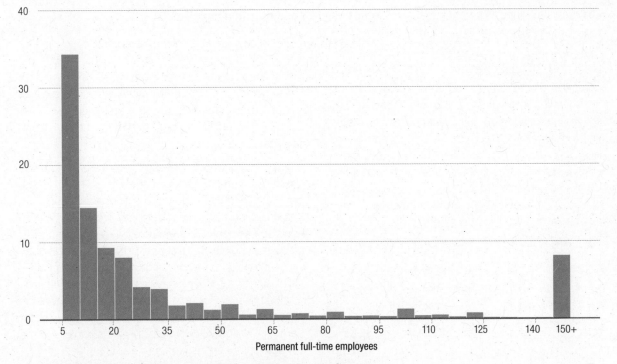

Permanent full-time employees

Source: UNCTAD secretariat calculations, based on data from World Bank Enterprise Surveys.

Notes: Data set comprises pooled firm-level data from World Bank Enterprise Surveys for 39 LDCs, covering the non-agricultural private economy, with only surveys conducted according to the standard global methodology of the World Bank included and only the most recent survey used for countries surveyed more than once; bin width is set at five permanent full-time employees.

Figure 2.21

Employment share by type of establishment

(Percentage)

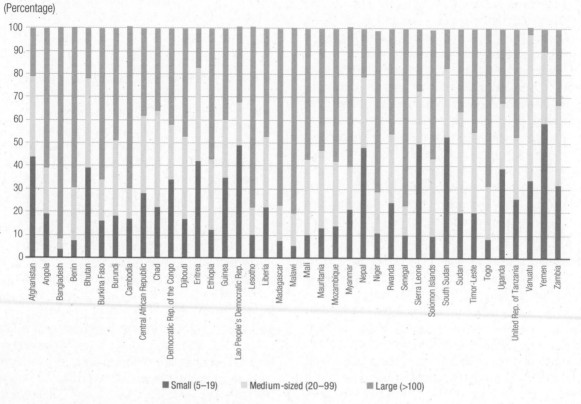

Source: UNCTAD secretariat calculations, based on data from World Bank Enterprise Surveys.
Notes: The employment share takes into account both permanent full-time employees and seasonal employees; the latter are considered pro rata, depending on the average duration of seasonal employment; sampling weights are considered in the estimation.

integrate into global value chains, either directly or as suppliers to larger exporters (see chapter 3).

SMEs provide a significant share of total employment in formal firms, although with wide variation between countries (figure 2.21). The median value of the employment share in all LDCs is 20 per cent for small enterprises, 30 per cent for medium-sized enterprises and 47 per cent for large enterprises. However, the net contribution of smaller firms to employment creation is likely to be more limited than their employment share, since the cross-sectional nature of the data implies that the net effects of firm exit are overlooked, and smaller firms tend to have lower survival rates (Page and Söderbom, 2015; Quatraro and Vivarelli, 2015). On average in all firm-level observations, women account for 27 per cent of full-time workers, with a higher incidence in SMEs (29 per cent of all full-time workers in small enterprises and 26 per cent in medium-sized enterprises) than in large enterprises (19 per cent). Temporary or seasonal workers represent some 6 per cent of total full-time equivalent employees, although again with wide variation between countries.

2. Empirical results

The effects of LDC firm characteristics on labour productivity growth and employment growth are discussed here, on the basis of the analytical methodology (box 2.2). Regression results are first reported for the full sample, then separately for subsamples of firms operating in the manufacturing and services sectors.

Table 2.2 presents the estimation results, focused exclusively on firm size and age, for the log of labour productivity growth and the log of employment growth as the dependent variable, specifying both firm size and age as continuous variables. The results suggest that the effects of firm size on labour productivity growth differ between sectors; they are positive and significant in the services sector, but negative, though non-significant, in the manufacturing sector. Older firms are found to experience significantly faster productivity growth, in both the full sample and the subsample of firms in the manufacturing sector.

The results indicate a significant positive relationship between firm size and labour productivity growth,

Table 2.2

Instrumental variable (two-stage least squares) regression results: Firm size and performance in the least developed countries

Dependent variable	Labour productivity growth			Employment growth		
	Full	**Manufacturing**	**Services**	**Full**	**Manufacturing**	**Services**
Models	*(1)*	*(2)*	*(3)*	*(4)*	*(5)*	*(6)*
Firm size	0.0098*	-0.0032	0.0269***	-0.0140***	-0.00725**	-0.0296***
(log of full-time employees)	(0.00516)	(0.0063)	(0.0101)	(0.00216)	(0.00289)	(0.00384)
Firm age	0.000811*	0.00143***	0.000123	-0.00108***	-0.00118***	-0.000876***
	(0.000435)	(0.000551)	(0.000695)	(0.000182)	(0.000253)	(0.000263)
Constant	3.771***	4.050***	3.697***	4.640***	4.629***	4.662***
	(0.0575)	(0.108)	(0.0743)	(0.024)	(0.0496)	(0.0282)
Observations	9070	4334	4736	9083	4345	4738
R-squared	0.193	0.17	0.214	0.081	0.069	0.119

Source: UNCTAD secretariat calculations, based on data from World Bank Enterprise Surveys.

Notes: The dependent variable is either the log of labour productivity growth (columns 1–3) or the log of employment growth (columns 4–6); columns 1 and 4 report results for the full sample; columns 2 and 5 for the subsample of firms in the manufacturing sector and columns 3 and 6 for the subsample of firms in the services sector; firm size and age are measured at t-3; values in parentheses represent the standard errors; *, ** and *** indicate a 10, 5 and 1 per cent significance level, respectively.

in both the full sample and the subsample of firms in the services sector. In the full sample, a 10 per cent increase in the number of full-time permanent employees is associated with a 0.1 per cent increase in labour productivity growth.

Conversely, both firm size and age have a significant depressive effect on employment growth, in both the full sample and the sectoral subsamples, indicating that smaller and younger firms tend to play a significantly stronger role in terms of employment creation. This finding may reflect a tendency towards greater labour intensity among small firms and/or the fact that younger firms may not yet have attained a minimum efficient scale and therefore remain in a process of expansion. The effect of firm age on employment growth is robust to an alternative definition of the former, namely a dummy variable that takes the value of 1 for firms in the first three years of activity (Valensisi et al., 2018).

Table 2.3 presents the result for a specification modified in three ways. First, the continuous measure of firm size is replaced with dummy variables for small, medium-sized and large firms based on employment in the year t-3. Second, additional control variables are introduced to account for firm characteristics; these are self-reported product and process innovations in the previous three years[22] and capital structure, with separate dummies for at least partial State ownership and foreign ownership. Finally, the analysis controls for access to finance, proxied by the availability of an overdraft facility; gender and years of experience of the top manager; export status; and whether or not the firm registered at start-up.

Even with these specifications, the significant and positive relationship between firm size and labour productivity growth is strongly confirmed. Firm age appears to have a positive yet weakly significant effect on productivity growth in the full sample, but not in the sectoral subsamples. Small firms have a significantly higher rate of employment growth than medium-sized and large firms, again in both the full sample and the sectoral subsamples. Firm age also appears to dampen employment growth significantly, as in the results shown in table 2.2. Overall, these findings are in line with those of Ayyagari et al. (2011), which show that in developing economies, controlling for firm age, small firms have significantly lower productivity growth than large firms.

The results reported in table 2.3 also suggest that innovation is positively and significantly associated with productivity growth in the subsample of firms in the manufacturing sector, and with employment growth in both the full sample and the sectoral subsamples. The involvement of government actors in ownership appears to have a significantly negative effect on productivity growth in the full sample, but not in the sectoral subsamples, and the involvement of foreign actors appears to have a positive effect on employment growth in the full sample and in the subsample of firms in the manufacturing sector, but not the subsample of firms in the services sector.

Access to finance consistently represents a significant boost to employment creation, while manager experience has — perhaps surprisingly — the opposite effect, although with a lower degree of significance and not for firms in the services sector.

Table 2.3

Regression results: Firm characteristics and performance in the least developed countries

Dependent variable	Labour productivity growth			Employment growth		
	Full	Manu-facturing	Services	Full	Manu-facturing	Services
Models	(1)	(2)	(3)	(4)	(5)	(6)
Medium-sized firm dummy	0.0367***	0.0340**	0.0396**	-0.0581***	-0.0696***	-0.0485***
	(0.0120)	(0.0166)	(0.0180)	(0.00517)	(0.00793)	(0.00721)
Large firm dummy	0.0563***	0.0577***	0.042	-0.0706***	-0.0742***	-0.105***
	(0.0164)	(0.0208)	(0.0347)	(0.00893)	(0.0116)	(0.0193)
Firm age	0.000734*	0.000838	0.000787	-0.000938***	-0.000746***	-0.00121***
	(0.000442)	(0.000549)	(0.000755)	(0.000203)	(0.000262)	(0.000318)
Innovation dummy	0.0173	0.0376**	-0.00633	0.0197***	0.0267***	0.0145*
	(0.0131)	(0.0170)	(0.0201)	(0.00533)	(0.00742)	(0.00755)
State owned dummy	-0.133**	-0.158	-0.103	-0.00599	-0.0153	0.0133
	(0.0662)	(0.100)	(0.0781)	(0.0214)	(0.0291)	(0.0309)
Foreign owned dummy	0.0191	0.0244	0.0095	0.0189***	0.0305***	0.00815
	(0.0166)	(0.0261)	(0.0216)	(0.00653)	(0.00966)	(0.00862)
Access to finance dummy	-0.0104	-0.00741	-0.00708	0.0190***	0.0237***	0.0121*
	(0.0122)	(0.0166)	(0.0180)	(0.00498)	(0.00737)	(0.00664)
Experience of top manager (years)	0.0000424	0.000589	-0.000726	-0.000418*	-0.000737**	0.0000703
	(0.000551)	(0.000686)	(0.000906)	(0.000247)	(0.000341)	(0.000366)
Female manager	0.0259**	0.0132	0.0360**	-0.0086	-0.00656	-0.0120*
	(0.0127)	(0.0182)	(0.0172)	(0.00561)	(0.00933)	(0.00699)
Exporter dummy	-0.0192	-0.0318	0.0102	0.0213***	0.0408***	-0.0295*
	(0.0174)	(0.0218)	(0.0314)	(0.00763)	(0.00875)	(0.0162)
Firm registered at start-up	-0.0288**	-0.0226	-0.0356*	-0.00419	-0.00121	-0.00692
	(0.0141)	(0.0197)	(0.0202)	(0.00557)	(0.00786)	(0.00782)
Constant	3.763***	3.953***	3.761***	4.601***	4.583***	4.599***
	(0.0473)	(0.113)	(0.0571)	(0.0174)	(0.0339)	(0.0224)
Observations	8676	4197	4479	8686	4207	4479
R-squared	0.197	0.174	0.219	0.084	0.09	0.102

Source: UNCTAD secretariat calculations, based on data from World Bank Enterprise Surveys.

Notes: The dependent variable is either the log of labour productivity growth (columns 1–3) or the log of employment growth (columns 4–6); columns 1 and 4 report results for the full sample; columns 2 and 5 for the subsample of firms in the manufacturing sector and columns 3 and 6 for the subsample of firms in the services sector; firm size and age are measured at t-3 and access to finance is proxied by the availability of an overdraft facility in the last three years; all regressions adopt an ordinary least squares approach, including regional and sectoral fixed effects; values in parentheses represent robust standard errors clustered at the country level; *, ** and *** indicate a 10, 5 and 1 per cent significance level, respectively.

Women are underrepresented in top management, as only 15 per cent of firms have a woman as the top manager. However, their presence is significantly associated with faster productivity growth, both in the full sample and in the subsample of firms in the services sector.[23] Exporter status appears to be significantly associated with higher rates of employment growth, in both the full sample and the subsample of firms in the manufacturing sector.[24] Finally, in line with Williams et al. (2017), the results reported in table 2.3 suggest that productivity growth is significantly faster in firms in LDCs that started as unregistered, compared with those that registered in the start-up phase.

The results highlight the different roles played by firms with different characteristics in structural transformation and thus the importance of taking full account of the heterogeneity of firms in policymaking, to best harness entrepreneurship for development. Smaller and younger firms are critical from the point of view of employment creation, yet the sustainability of their contribution is contingent on their surviving and thriving and this often requires greater skills and possibly different management structures (African Development Bank et al., 2017; Greiner, 1972). Conversely, larger firms appear to play a key role in capital deepening and productivity upgrading. Accordingly, while horizontal policies such as improving the business environment and widening access to finance undoubtedly have a role, structural transformation necessarily hinges on a well-balanced ecosystem that encompasses multiple types of firms, interrelated in a dense network of production linkages.

F. Concluding remarks

This chapter has outlined some stylized facts about enterprises in LDCs, which underline the importance of a nuanced understanding of entrepreneurship to policymaking in this area. Entrepreneurial activities, broadly defined, undoubtedly represent a major source of employment in LDCs, at nearly 70 per cent of the total, with self-employment as a proxy. This may signify substantial entrepreneurial potential, and helps to explain the prominence accorded to entrepreneurship in poverty reduction, notably for vulnerable populations such as women and youth.

A careful reading of the available evidence points to a more sobering reality, however, in particular from the perspective of structural transformation. The greater prevalence of necessity-driven entrepreneurs and low-productivity me-too businesses in LDCs suggests that much of the apparent entrepreneurial potential is likely to make at most a limited contribution to sustainable development. Instead, as high-productivity firms emerge and consolidate their positions, fuelling economic growth, the least productive entrepreneurs are more likely to discontinue their businesses in favour of better paid wage employment. The U-shaped relationship often posited between entrepreneurship and economic development suggests that, even in a successful country in this regard, a certain degree of upward consolidation in the entrepreneurial landscape is to be expected during the development process and is an important channel for labour reallocation towards higher productivity activities.

Similarly, while informality is associated with small-scale and necessity-driven entrepreneurial activities, informality and necessity-driven entrepreneurship can by no means be equated. Besides the cost and time burden of registration, a significant number of informal entrepreneurs see no potential benefits from formalization and there is growing evidence that some remain unregistered until they are confident that their business models will succeed after formalization. Therefore, while reducing registration costs and improving administrative efficiency may be beneficial, it is equally important to enhance the benefits of registration, by fostering a virtuous circle of growth and increasing productivity among formal firms, and to support young firms in cost discovery.

A more nuanced approach is also needed from an enterprise development perspective. Enthusiasm about start-ups and microenterprises and SMEs is understandable in terms of gross employment creation, but is often overstated. Microenterprises

Smaller and younger firms are critical for employment creation, yet larger firms appear to play a key role in capital deepening and productivity upgrading

and SMEs dominate the entrepreneurial scene in LDCs and undoubtedly play a key role in employment generation, not least because entrants with a suboptimal size need to expand to achieve economies of scale for survival. However, a large body of literature highlights remarkably low survival rates among start-ups, in particular smaller ones, implying substantial employment losses that are rarely accounted for due to the lack of longitudinal data. Larger firms also appear to perform better than smaller firms in terms of productivity growth, likely reflecting distinct economies of scale in different sectors, highlighting the importance of addressing the missing middle and promoting denser production linkages among a more balanced array of firms.

Start-ups can play a key role in structural transformation, notably by fostering competition, challenging incumbents and introducing innovations. However, in practice, only a limited proportion of start-ups can do so in a sustained way. Therefore, although universal policy measures, such as improving the business environment or enhancing entrepreneurship education, undoubtedly have some usefulness, effectively targeted support to enterprises with higher growth potential is equally critical in terms of sustainability. This point is further reinforced in LDCs given the serious resource constraints and the large number of potential beneficiaries of any implicit or explicit subsidization in the absence of adequate eligibility criteria.

Boosting the contribution of entrepreneurship to structural transformation thus requires – along with a careful and regular mapping of the entrepreneurship landscape across several complementary dimensions (for example along the lines of the OECD and Eurostat measurement framework), adapted to specificities in LDCs – a proactive industrial policy framework, including an incentive structure that nudges enterprises to improve performance, harnessing market discipline to foster innovation while limiting rent-seeking behaviour. It also requires bold approaches to harnessing international trade and investment to promote structural transformation.

Notes

1 This is not necessarily true for specialized surveys that focus on entrepreneurship, such as the adult population surveys carried out by the Global Entrepreneurship Monitor (GEM).

2 For these reasons, for example, the Organization for Economic Cooperation and Development (OECD) and Eurostat measurement framework avoids the use of a single synthetic indicator, and relies instead on an articulated set of measures to map entrepreneurship determinants, entrepreneurial performance and related impacts (Ahmad and Hoffman, 2007; Ahmad and Seymour, 2008).

3 See www.doingbusiness.org/data/exploretopics/entrepreneurship.

4 GDP per person employed is used in preference to GDP per capita to exclude the effect of cross-country differences in labour participation rates.

5 The postulated U-shaped relationship between the rate of entrepreneurship and GDP per capita (figure 2.2 (a) and (b)) may be at least partly explained by the parametric nature of the estimation. The specification of the fitted line in figure 2.2 (c) is also quadratic, as in (a) and (b), yet the coefficient of the quadratic term is close to zero and far smaller than the coefficient of the linear term.

6 The unweighted average values of the share of self-employment, total early-stage entrepreneurial activity and new business density in LDCs are 70, 30 and 0.78 per cent, respectively, compared with 37, 16 and 4.14 per cent, respectively, in other developing countries.

7 The main exceptions to this trend are conflict-affected countries such as Afghanistan and the Democratic Republic of Congo.

8 Eritrea represents a significant outlier, as the majority of self-employment is accounted for by employers, yet this is likely related to policies such as that on national service and their effects on the labour market (Kibreab, 2009; Human Rights Watch, 2017; Valensisi and Gauci, 2013).

9 The adult population surveys are administered by GEM national teams to representative national samples of at least 2,000 respondents in different countries, following a standard methodology, to measure the level and nature of entrepreneurial activity worldwide. The data collection process varies slightly between countries, but predominantly relies on landline telephone-based surveys, with some face-to-face and/or mobile telephone interviews in areas where landline telephone coverage is limited.

10 An unweighted average of 61 per cent of adults in LDCs perceive good opportunities to start a business, compared with 49 per cent in other developing countries and 42 per cent in developed and transition economies; and 70 per cent of adults in LDCs believe that they possess the required skills, compared with 59 per cent in other developing countries and 44 per cent in developed and transition economies.

11 An unweighted average of 35 per cent of adults in LDCs indicate that fear of failure would prevent them from setting up a business, compared with 33 per cent in other developing countries and 37 per cent in developed and transition economies.

12 The number of newly registered limited liability companies in LDCs has nearly doubled, from 31,896 in 2006 to 61,257 in 2016. The latter figure is comparable with the figures in Indonesia and the Netherlands.

13 Unweighted averages across country groups; findings do not change if median values are considered.

14 The sectoral classifications in this paragraph refer to those of GEM and differ from the standard categories of UNCTAD. The adult population surveys of GEM may underestimate rural entrepreneurship due to their reliance mainly on telephone interviews.

15 Business discontinuation is assessed by GEM through the following question: "Have you, in the past 12 months, sold, shut down, discontinued or quit a business you owned and managed, any form of self-employment or selling goods or services to anyone?" (see www.gemconsortium.org/wiki/1184).

16 The lack of gender equality patterns addressed here are consistent with those documented by GEM (2017) and GEM (2018), taking into account the differing country classification.

17 Angola (2010), Burkina Faso (2009), Democratic Republic of the Congo (2013), Madagascar (2009), Mali (2010), Myanmar (2014), Nepal (2009), Rwanda (2011).

18 The figures are Angola, 89 per cent; Burkina Faso, 60 per cent; the Democratic Republic of the Congo, 51 per cent; Mali, 79 per cent; Nepal, 50 per cent; and Rwanda, 56 per cent.

19 See www.enterprisesurveys.org/methodology.

20 The surveys for the Gambia (2006) and Guinea-Bissau (2006) were not used due to comparability concerns.

21 There have been separate surveys of microenterprises and informal enterprises in some countries, such as those referred to in section D, yet they are not comparable to the standard surveys as they follow different methodologies and often include country-specific features.

22 The corresponding dummy takes the value of 1 if the firm reported both a product and process innovation, in order to take a conservative approach.

23 One plausible explanation for this finding is related to the educational attainment of managers and the interplay with the pattern of women's participation in enterprise ownership and/or management. However, the lack of data impedes a formal test of this hypothesis. The presence of women owners and/or managers in the sample appears to be concentrated in a few countries (namely Bangladesh, Cambodia, the Lao People's Democratic Republic, Myanmar, Madagascar, and Zambia), with relatively higher and less gender-unequal levels of educational attainment than in other LDCs. Moreover, there is evidence suggesting that the impact of education on firm performance tends to be more pronounced in businesses owned by women than in those owned by men (De Vita et al., 2014).

24 The opposite is true with regard to enterprises in the services sector, but the associated coefficient hardly passes the 10 per cent-significance threshold.

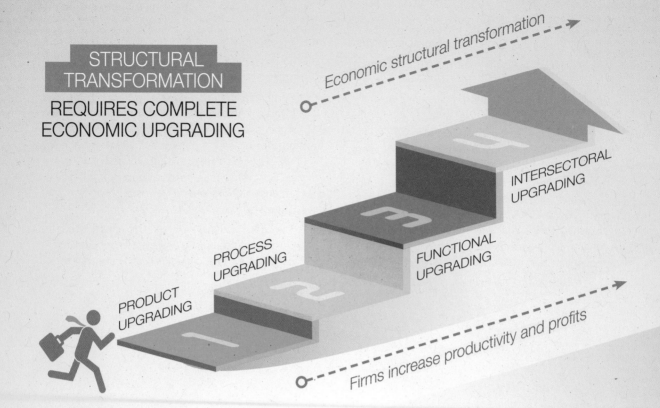

STRUCTURAL TRANSFORMATION
REQUIRES COMPLETE ECONOMIC UPGRADING

Economic structural transformation

PRODUCT UPGRADING

PROCESS UPGRADING

FUNCTIONAL UPGRADING

INTERSECTORAL UPGRADING

Firms increase productivity and profits

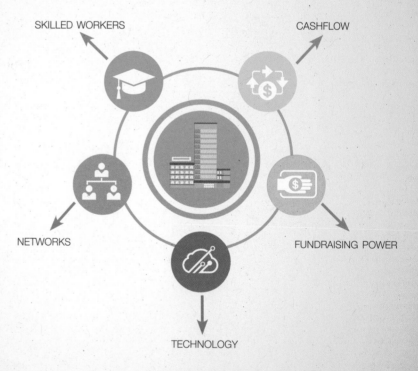

LARGER FIRMS
ARE BETTER AT ECONOMIC UPGRADING IN LDCs

They have superior internal and external resources

SKILLED WORKERS

CASHFLOW

NETWORKS

FUNDRAISING POWER

TECHNOLOGY

IDEAL

REALITY

FOR LDCs, HEIGHTENED COMPETITION IN GVCs MEANS ECONOMIC UPGRADING **CAN BE AN ELUSIVE GOAL**

The local entrepreneurship dimension of global production systems

CHAPTER 3
The local entrepreneurship dimension of global production systems

A. Introduction   **55**

B. Global value chains and entrepreneurship   **55**

    1. Interface between entrepreneurs and global value chains   55

    2. Upgrading within global value chains   56

    3. Competition and entrepreneurial engagement   57

C. Participation of the least developed countries in global value chains   **59**

    1. General patterns of least developed country participation   59

    2. Participation of the least developed countries in agricultural global value chains   61

    3. Participation of the least developed countries in textile and clothing global value chains   64

D. Global value chains and beyond   **69**

    1. Limitations of integration into global value chains   69

    2. The importance of enterprise   71

    3. The role of comparative advantage   72

    4. International competition for high-level skills and entrepreneurship   73

    5. Fostering intersectoral linkages: The example of tourism and agriculture   75

Notes   **77**

A. Introduction

This chapter explores whether shifting global production patterns stimulate entrepreneurship and industrialization in LDCs. International trade is now widely considered to be the primary source of developmental dynamism, and industrial policy has been largely replaced by trade policy in developing countries as the most predominant type of development policy. However, local entrepreneurship is essential to harness the benefits of trade for sustainable development and to generate the domestic resources LDCs need for investments in infrastructure, as well as skills and innovation that are necessary for achieving the Sustainable Development Goals.

International trade is increasingly defined by GVCs, which tend more and more to mediate the global division of labour and functional specialization in trade, giving rise to a growing disjunction between where goods are produced and where value is created and captured.[1] A critical developmental question for LDCs is therefore how the potential opportunities offered by GVCs can help stimulate the types of entrepreneurship that can drive structural transformation, particularly in the main resource-based traded sectors in LDCs (agriculture, extractives and manufacturing), on which initiatives aimed at structural transformation and wealth creation are increasingly centred. This chapter begins with a discussion on the nature of GVCs (section B) and of LDC participation in them. Greater detail regarding GVCs in agriculture and in textiles and clothing is provided in section C. Section D draws some conclusions from this discussion, raises related issues and suggests options for LDCs.

B. Global value chains and entrepreneurship

GVCs arise from the fragmentation of production processes into tasks that are dispersed internationally in borderless production systems spanning multiple locations in a system of sequential chains and complex global and regional networks. While GVCs are inherently sector specific, all are predicated on the quest by initiating firms to increase efficiency, lower costs and speed up production through the internationalization of operations. UNCTAD estimates that GVCs coordinated by transnational corporations account for some 80 per cent of global trade, much of it in intermediate goods such as parts, components and intermediate services (UNCTAD, 2013b). Trade in intermediate goods accounted for about 54 per cent of global trade in 2016 (United Nations, 2018).

There has been little research to validate the often-asserted advantages of GVCs in stimulating local entrepreneurship

---

GVCs are considered to offer important advantages, as they allow countries to specialize in particular functions or bundles of tasks, rather than in specific industries; they accelerate changes in comparative advantage (World Economic Forum, 2016), are open to new entrants and accommodate economies at any stage of development and skill. Therefore, integration in GVCs is often presented as an important way for LDCs to industrialize at much earlier stages of development, by bypassing the development of national supply chains involving the production of goods entirely in one country and generating opportunities for entrepreneurial engagement.[2]

Despite these asserted advantages, however, there has been surprisingly little research to validate the supposed advantages of GVCs in stimulating local entrepreneurship. Instead, the overwhelming emphasis of research is on employment gains, profit and learning opportunities for individual firms (Kowalski et al., 2015) and foreign exchange earnings. It is widely held that firms' participation in GVCs offers the potential for production at scale, specialization and access to international markets; their participation in GVCs is also considered to be an important source of technology, skills and capital in the form of direct investment, supplier credits and trade finance,[3] all of which are typically limited in LDCs. However, this view may be oversimplified, and few conclusions can be drawn about the potential benefits to entrepreneurship in LDCs without considering the ownership of beneficiary firms.

1. Interface between entrepreneurs and global value chains

Entrepreneurs and entrepreneurship can be considered to interface with potential market opportunities provided by GVCs through a process of opportunity discovery, evaluation, creation and exploitation (figure 3.1). Opportunity identification involves technical skills, such as financial analysis and market research, and creativity. Entrepreneurship is required to transform potential opportunities in GVCs into actual entrepreneurial opportunities embodied in three constitutive elements: products, customers and capabilities.[4] Opportunity discovery has an important subjective dimension: two entrepreneurs encountering

> Whether GVCs facilitate the development of entrepreneurship that promotes structural transformation is a critical issue

the same potential opportunity may well discover and create different concrete opportunities, according to their respective attributes and capabilities (Oyson and Whittaker, 2015).

Typically, discovered opportunities are exploited by firms — as the primary vehicle of action led by entrepreneurs — in a purposeful and deliberate process involving cognition and entrepreneurial action. In the current international environment, this process can occur much faster than when international trade was less liberalized, as globalization allows firms to internationalize at start up or soon thereafter without the need for accumulated experience and know-how in the domestic market.[5]

Potential opportunities for entrepreneurship engagement with GVCs exist both domestically and internationally. They may arise exogenously (through market conditions detected by entrepreneurs), endogenously (through actions of entrepreneurs), or both, through a process of recognition and development.

The key issue is whether participation in GVCs facilitates the emergence of a framework conducive to the development of entrepreneurship that promotes structural transformation. The literature suggests that GVCs promote economic upgrading by participating firms — seeking new competences

that allow them to develop more complex tasks and add more value — in response to the threat of new, low-cost competitors. Assessing the effects of GVC participation on entrepreneurship for structural transformation thus requires an understanding of the nature and underpinnings of such economic upgrading and of its linkages with entrepreneurship.

2. Upgrading within global value chains

The scope for firm-level economic upgrading within GVCs can be divided into four stages, linked to the segment of the chain in which a firm is active: process upgrading, product upgrading, functional upgrading and intersectoral/chain upgrading (table 3.1). While all are important, functional economic upgrading represents the tipping point for structural transformation, effectively locking in the shift from low- to higher-income activities. Intersectoral economic upgrading takes the process further, penetrating sectoral boundaries to initiate economy-wide innovation and diversification. These two stages can thus be considered the primary policy targets for structural transformation and the logical end goal of entrepreneurship policies in LDCs; process and product upgrading are the means to this end. Structural transformation requires the economic upgrading process to be completed either by progression or leapfrogging.

For individual firms, the gain from upgrading is the capture of a greater proportion of the value generated in a GVC. The greatest value in GVCs is generally in upstream activities, such as design, product development, research and development, and the manufacture of key parts and components; and in downstream activities such as marketing, branding and customer service. The roles of different economic

Figure 3.1

Entrepreneurial path to opportunity discovery and exploitation

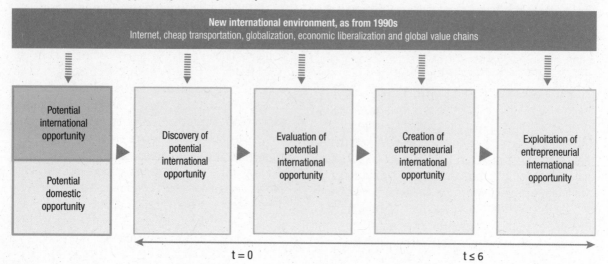

Source: Adapted from Oyson and Whittaker, 2015, figure 2.

Table 3.1

Types of economic upgrading in global value chains

Process upgrading	More efficient production by introducing superior technology or reorganized production systems
Product upgrading	Knowledge and competency acquisition by transitioning to more sophisticated products lines
Functional upgrading	Value addition by acquiring new functions or abandoning existing ones to increase overall skill and value content of activities (moving up the chain)
Intersectoral/chain upgrading	Leveraging knowledge acquired in one sector to achieve horizontal moves into new sectors and productive activities

Source: Humphrey and Schmitz, 2002.

actors and countries in GVCs are thus depicted by the smile curve (figure 3.2), which illustrates the global division of tasks and functions in GVCs and the benefits derived by participants. Activities at both ends of the value chain are intensive in knowledge and creativity, while manufacturing and standardized services are in the lower-value trough of the curve (Mudambi, 2008).

Governance patterns and power relations within GVCs are critical. Lead firms that undertake the functional integration and coordination of internationally dispersed activities determine the allocation and flows of financial, material and human resources within a GVC (Humphrey and Schmitz, 2002). By controlling information flows and knowledge acquisition within GVCs, lead firms have a major influence on upgrading – which is dependent on knowledge that flows through the chain — and on instigating product upgrading through the allocation of new tasks, for example when a supermarket chain induces producer customization by launching new product lines or introducing more sophisticated processing and packaging (Humphrey and Memedovic, 2006).

Thus the pathways to economic upgrading are not only specific to each GVC; they depend on the balance of power within the chain, which is overwhelmingly skewed in favour of the lead firm. A further layer of uncertainty and complexity is added by the prospects for the future evolution of GVCs, given the context of protectionist pressures and digitalization (box 3.1), whose implications are likely to differ markedly between GVCs for different products.

3. Competition and entrepreneurial engagement

The location of fragmented production processes according to the availability, cost and quality of the necessary skills and materials stimulates competitive pressure between economies and locations. As a result, GVCs are associated with heightened competition, which varies between sectors, types of value chains and products. Competitive conditions also change, as GVCs are continuously reconfigured (De Backer and Miroudot, 2013), for example in response to changes in relative labour and capital costs between countries.

Figure 3.2

Stylized smile curve of upstream customization-led global value chains

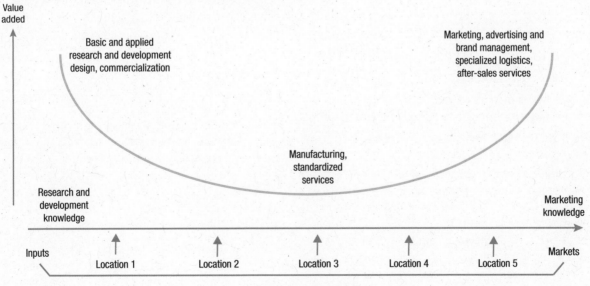

Source: Mudambi, 2008.

Box 3.1 **The future of global value chains**

GVCs are currently buffeted by opposing forces, some of which favour their expansion and increased complexity, while others might lead to their realignment or decline. Following a limited consolidation of GVCs during the economic crisis of 2008–2009, declining trade-to-GDP ratios globally suggest that GVCs have lost momentum. In 2017, their growth came to a halt for the first time in 30 years, as the share of foreign value added in exports fell to 30 per cent. It remains to be seen whether this represents a natural correction to an overshooting of international fragmentation as a result of overexuberant company sourcing and production strategies. However, digital technologies and the "fourth industrial revolution" may make production that is close to final markets more attractive, while facilitating rapid responses to changing consumer preferences. Rising trade costs and protectionism also render international production more expensive.

It is uncertain whether the aforementioned factors will outweigh those promoting the further expansion of GVCs: the liberalization of trade and investment, rapid advances in ICTs, the entry of new low-cost producers in manufacturing, increasing efficiency and wider international availability of services, and new markets in emerging economies. Indeed, some impending developments may have opposing effects. Some ICT improvements reduce the benefits of specialization, while others reduce its costs. Equally, while robotization could erode the competitive advantage of cheap labour, contributing to the further concentration of manufacturing in a few locations, some sectors may be largely unaffected, as the technical feasibility of automation may not be matched by profitability. Rapid technological progress could also generate efficiency gains within companies, facilitating functional and intersectoral upgrading and contributing to employment growth and structural transformation.

Sources: African Development Bank et al., 2017; De Backer and Flaig, 2017; UNCTAD, 2017b; UNCTAD, 2018b.

Therefore, the impact of globalization on entrepreneurship is not straightforward and may be positive or negative (Verheul et al., 2001). Opportunities for entrepreneurial engagement may not diminish if developments in GVCs continue to favour LDCs as production locations. However, it is likely that competitive conditions will change, and the ability of LDC entrepreneurs to exploit these opportunities or adjust to changes in GVCs is open to question.

A firm's location within a value chain is important, as competitive pressures are most intense in those parts of the production process with the lowest entry barriers. This affects both the precariousness of a firm's financial position — accentuated by advances in ICTs and technological disruptions — and the lead times a firm has to learn, adapt and innovate.

The intense competition characteristic of the GVC segments most accessible to LDCs can, in principle, be a stimulus for entrepreneurship. Yet it can also be a deterrent or promote destructive entrepreneurship (Baumol, 1990; Wiegratz, 2016). In integrating into GVCs, LDC firms are exposed to competition with firms elsewhere, which may have different characteristics and local conditions more conducive to reacting to GVC challenges and adopting upgrading strategies.

Perceptions and responses of SMEs to market signals are affected by various resource constraints linked to supply and demand, including finance (van Burg et al., 2012). These constraints direct an entrepreneur's attention towards fewer opportunities within his or her constrained domain, with positive or negative effects on the identification of opportunities. LDC entrepreneurs may thus respond differently from, and less innovatively than, their counterparts in more developed economies, in identical competitive conditions within GVCs, missing out on promising opportunities outside their limited domains.

GVCs also tend to amplify the effects of trade barriers, such as border bottlenecks and diversity of standards in final goods trade (Criscuolo and Timmis, 2017), so that the lack of a supporting environment can lead firms with high growth potential to adopt suboptimal expansion strategies in the face of higher production and trade costs (OECD and World Bank Group, 2015).

Despite potential gains in terms of export growth, the potential benefits of GVCs for LDCs are thus limited by barriers to entrepreneurship. Even entrepreneurs with the necessary attributes for GVC integration cannot escape credit constraints, high transaction costs, inadequate infrastructure and inefficient administrative procedures for international trade.

The types of enterprise that thrive in a GVC environment are an important consideration. Economic upgrading requires firms that are both entrepreneurial (opportunity-seeking) and strategic (advantage-seeking) in their approach (Hitt et al., 2001). While firms that lack these attributes may succeed in entering a GVC, they are unlikely to sustain and improve their position in it. These are key characteristics of high-impact, innovation-driven and market-creating entrepreneurship, as opposed to the survivalist entrepreneurs that typically predominate in LDCs (chapter 2).

An important policy objective in LDCs is thus to develop the critical mass of such entrepreneurs that is needed to drive structural transformation. A key issue is finance, as upgrading by high-impact entrepreneurs — those with the greatest potential to have an impact on innovation and customer benefits, job creation, wealth creation and society — requires long-term credit for investment and innovation. According to the life-cycle framework (World Economic Forum, 2014), high-impact ventures undergo five stages of growth, each requiring different levels and types of finance. At the *launch* (pioneering and growth) stage they distinguish themselves from other types of entrepreneurial venture through a clear strategy and vision, coupled with strong product or service differentiation. Their long-term potential is underpinned by solid business strategies and differentiated offerings during the *build* (high-growth) stage. During the *run* (mature growth) stage, they attain maturity by leveraging capabilities built in the previous two life stages to embed efficient operations and generate sustainable profits. Having reached their fully adult life stage, they will often renew and reinvent themselves to stay dominant and maintain high-impact and growth.

Long-term credit is particularly limited in developing countries (OECD, 2018), although there is evidence that high-impact opportunity-driven entrepreneurs are less affected by credit constraints than their necessity-driven counterparts (van der Zwan et al., 2016).

C. Participation of the least developed countries in global value chains

This section presents an assessment of LDC participation in GVCs, using case studies of the agriculture and garment manufacturing sectors to shed light on the nature of the entrepreneurial opportunities they offer. It further develops an analysis of the topic undertaken for *The Least Developed Countries Report 2007* (UNCTAD, 2007).

As well as their significance as sources of foreign exchange earnings, the agricultural and textiles and clothing sectors are poster children for job creation, inclusive business and women's empowerment. It has been suggested that growth generated by agriculture is up to four times as effective in reducing poverty as growth in other sectors (International Institute for Environment and Development and Sustainable Food Lab, 2011), and that reaping full benefits in poverty reduction is contingent on the growth of SMEs, which generally include smallholders and small family farms (Humphrey and Memedovic, 2006).

The trend in LDC exports indicates increased concentration of both products and partners

---

Both sectors also have a long-standing association with the participation of women and remain battlegrounds for gender equality. For example, 82 per cent of all garment industry jobs in Lesotho are occupied by women (*Origin Africa*, 2017). In the agricultural sector, gender inequality in terms of land ownership and value capture is a major challenge. Equally, while textiles and clothing have been traditionally associated with gender empowerment on the basis that job creation tends to favour women whose opportunities were previously limited to the household or the informal sector (Keane and te Velde, 2008), new issues arise from informal operations, low wages, gender pay gaps and poor working conditions.[6] Rather than challenging or dismantling gendered job segregation, it has been argued, GVCs recruit women at a lower cost by casting particular skills or functions as "feminine", while the benefits from upgrading accrue disproportionately to men (International Centre for Trade and Sustainable Development, 2016; UNCTAD, 2014g; UNCTAD, 2018c).

1. General patterns of least developed country participation

The share of LDCs in global trade is less than 1 per cent, a relatively constant trend since 2008. In contrast, their export-to-GDP ratios average about 25 per cent, substantially below the developing country average of about 35 per cent, showing a clear downward trend since 2011. This highlights the intractable obstacle to the competitiveness and development of LDCs that their structural impediments represent (UNCTAD, 2017c). The trend in LDC exports indicates an increasing concentration of both products and partners (UNCTAD, 2018d). In addition to inadequate infrastructure and poorly functioning trade-related institutions, many LDCs face specific trade-related obstacles such as landlocked positions, distance from large and dynamic markets, and small domestic markets that limit potential economies of scale. The changing circumstances for LDCs' development over successive decades have compounded the difficulty of escaping the underdevelopment trap (UNCTAD, 2016b).

The participation of LDCs in GVCs is significantly affected by trade and investment agreements. Tariff

Predominant mode
of LDC **entry** into
global value chains is

foreign direct investment

these markets. Trade agreements and associated preferences are often regional, favouring intraregional over interregional trade. However, regional trade agreements vary in their ability to promote trade, and by extension, entrepreneurship.

The predominant mode of LDC entry into GVCs is foreign direct investment (FDI), though with a more limited role in agriculture (box 3.2). Despite a declining trend since 2012, FDI represented 21 per cent of total inward financial flows in LDCs in 2013–2017 (UNCTAD, 2018b). According to the UNCTAD Investment Policy Hub database (http://investmentpolicyhub.unctad.org/), virtually all LDCs are parties to bilateral investment treaties or treaties with investment provisions.

While LDCs' export volumes increased by 276 per cent between 2000 and 2016, LDC participation in GVCs remains limited, having grown by only 2 per cent annually between 2010 and 2017. Further, the share of foreign value added in their exports — 9 per cent — is the lowest among developing countries (UNCTAD, 2018b). LDCs are a predominant source of inputs for other countries' exports in several sectors. That is to say, their downstream (forward) integration is greater than their upstream (backward) integration (figure 3.3), largely reflecting their dependence on primary exports, including ocean-based primary commodities in the case of island LDCs. However, island LDCs have greater upstream integration because of the predominance of services exports,

escalation[7] is a major barrier, both to the processing of agricultural products and to manufacturing, and tariff peaks continue to affect important sectors such as agriculture, apparel, textiles and leather goods. This makes preferential market access critical. LDCs benefit from preferential treatment under bilateral, unilateral or international trade agreements such as the Everything but Arms initiative of the European Union, as do some under the African Growth and Opportunities Act of the United States of America.[8] However, the proliferation of multilateral, regional and bilateral trade agreements erodes preferential margins over time, limiting competitiveness in

Box 3.2 **Trends in foreign direct investment inflows to the least developed countries**

Foreign direct investment represented 21 per cent of total capital flows to LDCs in 2017, a proportion that has been declining since 2012. While FDI flows to LDCs as a whole fell by 17 per cent in 2017, those to Asian and Island LDCs grew by 20 per cent; the fastest growth was achieved by Myanmar (45.2 per cent) and Cambodia (12.5 per cent). In comparison, flows to the Lao People's Democratic Republic declined for a second year, by 18 per cent, due to a reduction in Chinese investment. Though aggregate flows to African LDCs and Haiti declined by 31 per cent, largely because of deep contractions in investments in the extractive sectors in Angola and Mozambique, prospects for FDI appear favourable for African LDCs. While FDI inflows to LDCs represent a small proportion of FDI to all developing countries (4 per cent in 2017), they are often large relative to GDP, which was the case in Cambodia, Djibouti, Lesotho, Liberia and Sierra Leone in 2016.

Box figure 3.1

Top five least developed country recipients of foreign direct investment by (a) value, in billions of dollars, 2017 and (b) share, in percentage, of gross domestic product, 2016

(a)

| 4.3 | 3.6 | 2.8 | 2.3 | 2.2 |

■ Myanmar
■ Ethiopia
■ Cambodia
■ Mozambique
■ Bangladesh

(b)

Lesotho	7
Djibouti	8
Cambodia	10
Sierra Leone	13
Liberia	20

Sources: UNCTAD, 2018b; UNCTAD, 2018d.

Figure 3.3

Integration of least developed countries into global value chains, by country grouping, 2017

(Percentage of total exports)

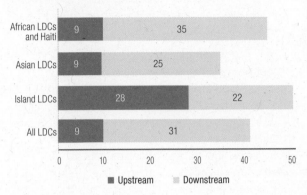

Source: UNCTAD-EORA database.

primarily tourism. Proximity to "factory Asia" (the regional GVC production hub) — in particular the China growth pole — can be expected to accelerate the integration of Asian LDCs into regional and global value chains, as firms from China, Japan, Thailand and Viet Nam are increasingly propelled by rising labour costs or labour shortages to relocate or outsource operations to lower-cost countries. However, GVC production in Asian LDCs remains heavily dependent on foreign firms, and their role is largely downstream, suggesting limited benefits from integration. There are no signs of a comparable "factory Africa" emerging, reflecting more limited GVC integration among African LDCs, many of which remain effectively locked into low-value upstream segments of the supply chain.[9]

A common source of instability arising from LDCs' participation in GVCs is its concentration in the production of traded goods that are disproportionately postponable,[10] which makes them particularly vulnerable to global demand shocks (Baldwin, 2009; ILO and World Trade Organization, 2011).

2. Participation of the least developed countries in agricultural global value chains

The agricultural, forestry and fishing sector is the main source of employment in LDCs, in some cases increasingly so (UNCTAD, 2015a). Though not generally an important driver of exports, it is often the leading source of livelihoods (UNCTAD, 2015a; UNCTAD, 2017i). In Cambodia, for example, agriculture accounts for one third of GDP and 80 per cent of employment (International Finance Corporation, 2014). Similarly, 77 per cent of households in Vanuatu are engaged in artisanal fishing.[11] Fishing, a mainstay of island LDCs, is mainly undertaken by artisanal

fishers. Industrial-scale fishing, carried out by foreign fleets and sometimes processed by domestic industries, is unlikely to be viable in most island LDCs. In Vanuatu, 77 per cent of households are engaged in artisanal fishing. In contrast, the fishing industry in Bangladesh contributes 4.4 per cent to GDP and directly or indirectly sustains 15 million people (UNCTAD, 2017i). Agriculture is the sector where local participation in value added is greatest in LDCs. However, notwithstanding differences across LDC regions, it is generally characterized by low productivity. Even Asian LDCs, which have the highest agricultural productivity, remain well behind most other developing countries in Asia by this measure. Agricultural labour productivity in island LDCs, though historically higher than in Asian and African LDCs, is declining (UNCTAD, 2015a).

Agribusiness and agro-industry encompass the commercialization and value addition of agricultural and post-production enterprises, and the building of linkages among agricultural enterprises (FAO, 2013a). Agribusiness denotes all business activities performed "from farm to fork", from agricultural input suppliers, producers, agroprocessors, distributors, traders and exporters, to retailers and consumers.[12] Agro-industry refers to the establishment of linkages between enterprises and supply chains to develop, transform and distribute agricultural inputs and products.

While GVCs play a more limited role in agribusiness and agro-industries than in other sectors, their importance is increasing, a reflection of rising global food prices stemming from and resulting in a redistribution of global economic activity towards developing countries. Their association with manufacturing and agriculture makes agrifood GVCs particularly pertinent to entrepreneurship and structural transformation in LDCs.

GVC dynamics in agriculture vary widely between products and countries, limiting the potential for generalization across the sector or across LDCs. Identifying LDC participation in agricultural GVCs is also hampered by the uneven coverage of country and product case studies, the limited information they provide on entrepreneurship and their focus on trends in upgrading in low-technology industries (DiCaprio and Suvannaphakdy, 2017).

Nonetheless, despite the importance of agriculture in LDCs and their apparent comparative advantage in agricultural production, their participation in GVCs appears generally to be more limited than in other sectors (Asian Development Bank, 2013). Data from the Observatory of Economic Complexity (2016) and regional and country case studies[13] suggest that LDC value chains in agriculture tend to be primarily domestic and regional, partly reflecting the predominance of smallholder and subsistence agriculture and of artisanal activities. Asian LDCs tend to supply primary inputs to regional value chains centred in developing Asia, reflecting the region's status as the world's largest food market (Timmer, 2013). A similar pattern, though less marked, is also evident in Africa. The geographical isolation of island LDCs limits both the development of regional value chains and their integration into GVCs, while their small populations compound structural obstacles to competitiveness and attractiveness to FDI.

This may in part reflect distinctive product characteristics and policies (OECD, 2017c). Globally, agriculture is the beneficiary of significant public support, despite contestation of the cost–benefit of such support,[14] and LDCs are seriously disadvantaged by resource constraints in providing such support. Agricultural products are also likely to be processed in export markets for re-export (OECD, 2017c).

Despite widespread reference in the literature to the potential for beneficiation, LDC participation in agricultural GVCs is generally characterized by short domestic value chains and limited domestic

processing; agriculture is typically dominated by small family farms with limited upgrading, as demonstrated by the domestic value chains of key export products from the four food- and agricultural-exporting LDCs (box 3.3). Success in GVC integration is thus mostly measurable in terms of increasing quantities of exports.

Policy and government support can have a significant effect on agricultural value chains, as shown by the success of Rwanda in repositioning its coffee from commodity grade to high-value speciality grade (World Bank, 2016a). Conversely, in Guinea-Bissau, despite the economic importance of cashew nuts, development of the sector has been held back by the absence of a legislative and regulatory framework to structure the market (Catarino et al., 2015).

Trade preferences are particularly important for LDC participation in agricultural GVCs, as tariffs on agricultural produce are generally much higher than those on manufactures and natural resources. Agricultural trade, especially in high-value niche segments of interest to LDCs, is particularly affected by non-tariff measures such as hygiene and health standards, private and national ethical and environmental standards, traceability requirements and regulations relating to product size, form and colour. Opportunities for product differentiation are

---

Box 3.3 **Domestic value chains for major agricultural exports in food and agricultural exporting least developed countries**

Guinea-Bissau

Coconuts, Brazil nuts and cashew nuts accounted for 40.5 per cent of total exports in 2016. Cashews are produced mainly by small family farms and producer cooperatives or growing companies. They are bought by a network of up-country buyers linked to urban buyers and sent either to warehouses, where they may be dried, bagged and consolidated in loads, or directly to exporters in the capital. Cashews are almost entirely exported raw to China, India and Viet Nam for processing and sale to developed markets.

Malawi

Raw tobacco leaf, produced mainly by smallholder and tenant farmers, accounted for 29 per cent of total exports in 2016. Tobacco is purchased by international leaf merchants through auctions or direct contracts governed by long-term arrangements with different forms of governance in relations with tobacco farmers and thus with different implications for product and process upgrading.

Solomon Islands

Rough wood accounted for 37 per cent of exports in 2016. Planted high-value teak is a major potential resource, and estimates of participation rates in teak planting since it began in the 1980s suggest that smallholders are likely to remain the significant source alongside State and large commercial plantations that date back to the 1960s. Teak is mainly exported raw to manufacturers in China, India and Viet Nam through a network of international buyers. A small proportion of wood undergoes limited processing by local companies and is exported by traders for further processing in destination markets. The Solomon Islands are also the world's second largest exporter of copra (dried coconut), after Indonesia. Coconut production is overwhelmingly a smallholder crop.

Somalia

The primary export is livestock for food, mainly produced by pastoralists. Exports of chilled meat are facilitated by a network mediated by brokers, who provide the main link between producers, small-scale traders and exporters' agents.

Sources: Australian Centre for International Agricultural Research, 2015; Catarino et al., 2015; FAO and International Bank for Reconstruction and Development/World Bank, 2018; Moyer-Lee and Prowse, 2012; Negassa et al., 2012; news24, 2017; Unfairtobacco, 2016.

often conditioned by non-tariff measures linked to certification (Humphrey and Memedovic, 2006; UNCTAD, 2015b).

Non-tariff measures in agriculture, which lead to compliance costs for local entrepreneurs that can be addressed by technical assistance and the use of modern technology, also have implications for GVCs. The global agrifood business is increasingly dominated by vertically coordinated GVCs akin to those traditionally associated with manufacturing, using various forms of coordination. These include outgrower schemes, contract farming, category management by supermarket suppliers and marketing contracts (Humphrey and Memedovic, 2006). This can aggravate the risk of market power abuse. For example, accurate and timely traceability of products has become an important factor, and lead firms exercise power over producers in the implementation of compliance. In Malawi, where the tobacco sector is dominated by smallholder production, leaf merchants' efforts to contain the costs of compliance and secure guaranteed traceability have created a tendency towards vertical integration (Moyer-Lee and Prowse, 2012). Leaf merchants have also lobbied for the abolition of the country's vibrant and competitive auction system, which ensures higher prices for farmers, in favour of a sector operated by contract farming.

Supermarkets and other major retailers are playing an increasing role in agricultural GVCs, leading to considerable growth of contract farming as a response to high transaction costs in the thin and imperfect markets and weak market institutions common to LDCs. Contract farming is a highly controversial topic, and there are concerns about the potential for abuse of small farmers' weak bargaining positions, exploitation of producers by middlemen (traders, brokers and buyers) and the potential of GVCs to promote destructive entrepreneurship. Responses to such concerns have included attempts to shorten domestic value chains by linking producers directly to exporters or manufacturers and to promote producer cooperatives (International Institute for Environment and Development and Sustainable Food Lab, 2011; Sustainable Organic Agriculture Action Network, 2013; Struthers, 2017; Wiegratz, 2016).

The prevalence of contract farming varies widely between commodities, destination markets and types of buyer (Minot and Ronchi, 2014). The high fixed costs of contracting, coupled with the economies of scale characteristic of some crops, favour medium- and large-scale farmers. However, the delicacy of some high-value products complicates mechanization, potentially favouring

Increased concentration at all stages of the agriculture value chain has implications for entrepreneurship and the balance of power

smallholders (Bamber et al., 2014), and there is evidence of small farmers benefiting from contract farming through more secure access to inputs such as seeds and fertilizers.[15] Nonetheless, challenges remain. The poorest and most marginalized rarely benefit or successfully upgrade and are vulnerable to exploitation by unscrupulous third-party contractors, giving rise to concerns that GVCs may facilitate destructive entrepreneurship (Bamber et al., 2014; Women in Informal Employment: Globalizing and Organizing, 2013; Dihel et al., 2017; Ethical Trading Initiative, 2005; Wiegratz, 2016).

Since larger firms are generally more technically efficient and are better able to meet public and private standards, this helps increase concentration at all stages of the value chain, with implications for entrepreneurship and the balance of power. Concentration at the inputs stage is related to lead-firm strategies for control over intellectual property. With some exceptions, notably coffee and cocoa, where farm production appears to be more and more fragmented and small scale in nature, concentration at the processing stage promotes an increase in scale of production units. Concentration at the processing stage provides a justification for production contracts or direct ownership of production units (vertical integration), and concentration in retailing contributes to increasing oligopoly. Moreover, concentration appears to have a ripple effect throughout GVCs – consolidation at one point giving rise to consolidation at another. The growing importance of standards in agribusiness accentuates this trend (Humphrey and Memedovic, 2006).

Although the scale of potential benefits is difficult to establish, a more positive trend is the potential of some high-value crops to stimulate entrepreneurship in LDCs to exploit niche markets. Examples of direct exports by LDCs in high-price, but often low-volume niche markets include tea and coffee (Nepal and Timor-Leste), organic cocoa (Sao Tome and Principe and Vanuatu), spices (the Comoros, Madagascar and Nepal), exotic fruit (Afghanistan and Madagascar), and Fairtrade and organic cotton (Benin, Burkina Faso, Chad, Mali and Zambia). Madagascar supplied 80 per cent of lychee imports to Europe in 2016 (Centre for the Promotion of Imports from Developing

There is little sign that LDC entrepreneurs will be able to follow the same trajectory as East Asian strategic suppliers

Countries, 2016) and 80–85 per cent of the world's natural vanilla (*The Economist,* 2018a). However, many LDC entrepreneurs may find it challenging to meet the more stringent quality standards, including labour and environmental standards, that are typical of such markets, as well as to overcome high transaction costs, lack of skills and infrastructure.

Agriculture is the highest sectoral priority for African countries in bilateral investment treaties and other agreements with investment provisions, while several agricultural and agro-industrial subsectors are major priorities for Asian LDCs (UNCTAD, 2013a). The share of agriculture in global FDI is small but growing (UNCTAD, 2012b): food, beverages and tobacco accounted for only 3 per cent of FDI in 2012–2014 (Fiedler and Iafrate, 2016). As in other sectors, FDI in agriculture in LDCs is more limited than in other developing countries. However, it is concentrated in a few countries, partly reflecting policy differences, for example in Ethiopia, whose development policy focuses on the commercialization of agriculture. There were relatively large flows of agricultural FDI to Cambodia, Ethiopia, Mozambique, Uganda and Vanuatu in 2009–2011, and significant stocks thereof in Cambodia, Malawi, Uganda and Zambia during the same period (UNCTAD, 2012b). However, assessment of the impact of such investment on local agriculture entrepreneurship is hindered by data availability and issues of confidentiality, comparability and reliability.

As a strategic sector, agriculture is often subject to restrictions on foreign ownership (UNCTAD, 2013b). However, such restrictions are not always implemented in LDCs. For example, the High Commission on Investment of Afghanistan has yet to exercise its authority to limit the share of foreign investment in certain sectors, industries and companies (Export.gov, 2016), while a moratorium on concessions greater than 1,000 hectares in the Lao People's Democratic Republic has proven ineffective and unenforceable (International Institute for Sustainable Development, 2012).

In contrast with historical experiences, there is evidence that new forms of FDI in agriculture are increasingly directed towards gaining access to natural resources of land and water, often emphasizing the production of basic foods or animal feed for export to the investing country (FAO, 2013b). This type of investment limits the scope for looser forms of association with local producers, which are more conducive to local entrepreneurship.

3. Participation of the least developed countries in textile and clothing global value chains

The textiles[16] and clothing sector is widely considered to offer good opportunities for industrialization, because of its labour intensity and requirement of large numbers of unskilled workers. It encompasses several stages of production (fibres, yarns, fabrics, finishing, knitting and so forth), a considerable variety of production processes and a multiplicity of end-products. The sector is shaped predominantly by large companies that decide what is produced, where and by whom; production moves quickly between countries and regions, largely in response to production costs, in particular those relating to labour.

Strategic suppliers and coordinators in East Asia have enjoyed resounding success. The key to this positive outcome was the ability of East Asian companies to progress from the assembly of imported inputs that were traditionally associated with export-processing zones to full-service package suppliers, a more domestically integrated form of exporting that generates greater value added (Gereffi, 1999). This is illustrated in figure 3.4 on the use of combined strategies of proactive upgrading and responsiveness to buyer strategies to reallocate tasks and risks within their GVCs. These transformed East Asian suppliers have now established their own triangular production networks into which LDCs are increasingly being integrated.

As yet, however, there is little sign that LDC entrepreneurs will be able to follow the same trajectory. While LDCs have benefited from GVCs, including regional production networks organized by regionally embedded investors, value addition remains elusive for most, with only the cut-make-trim segment having the room to accommodate additional entrants. For LDC entrepreneurs to emulate Asian strategic suppliers would require regional supplies of inputs, upgraded capacity — including in ICT — and greater speed and flexibility in reaching markets. Crucially, it would require entry by way of independent locally owned investors and a direct relationship with GVC buyers.

All LDCs are active in some way in one or more textiles and clothing segments. Several LDCs have a long tradition of cotton cultivation, dating back to 1904 in the United Republic of Tanzania, for example

Figure 3.4

Towards greater value addition in developing country textile and clothing industries

CUT, MAKE AND TRIM	Contractor carries out basic assembly using fabric sourced and owned by buyer or brand owner; payment based on processing fee (marginal supplier)
ORIGINAL EQUIPMENT MANUFACTURING	Contractor entrusted with whole manufacturing process by brand buyer and owner, including functional upgrading into logistics, i.e. sourcing and delivery of fabric in line with buyer specifications; design and brand belong to buyer (preffered/niche supplier)
ORIGINAL DESIGN MANUFACTURING	Contractor entrusted with some pre-production functions, i.e. design, testing (research and development) and whole production of garment; may include functional upgrading into distribution to final consumer for brand owner; brand belongs to buyer (strategic supplier)
FULL PACKAGE SERVICE PROVIDER	Contractor coordinates supply chain, contract manufacturing or invests in production in foreign markets for buyer or brand (coordinator/foreign investor)
ORIGINAL BRAND MANUFACTURING	Contractor retails own branded products; exercises post-production capabilities in product development, branding, marketing, retailing and consumer research (may retain coordinator role or sever ties to become lead firm)

Source: Esho, 2015; United Nations, 2005.

(International Trade Centre, 2015a) — and 19 LDCs export raw cotton, although cotton exports are a substantial share of exports and significant relative to the global market only in Benin, Burkina Faso, Chad and Mali, known as the "Cotton 4" countries. They export mainly to major textile industry centres in Asia and to Europe, suggesting that, like other LDCs, they are integrated into clothing GVCs, if only informally. Cotton production in LDCs is generally dominated by smallholders, and despite a significant decline across the board, remains a significant source of livelihood for many.

At least 12 LDCs across all geographical groups export prepared cotton, woven cotton and natural or synthetic yarn or textiles. LDC textile industries have suffered similar historical declines, struggling to compete with China following the expiry in 2004 of the Arrangement regarding International Trade in Textiles, also known as the Multi-fibre Arrangement, and in the new context of GVCs. However, the spinning industry

is showing resilience in some LDCs, and several hope to retain capabilities in initial processing, such as woven cotton and yarn, and to rekindle the textile industry.

It is in the garment sector that LDCs are most active, variously seeking to launch, expand or retain export-oriented garment industries. This sector has shown a potential for rapid growth. In Ethiopia, the garment industry grew by 51 per cent per year in 2010–2016 (van der Pols, 2015) and in Cambodia, garment and footwear exports, by 10.8 per cent per year in 2014–2016 (ILO, 2017b). In comparison, employment in the garment sector in the Lao People's Democratic Republic grew from 800 workers at its inception in the early 1990s to some 30,000 workers in 2012 (Nolintha and Jajri, 2015).The origins and evolution of the global garment industry and the role of LDCs in that industry's GVCs has been the subject of extensive study (Gereffi, 1999; ILO, 2014; Kaplinsky, 2005). At least 20 LDCs exported garments in 2016.

Garments are a leading export of Bangladesh, Cambodia, Haiti, Lesotho and Madagascar, and of increasing importance to several others, for example Afghanistan, the Comoros, Ethiopia and Sao Tome and Principe. In other LDCs, the sector remains nascent but is receiving government attention. Several LDCs have designated the sector strategic, or a national development priority, providing generous investment incentives and/or public support.

The scope for upgrading within garment GVCs in LDCs is affected by the positioning of strategic suppliers, which in part reflect investor and export market profiles, and by local dynamics at the time of integration into GVCs. An important driver of the inclusion of LDCs in textile and clothing GVCs is tariff hopping by strategic suppliers in response to shifting trade preferences. LDCs' duty-free access to major markets has influenced the geographical distribution of textile and clothing production and trade. This has contributed to a restructuring of GVCs to include LDCs in the low-value cut-make-trim manufacturing segment, but also in relatively short domestic value chains, mainly limited to primary production or low-value cut-make-trim processes relying on imported fibre, yarn and fabric to assemble finished garments for re-export. Some LDCs have, however, developed a degree of specialization; for example, the United Republic of Tanzania specializes in mosquito nets for the regional market. Some island LDCs specialize in awnings, sails and tents or in-home and lifestyle textiles; Sao Tome and Principe, in synthetic fibres; and several LDCs, in knitwear. In Ethiopia, the sector holds significant promise, as it produces a range of products, from natural and human-made yarns, fibre, threads and textiles, to various garments, carpets and home textiles (International Trade Centre, 2015b).

Since trade liberalization gives rise to a constant threat of preference erosion, compounded by the possibility of such preferences being extended to other developing countries,[17] the tariff-hopping motivation adds a further layer to the uncertainty that characterizes GVCs (section B).

Policy space is also an important issue in the context of trade, and LDCs generally have more policy space than other developing countries under World Trade Organization agreements (UNCTAD, 2015b). However, policy space issues also arise in a bilateral context. The Zambia–China agreement, for example, allows China, which has a competitive, advanced textile industry, tariff-free access to the Zambian market against that country's exports of raw cotton. This poses a major challenge to the development of the Zambian textile industry (Wang and Brown, 2013). Growing interest in recycling, a reflection of increasing concern with environmental issues, has contributed to a boom in used-clothing exports from developed to developing countries (Baden and Barber, 2005; Waste and Resources Action Programme, 2016). The proposal of the East African Community[18] to place an import ban on used clothing and shoes, aimed at encouraging local production and development, was reversed following a threat of retaliation from the United States — the world's largest exporter of used clothing (BBC News, 2018; The Conversation, 2018). The United States had carried out a similar threat against Rwanda when it raised tariffs on imported used clothing in 2016.

Garment sectors in LDCs are heavily dominated by FDI, with a poor record of upgrading and fostering local entrepreneurship: Bangladesh, Ethiopia, Haiti and Madagascar are among the few LDCs that exhibit significant local ownership and entrepreneurship. Together with the relative capital intensity of the textile and clothing sector, with an investment-to-turnover ratio of 1:1 for spinning, 1:1.5 for fabric production and 1:4 for clothing production (International Trade Centre, 2015a), tariff hopping has contributed to intense competition among LDCs for such investment.

Investment and trade patterns in GVCs are closely linked and combine with local market dynamics to exert a major influence on the potential for upgrading. Rather than adopting global investment and sourcing strategies, investors generally base investment decisions on geographical and cultural proximity to allow greater interaction and a more flexible division of labour. Investments outside an investor's region are primarily motivated by lower labour costs or tariff advantages. The emergence of developing countries in Asia as a global centre for textile and garment production has thus benefited Asian LDCs, which play a complementary role in the GVC strategies of strategic global suppliers in the region. LDCs in Southern Africa are benefiting from the GVC strategies of Mauritian strategic suppliers and strategies of South African manufacturers and retailers to withstand competition from China in their domestic market. For example, the garment industry in Lesotho, though initially driven by Asian FDI seeking access to the United States market, is now dominated in terms of number of firms, not export value, by producers for the South African market. This had led to a diversification of exports (Origin Africa, 2017). In both regions, nearshoring strategies are facilitated by a mix of headquarter and factory economies.

In Southern African and Asian LDCs, nearshoring has delivered qualitatively superior outcomes regarding skills development and functional upgrading, although this has not proved transferable to other regions, as local and regional embeddedness is critical to this success. For example, Staritz et al. (2016) identify different strategies adopted by firms in Lesotho and Madagascar to fulfil end-market and buyer requirements. Asian-owned firms that are part of established triangular networks supplying mainly standardized high-volume products to the United States market are often compelled to use inputs from investors' established input and services networks, limiting the potential for economic upgrading. In contrast, more regionally embedded investors from Mauritius and South Africa tend to service small orders of shorter-run products with higher fashion content and less upstream customization, mainly to Europe and South Africa. While maintaining close relationships with suppliers in Mauritius and South Africa, their strategies tend to favour small entrepreneurs and skills upgrading.

The proximity of Madagascar to Mauritius has also allowed the development of closer relationships with investors in these countries, facilitating knowledge and skills transfer. Likewise, South African investors increasingly employ local managerial staff in Lesotho, while Asian investors are hampered from doing so by the concentration of decision-making in their head offices and high upstream customization. Language barriers are also cited by case studies as a contributing factor to the use of expatriates in Africa and Asia. Regional investors have shown greater interest in moving higher-value-added functions to local firms. Asian investors engage less in training and innovation, and training is generally limited to basic production. This generates a pattern of widespread use of expatriates to fill skill gaps and in turn, an environment characterized by the following factors: limited career progression, high labour turnover, few incentives for local investment in specialized education, lack of public investment in industry-specific institutions and weak linkages between industry and educational institutions.

The findings on the differences in GVC governance structures and their implications for economic upgrading are confirmed by country case studies across developing regions (Staritz and Morris, 2013; Staritz et al., 2016; World Bank, 2011).

A further impediment to upgrading in many LDCs is the absence of integrated domestic value chains and local entrepreneurs in the sector. Local market dynamics substantially affect prospects for upgrading. In Madagascar, the distinction between domestic and local entrepreneurship is an important consideration, as investment and entrepreneurship in the sector have been led by investors who have European citizenship but are long-term residents and are embedded in

Regionally embedded investor strategies tend to favour small entrepreneurs and skills upgrading

the national economy. These investors' strong links with European markets played an important role in sustaining the industry during the loss of privileges under the Africa Growth and Opportunity Act in 2010–2014. In Bangladesh, where export-oriented garment manufacturing is a major driver of industrial development, the historical presence of a large local textile industry and a relatively complete supply chain contributed to resilient local entrepreneurship in the face of large-scale FDI, in export-processing zones and beyond, despite the predominance of artisanal SMEs and the reliance of the garment supply chain on the modern textile sector (UNCTAD, 2012c). In Haiti, apparel firms, which have traditionally serviced the United States market for high-volume standardized commodity apparel, also include those with roots in the local business community and more recent start-ups launched by or with foreign investors.

Subcontracting, driven by factors linked to GVCs, the phenomenon of fast fashion and the business-enabling environment, including access to credit and trade-facilitation bottlenecks (Centre for Research on Multinational Corporations, 2015), occurs to varying degrees in some LDCs, but primarily in the informal sector. Subcontracting activity and local linkages in Lesotho remain negligible (*Origin Africa*, 2017). In Cambodia, by contrast, subcontracting is a practice that occurs in all parts of the garment production process, primarily in relation to enterprises operated from private homes, warehouses or industrial buildings but their activities go largely unrecorded (ILO, 2017c), which may be indicative of informal operations. The implications for earnings, including effects on formal sector wages, may be negative and require further research. This is not suggestive of the benefits typically associated with subcontracting and linkages in industry cluster approaches to entrepreneurship.

Further constraints to upgrading arise from LDCs' early stage of development. Weaknesses in infrastructure and support services can undermine competitiveness, and limited access to credit and foreign exchange shortages can delay or prevent imports of intermediate inputs. Though a priority of the FDI-led industrialization strategy of Ethiopia, expansion of its garment sector may ultimately be hindered by a foreign exchange shortage (*Financial Times*, 2018). Some LDCs have responded to the

LDCs are potentially direct competitors to Asian strategic suppliers and coordinators

industry's high import dependence by making tax incentives conditional on exporting. In Madagascar, for example, tax incentives are conditional on 95 per cent of production being exported.

The absence of direct linkages with buyers and retailers in major markets and the substantial investments needed to establish such linkages are also obstacles to upgrading. Moreover, LDCs are potentially direct competitors to Asian strategic suppliers and coordinators, and this could be a source of tension. Bangladesh, however, may have the advantage of purchasing and distribution capabilities, while the Lao People's Democratic Republic benefits from having attracted FDI across several segments of the supply chain (Nolintha and Jajri, 2015).

The prospects for LDCs securing a role in garment GVCs is uncertain. Such chains are evolving in response to growing pressures at the retail end of the chain, as customers in developed markets are increasingly unwilling to pay higher prices for clothing and footwear, intensifying pressures for upgrading to full-package services and cost reduction (The Fung Group, 2016). Further, the industry is increasingly compelled to employ postponement strategies in the face of rapidly changing consumer tastes and preferences (Azmeh and Nadvi, 2014). While LDC garment industries could potentially gain from the pressure to create strategic partnerships, these conditions favour established players and preferred input suppliers and distribution networks. They could also result in industry consolidation, as suppliers seek to increase volume capacity to meet large and unpredictable buyer requirements in United States markets. In an industry that is already highly competitive, with narrow margins, LDCs operating in the cut-make-trim segment might struggle to maintain competitiveness.

The participation of some LDCs in electronics GVCs has similar characteristics to their participation in textile and clothing GVCs, as illustrated by the case of Cambodia (box 3.4).

Box 3.4 **Cambodia in the electronics global value chain**

GVCs are pervasive in the electronics industry, with production hubs centred in Asia, Europe and North America. The Asian hub is dominant, and most other Asian countries are linked to its two central players: Japan, as lead manufacturer of parts and components; and China, as contract manufacturer. The fragmentation of production processes is promoted by the high-value/low-weight nature of electronic components, which facilitates rapid and inexpensive air shipments globally, and a high degree of standardization, codification, computerization and interoperability.

In comparison, agriculture and garment GVCs are characterized by upstream customization, so that profits are derived mainly from marketing, branding and retailing activities. In electronics GVCs, more complex products and downstream customization mean that profits mainly take the form of economic rents from proprietary knowledge or technology and are driven by scale, volume and technological advances. Governance structures and specific features or electronics GVCs generate specific types of technological spillovers and opportunities to increase value added, leading DiCaprio and Suvannaphakdy (2017) to describe the sector as "propulsive".

Cambodia, a downstream assembler in electronics, has experienced explosive growth in FDI-driven electronics exports, which have more than tripled since 2010. Japanese manufacturers, in particular, have taken advantage of special economic zones in Cambodia for electronics and automotive-related production.

Cambodia has the advantage of proximity to Thailand, which is transitioning from hard drives to integrated circuits and radio frequency identification, and Viet Nam, which has secured a manufacturing niche in mobile phones, printers, and copiers. However, none of these countries is engaged in higher-level electronics design. In Cambodia, the lack of knowledge in physics, chemistry and materials science is a serious obstacle to advancement beyond assembly activities. As in the LDC garment industries, there is a vicious cycle in skills development: limited electronics education is both a cause and an effect of limited upgrading, and there is both a shortage of skilled engineering graduates and few employment opportunities for them. In the absence of opportunities for design work, most university graduates become technicians, while most technical and vocational education and training graduates become assembly workers.

Sources: De Backer and Miroudot, 2013; DiCaprio and Suvannaphakdy, 2017; Kaplinsky, 2005; RTI International, 2016; Sturgeon and Kawakami, 2010.

D. Global value chains and beyond

1. Limitations of integration into global value chains

A full assessment of the benefits of GVC participation for LDCs is not possible without additional data, particularly on spillover effects from GVC investors, which are often imprecisely measured and where tangible evidence is lacking or unclear. New data could rewrite the narrative on this issue, particularly with respect to local entrepreneurship. Nonetheless, while caution is needed in interpreting analysis based on a limited number of country and product case studies, the foregoing discussion suggests some useful insights.

Since a country's participation in GVCs largely reflects its structural characteristics (OECD, 2015a), LDCs attract mainly low-wage-seeking GVCs. While participation by LDCs in lower-end activities in GVCs has direct and visible short-term effects on the presence of FDI, employment and export growth, its longer-term impact on capacity-building, and the sustainability of the local industrial base is less apparent. Understanding of the wider economic effects of participation in low-value segments of GVCs is limited by a lack of systematic research on the linkages between GVCs and local entrepreneurship.

While low-value segments of GVCs have low entry barriers, their potential benefits are conditional on prior entrepreneurial engagement and are dissipated by acute competitive pressures (UNCTAD, 2016b). In LDCs, this form of participation in GVCs is not generally proven to be conducive to such engagement. There are numerous factors that limit opportunities for such engagement in LDCs; unless these other dimensions are addressed, LDC efforts to promote upgrading are likely to prove ineffective at best. For example, the case studies in this chapter show little sign of significant transfers either of technology or of tacit knowledge. When the knowledge needed to upgrade does not flow smoothly within the chain, the quality of national innovation systems can be a binding constraint on upgrading.

Based on 44 studies of developing country participation in GVCs, Choksy et al. (2017) find that suppliers lacking the necessary resources and capabilities rarely achieve functional upgrading. They also note that the occurrence of functional or other upgrading does not necessarily enhance such suppliers' ability to capture higher profits, and their strategies to improve profit margins may include downgrading.

> **Sustainability of the local industrial base is less apparent from the participation by LDCs in lower-end activities in GVCs**

The move towards more dynamic activities is largely determined by a country's production experience (United Nations, 2017a). A broader mix of capabilities and economic activity enhances the growth-pulling potential of the economy (UNCTAD, 2016b) to attract GVCs with different degrees of economic upgrading potential, broadening the range of product supply chains and the scope of entrepreneurship opportunities. Empirical evidence suggests that domestic supply chains and proximity to GVC hubs can reduce fragmentation costs (Beverelli et al., 2016), potentially helping LDC entrepreneurs to overcome some of the obstacles to increasing value capture inherent in GVCs. The same study also finds that strong domestic value chains may discourage GVC integration in sectors with high switching costs and low fragmentation costs. Countries with greater economic complexity (the capabilities to produce a diverse range of products, including niche products) tend to capture a larger share of value added from GVCs (International Monetary Fund, 2015; Kowalski et al., 2015). New interpretations of economic complexity also confirm that greater complexity is associated with less income inequality and that growth and development outcomes are affected by types of exports and related productive capabilities (Hartmann et al., 2017; Mealy et al., 2018; Pugliese et al., 2017).

While the ambition of developing countries to capture and retain more value from GVC participation has been questioned (Kowalski et al., 2015; United States Agency for International Development and East Africa Trade Investment Hub, 2017), such concerns may be misplaced. LDCs face enormous costs to achieve the Sustainable Development Goals (UNCTAD, 2017a) and are under pressure to provide social security nets but there is relentless pressure on them to reduce aid dependence and to undertake further trade liberalization (reducing revenues from trade taxes), while insertion in GVCs relies heavily on generous tax exemptions and incentives to attract FDI. Equally, GVC participation is heavily dependent on foreign exchange for intermediate imports (UNCTAD, 2013b) but implementation of trade support commitments by development partners has been inadequate, including relating to technology transfer. Increasing value retention from GVCs is essential to the domestic

Lead-firm strategies may exacerbate structural deficits in LDCs

resource mobilization required to reconcile these contradictions, in light of the demonstrable failure of GVC participation to unleash local entrepreneurship and the associated concentration of value capture by foreign investors.

Understanding GVC power structures is essential, both for entrepreneurs to identify opportunities for upgrading and for policymakers to devise appropriate policies. However, the effect of power imbalances in GVCs in limiting choice for LDC entrepreneurs is often overlooked in the GVC literature. There is evidence of potential conflicts between policies towards entrepreneurship and upgrading and lead-firm strategies, which, far from serving as an engine for entrepreneurial growth, may exacerbate structural deficits in LDCs.

As well as seeking to arbitrate labour cost differentials across countries,[19] the evidence suggests that lead firms predetermine the location and direction of value capture (Rakhmatullin and Todeva, 2016) and take defensive action against suppliers that might grow to become competitors (Gereffi, 2014). They are able to use their power within GVCs to distribute exposure to risk in their own favour and are increasingly shifting the consequences of uncertainty and the costs of adaptation to unforeseen circumstances to suppliers in developing countries. This issue is of particular significance in LDCs.

This suggests a need for concerted action at the global level to address the more insidious aspects of the GVC trade model. For example, digital and other technological innovations, though unquestionably positive, help lead firms to create and capture new value (Hagel et al., 2015), entrench their market power and disproportionately assign risk to developing countries and firms at the lowest levels of the value chain.

At best, the purported potential of the GVC model to deliver rapid industrialization and flourishing entrepreneurship remains unproven. GVCs have the potential to constrain structural transformation, as well as to widen opportunities (UNCTAD, 2016b), and GVC participation may compound the risk of LDCs graduating without the structural transformation required to sustain development progress (UNCTAD, 2016a). GVCs can also exacerbate existing structural problems such as gender inequality (International

Centre for Trade and Sustainable Development, 2016). IZA World of Labour (2016) highlights the dependence of large-scale job creation in GVCs on low wages, so that labour and skills upgrading may worsen both inequalities and outcomes for low-skilled and women workers.

Yet disappointing evidence on the developmental impact of GVCs is not limited to LDCs. The experiences of other developing countries suggest that economic upgrading is still constrained by a glass ceiling, although particular GVC products or services can provide pockets of excellence in a broader context of productivity-reducing structural change, stalled industrialization or premature deindustrialization as a result of globalization, trade liberalization and the retreat of the developmental State (ILO and World Trade Organization, 2011; UNCTAD, 2016b). This suggests that GVCs cannot guarantee the prospects of economic upgrading.

The opportunities and challenges of GVC participation also highlight the importance of a balanced mix of enterprises of different scales, rather than an excessive emphasis on micro and small enterprises. Scale economies are critical to lowering costs and maintaining competitiveness as profit margins narrow (Audretsch and Thurik, 2001; Kowalski et al., 2015). Larger firms are generally better placed to absorb the cost disadvantages of LDCs (Criscuolo and Timmis, 2017), critical in GVC trade, where low transaction costs are essential; and to meet quantity requirements and quality and safety standards at low production costs, which were identified by a World Trade Organization survey of LDC firms as the most important factors in connecting to GVCs (World Trade Organization, 2013). Equally, high levels of informality and self-employment hamper the ability of LDC firms to capitalize on GVCs (OECD and World Bank Group, 2015), while locally embedded large firms often serve as incubators for entrepreneurial talent and the transfer of tacit knowledge.

This discussion also raises questions about widely used policy instruments. LDC integration into GVCs occurs principally through FDI (Criscuolo and Timmis, 2017; UNCTAD, 2013a), and arguably, investment incentives play a more significant role in LDCs than in other developing countries, where firm competitiveness is of greater importance. However, such incentives can degenerate into measures to avoid FDI relocation, and may divert attention away from the higher priorities of building productive capacities and facilitating local entrepreneurship (Auerswald, 2015; UNCTAD, 2000). Similarly, special economic zones, which are often used to offset high transaction costs, can become enclaves or create dual economies in which a dynamic modern economy coexists with a more stagnant informal economy (Taglioni and Winkler, 2017; UNCTAD, 2016b). They may have explicit or de facto barriers to domestic investors, allowing disproportionate capture of policy rents by FDI (Kaplinsky, 2005; Taglioni and Winkler, 2017). In addition, they often lead to oligopolistic local market structures that impede the flourishing of transformative entrepreneurship (Bamber et al., 2014; Dihel et al., 2017; Ethical Trading Initiative, 2005; Wiegratz, 2016; Women in Informal Employment: Globalizing and Organizing, 2013).

2. The importance of enterprise

The issues surrounding LDC participation in GVCs reinforce the importance of high-impact entrepreneurs with the ability to overcome the obstacles to upgrading that bedevil LDCs. Despite the formidable impediments to entrepreneurship in LDCs, including infrastructure deficits, underdeveloped logistics industries, high trade transaction costs, underdeveloped input markets and climate risks (chapter 4), there are striking examples of individual entrepreneurs overcoming such obstacles in LDCs, as well as in other developing countries (box 3.5). The demonstration effects of such ventures can help unleash transformational entrepreneurship, and stimulate policy innovation and crowding in public investment.

What distinguishes the entrepreneurs described in box 3.5 is their ability to engage in opportunity discovery. The case studies also highlight the role of experience and knowledge in effectively overcoming entrepreneurship challenges and recognizing market opportunities, while the intersectoral mobility of some of the entrepreneurs suggests that lack of specialized training in agriculture or in entrepreneurship is not an insurmountable obstacle.

A commonality of the LDC cases, in particular, is young, well-educated, opportunity-driven entrepreneurs with exposure to modern business. Shambani Graduate Enterprise appears to have been motivated by a combination of necessity and opportunity, which may not be unusual. A study of high-growth women entrepreneurs (Neill et al., 2017) has found that most of them engaged in both discovery and creation of

Box 3.5 **Entrepreneurship against the odds**

Shambani Graduate Enterprise, established by three unemployed agriculture graduates, supplies retail outlets in Morogoro municipality, United Republic of Tanzania, and in the capital, some 200 km away, with fresh, cultured and flavoured milk. It has grown from an initial processing capacity of 30 litres with a single small supplier to a processing capacity of more than 1,000 litres of milk, supplied by 300 Masai cattle owners. The Enterprise has successfully established a viable supply chain, allowing existing producers to become profitable and creating jobs.

A graduate of business administration with practical experience at Ethiopian Airlines founded Green Ethiopia Exports in 2012. The company produces and exports popular Ethiopian spice blends such as shiro, mitmita, korarima and berbere, initially serving the country's sizeable diaspora in Europe and the United States, before expanding into African markets.

A former epidemiologist now owns and runs Fresh Direct Produce and Agro-allied Service, a leading company that grows fresh vegetables and distributes meat across the country. She moved her farm to the capital Abuja — cutting fuel costs and reducing the amount of produce ruined on the way to market — by turning to organic container farming. Before switching to farming, she worked as a research consultant in the Economic Development and Partnership Office of Osun State and research analyst for the Government of Nigeria. She also served as Special Assistant to the President on Wealth Creation and to the Coordinator of the National Poverty Eradication Programme. In the course of this work, she learned about hydroponics.

Taobao, founded in 2003 and owned by Alibaba, is the largest e-commerce marketplace in China and is increasingly important to rural economies across China. Online stores can be established on Taobao with little more than a good Internet connection and a logistics chain (often motorcycle delivery), and millions of rural people now sell goods at low cost online through Taobao villages, including mass-produced manufactured goods sold from villages near factories. This has helped to ease some of the push factors underlying rural-urban migration. Besides the size of the Chinese market, Taobao's success as an online platform is largely attributable to the attention given to building an appropriate ecosystem by taking proactive steps to create trust; build missing infrastructure, including a network of logistics providers; and develop a payment system.

One village in the southern province of Guangdong has taken a step further, opening a Taobao university that offers courses in online sales. The local government of Junpu was proactive in supporting the Taobao concept with free wireless Internet for residents, tax credits and free store space for residents and non-residents setting up physical shops for their inventory. Local officials also opened a free Taobao vocational school. Students are motivated by the wealth amassed by Taobao sellers.

Sources: Agriculture for Impact, 2014; BBC News, 2018a; Food, Agriculture and Natural Resources Policy Analysis Network, 2012; NaijaGists.com, 2017; Strategyzer, nd; Strategyzer, 2017; *The Economist*, 2014b.

The critical role of agriculture in LDCs makes policymaking in this area particularly complex

opportunity, suggesting that entrepreneurs taking this dual approach were most likely to leverage experience and learning in cognitive leaps and were confident in their ability to succeed. However, an entrepreneur's measure of self-belief is not a reliable indicator of entrepreneurial contributions to structural transformation. Despite more limited experience, less successful necessity-driven counterparts exhibited even greater belief in their own ability to succeed.

The case studies also demonstrate that entrepreneurship relevant to rural transformation need not originate in rural areas or entail action primarily at the producer end of the supply chain. As the Taobao case demonstrates, opportunity-driven entrepreneurs can play a catalytic role in channelling policy initiatives and investments. Evidence from countries such as Indonesia, Kenya, Peru and Uganda also suggests a clear divide between older and younger farmers, the latter generally bypassing traditional crops and showing a greater proclivity for technology and higher-value crops, for example in horticulture and greater responsiveness to increasing demand from the middle class (ILO, 2017a).

The critical role of agriculture in LDCs makes entrepreneurship in agriculture particularly important but makes policymaking in this area particularly complex.[20] Agriculture plays a major role in LDCs, economically, socially and in political economy, and is central to rural development, food security and poverty reduction, as well as structural transformation. It is also closely linked with environmental sustainability and gender equality.

This makes it difficult to distinguish and align economic and social objectives. While social objectives such as poverty reduction and food security often imply a focus on the most disadvantaged, promoting entrepreneurship in the sector requires attention to those best able to establish viable and thriving businesses. These are typically those already privileged by factors such as proximity to urban centres, education and access to specialized knowledge, capital, infrastructure and networks. Thus, International Institute for Environment and Development et al. (2012), for example, wonder whether a focus on value chains could narrow development vision to the top of the pyramid of small

producers — the top 1–15 per cent of producers — raising the risk of a new elitism in development policy, contrary to the tenets of inclusiveness.

While a detailed discussion is beyond the scope of this report, reconciling these tensions and ensuring that the single-minded pursuit of social goals does not undermine economic objectives and vice versa, is essential to structural transformation, including in rural areas. A first step is recognizing that the interdependence of the two goals is central to sustainable development (UNCTAD, 2016a).

3. The role of comparative advantage

A growing body of GVC literature offers policy recommendations relevant to making GVCs work for development in LDCs (Keane and Baimbill-Johnson, 2017; Taglioni and Winkler, 2017). In particular, Taglioni and Winkler (2017) present comprehensive and detailed practical guidance on the nature and potential of GVCs, their pitfalls and means of leveraging them for development. However, this literature generally relies on revealed comparative advantage,[21] as identified by standard trade theory, as the basis for the design of GVC engagement strategies. For most LDCs, this would imply seeking or maintaining specialization in low-skilled and low-value manufacturing as the basis for industrialization. Such a specialization would increase their productivity, lower unit production costs, and ultimately benefit global trade.

However, while revealed comparative advantage may be a useful indicator and policymaking tool, the overriding objective is to ensure an evolution of the revealed comparative advantage and develop dynamic comparative advantage in line with the goal to achieve sustainable development in LDCs. Since the weakness of local entrepreneurship in LDCs creates barriers to capturing the gains from GVC engagement, this implies a need to disrupt the revealed comparative advantage to launch the process of structural transformation. Trade theory predicts that a strategy based on static revealed comparative advantage would maximize the overall benefits of global trade, but not that such benefits would be evenly distributed or accrue to all participants. Rather, the evidence strongly suggests that LDCs would be among the losers under this model, as an exclusive focus on leveraging their current revealed comparative advantage would make it difficult to engineer the necessary evolution of their revealed comparative advantage for an upward progression in development and industrialization.

A sustainable development perspective thus indicates the need for a more nuanced approach to the application of revealed comparative advantage in order to enhance coherence and consistency and prioritize developmental goals rather than entry into GVCs based on a country's current revealed comparative advantage.

An important part of good development governance is aligning policies with desired developmental outcomes (United Nations, 2017). An active FDI policy (development-led engagement) aimed at changing a country's industrial structure can be expected to be more effective than passive FDI and trade policy (GVC-led engagement) in preventing adverse development outcomes arising from contradictions between GVC investors' competitive strategies and national development objectives. Under restrictive patterns of GVC governance, the latter approach is more likely to generate static entrepreneurship and export patterns defined by current industrial structures.

The possibility that revealed comparative advantage may evolve in a way that allows the predominance of traditional low-skilled labour-intensive exports to persist[22] suggests that LDCs may be better served by an eclectic industrial strategy that simultaneously targets low and high-skill sectors, and by non-equity modes of GVC integration. The probability of positive spillovers from arm's-length trade and non-equity modes of GVC involvement are known to be higher than other modes (Taglioni and Winkler, 2017; UNCTAD, 2013a). An eclectic approach better reflects LDCs' multiple policy objectives of macroeconomic stability, job creation, poverty reduction, industrialization and structural transformation.

GVCs require government coordination at the micro level (Taglioni and Winkler, 2017) and have exposed the limitations of past development strategies that did not prioritize strong developmental States. Indeed, GVCs have contributed to the global revival of industrial policy, while also highlighting parallels between more recent strategies and the failures of past industrial policies — indiscriminate FDI incentives, mirroring unselective subsidies to local firms; the tendency to establish enclaves; a disproportionate focus on incumbents; oligopolistic market structures; and limited capacity to generate feedback between policy design and implementation. While these problematic aspects of industrial policy remain, they can be moulded and rendered less binding through appropriate institutional design (Rodrik, 2008).

LDCs need to strategically reframe policy

to unlock potential opportunities of GVC

4. International competition for high-level skills and entrepreneurship

One consequence of the rise of GVCs in both developed and developing economies is job polarization: a shift of employment from middle-wage to high- and low-wage jobs (United Nations Department of Social and Economic Affairs, 2017; World Bank, 2016b;). There has been a tendency to assume that the risk of job polarization in LDCs is limited by the potential for GVCs to tap mainly abundant unskilled labour. Nonetheless, in 2016, there was evidence of job polarization in some, though not all, LDCs — in Uganda and the United Republic of Tanzania, but not Ethiopia, for example (World Bank, 2016b); this lack of uniformity could reflect differences in degrees of integration into GVCs and/or lagged effects.

Job polarization arises in part from the growing role of GVCs in increasing competition for highly skilled workers. International mobility of highly skilled human capital has increased substantially, in tandem with the expansion of the knowledge-intensive economy that is the hallmark of contemporary globalization.[23] There is evidence of a strong correlation between high-skill migrant concentration and the ability of destination countries to maintain a competitive edge academically and economically (Kerr et al., 2016); the desire to leverage multiplier effects generated by skill agglomeration has resulted in fierce competition, mainly among developed countries, to attract highly skilled migrants. Like GVC production hubs, the geographical distribution of high-skill migration is

Competition for high-skill human capital has been transformed to encompass the targeting of talented and high-impact entrepreneurs and innovators

significantly concentrated, and such migration to OECD countries is growing at staggering rates. The agglomeration of skills is also evident in the pattern of high-skill intraregional migration within developing regions (UNCTAD, 2018e).

Competition for high-skill human capital has been transformed to encompass the targeting of talented and high-impact entrepreneurs and innovators. The intensity of this competition, which partly reflects the disparity in rents across GVCs indicated by the smile curve (section B.2), is demonstrated by the establishment by several developed and developing countries of entrepreneurship visa programmes in addition to traditional high-skill visa or immigration schemes. These include Australia, Chile, Denmark, Germany, Ireland, Italy, New Zealand, Singapore, Sweden and the United Kingdom. Other countries, such as Qatar and the United Arab Emirates, have policies with the same aim, based on inviting potential entrepreneurs to "come here, build here and we will help you succeed". Others, such as Spain, offer an automatic second residency for entrepreneurs that set up businesses locally. Following the mass emigration of graduates in the wake of near bankruptcy in 2010, Greece has followed the example of Israel and its venture capital model of investing in Israeli and Israeli-linked businesses to reverse the brain drain. The Government of Greece has entered into partnership with the European Investment Fund and the European Investment Bank to capitalize Greek entrepreneurs abroad, provided they set up businesses in Greece (BBC News, 2018b).

Such programmes are qualitatively different from traditional policies in recognizing differences in the ability of various types of human capability to translate knowledge into commercial value and seeking to leverage potential high-impact entrepreneurs to achieve cognitive leaps in business that create a ratchet effect. However, while some programmes are considered successful, such as that of Chile (chapter 5), their efficacy across the board is unclear, and evaluation is hindered by gaps in data (ICF International, 2016).

Adapting migration strategies to these developments is a high priority in LDCs. Migration clearly raises world output, and there is conclusive evidence of large benefits in other dimensions of human development, such as education and health (International Organization for Migration, 2018; UNCTAD, 2018e). However, the evidence also indicates a need for selectivity in LDCs seeking to transform or construct revealed comparative advantage through entrepreneurship.

While they cannot hope to match the generous incentives offered by developed countries and other developing countries, LDCs cannot afford to be bystanders, because demonstration effects contribute to increasing emigration (International Organization for Migration, 2018), and differences in the returns to skills are a major driver of international migration (Rosenzweig, 2005; UNCTAD, 2018e). The emigration of skilled workers may also have a negative impact on the returns to expenditure on education for individuals and the economy, in the contexts of GVCs, as in the case of university and technical and vocational education and training graduates in the electronics industry in Cambodia (box 3.4). Related concerns are the implications for individual occupational choices, and associated concentrations in educational investment. For example, while India leads the world in the number of students obtaining Bachelor's degrees in science, technology, engineering and maths, this demand is driven in large measure by workforce needs and measures to attract highly skilled migrants in the United States (UNCTAD, 2018f).[24] The influence of migration prospects on individual educational choices may limit the ability of LDC policymakers to harness scarce education resources effectively for sustainable development.

LDCs may benefit from policies aimed at offering more opportunities and incentives for temporary or permanent highly skilled migrants and high-impact entrepreneurs to return from more developed destination countries. Since skill acquisition is likely to be more important for more educated and higher-skilled migrants with a higher probability of working in dynamic sectors (Rosenzweig, 2005; UNCTAD, 2018e), targeted, rather than generalized, schemes may be more conducive to harnessing return migration to close technology gaps (International Organization for Migration and Migration Policy Institute, 2012) and construct revealed comparative advantage. The latter outline the sequence of steps needed to identify goals, build institutions, and design and implement calibrated strategies in line with policy goals, including strategies specific to entrepreneurship. Cost-effective options range from general frameworks such as dual citizenship,[25] to more intensive institutional activities such as the establishment of skilled migrant registries and matchmaking activities, starting with the mapping of networks, interests, expectations and available resources among expatriate communities.

Some destination countries partner with countries of origin on such programmes. For example, the Ministry of Foreign Affairs of Italy has assisted Ethiopia in registering migrant associations and creating a national database of Ethiopian migrants, and in assessing SME proposals by potential returnees.

LDCs with sovereign wealth funds, such as Angola, Kiribati, Mauritania and Senegal, might be able to emulate enterprises based in other developing countries that have acquired firms or plants from industrialized countries for their technology and have relocated their operations. Examples include the acquisitions by Tata, an Indian company, of Land Rover in the United Kingdom and by Hangang, a Chinese company, of the Kaiserstuhl III coking plant in Germany (*The New York Times*, 2007). Asian platform brands have had notable success in using strategic acquisitions alongside investment in research and development to overcome constraints on upgrading in electronics GVCs.

5. Fostering intersectoral linkages: The example of tourism and agriculture

The service exports of LDCs are overwhelmingly concentrated in tourism, which represents 7 per cent of their total exports and 10 per cent of exports of non-oil exporters (World Tourism Organization et al., 2017). Tourism is also featured as an explicit target in Sustainable Development Goals 8, 12 and 14. Fostering strong and diverse linkages between tourism and other sectors could generate synergies and multiplier effects and increase opportunities for local entrepreneurial engagement. Strengthening linkages with agriculture and creative or cultural sectors, in particular, can be an effective strategy to promote entrepreneurship and structural transformation. In Ethiopia, for example, government restrictions on food imports help cultivate strong backward linkages between tourism establishments and smallholders, increasing local procurement, so that 44 per cent of hotel spending on food accrues to local producers (UNCTAD, 2017d).

However, tourism development in LDCs is oriented primarily towards satisfying export markets rather than promoting local value added, giving rise to enclave issues similar to those found in the manufacturing sector, including heavy reliance on imported inputs and FDI. Exploring new and innovative approaches to leveraging intersectoral linkages in a concerted

Opportunities exist for LDCs to revitalize tourism and entrepreneurship around unique agricultural produce and traditional products

and comprehensive way could play an important role in increasing the potential for local entrepreneurial engagement, plugging economic leakages, increasing production volumes and stimulating upgrading, as well as improving livelihoods, including in rural communities.

Linkages between agriculture and tourism can be strengthened through the establishment of local supplier clusters and supply chains, as well as agricultural supplies for tourism. Coupled with a well-coordinated branding strategy, including the use of geographical indications and other reputational and quality schemes, as well as an organized marketing campaign that taps consumer values, such an approach could generate multiplier effects in terms of investment, upgrading and beneficiation. Food festivals and tours can also expand agriculture–tourism linkages.

UNCTAD research and technical assistance on geographical indications highlights the astonishing array of often unique agricultural produce and traditional products available in LDCs, which have begun to valorize and market these products internationally (UNCTAD, 2015c). Opportunities thus exist for LDCs to revitalize tourism and entrepreneurship around these products. By addressing domestic and export objectives and supporting territorial food supply chain strategies, intersectoral linkages can also contribute to inclusivity and food security

Several developing countries have engaged in deliberate efforts to leverage cuisine as a recognizable national brand. The case of Peru offers useful insights on a national strategy assigning commercial value to local food culture (box 3.6). Peruvian cuisine has been used as a vehicle to foster national identity, social inclusion and economic development. As well as increasing the dynamism of an already successful tourism sector, the strategy spawned Peruvian entrepreneurs in the restaurant sector. The Government of Peru played a central role in gastronomy-centred campaigns to attract global attention and successfully rebranded the country's image following a period of political instability.

Box 3.6 **The Peruvian gastronomic revolution**

Peruvian cuisine has received international acclaim and is the subject of an application by the Government of Peru for designation by the United Nations Educational, Scientific and Cultural Organization as intangible cultural heritage. In its promotion of Peruvian cuisine as a symbol of a common national cultural identity, the Government declared it national heritage in 2007, triggering a gastronomic revolution. As a result, Peruvian cuisine became an export commodity and a source of dynamism for the tourism sector. Peruvian food exporters have leveraged geographical indications and other quality schemes, while extensive media campaigns have raised the local and international profile of the cuisine. Parallel campaigns marketing Peru as a culinary travel destination, alongside its iconic ruins and landscapes, have led to a boom in tourism and have inspired Peruvian entrepreneurs to establish Peruvian restaurants at home and abroad. This has generated wider benefits for local producers and promoted the development of related agricultural and tourism supply chains.

Sources: Bannister, 2017; Santilli, 2015; *The Economist*, 2014a.

Notes

1   Dai, 2013; Phillips, 2017; ILO, 2011; ILO and World Trade Organization, 2011; Rakhmatullin and Todeva, 2016; UNCTAD, 2013b; UNCTAD, 2013c; UNCTAD, 2016b; World Bank Group et al., 2017.

2   Hartog et al., 2010; Ponte and Sturgeon, 2017; Thurik et al., 2002; Verheul et al., 2001.

3   CUTS International, 2016; International Trade Centre, 2013; World Bank Group et al., 2017.

4   Angelsberger et al., 2017; Neill et al., 2017; Oyson and Whittaker, 2010; Oyson and Whittaker, 2015.

5   Barkema and Drogendijk, 2007; Shaw and Darroch, 2004; Verbeke et al., 2014.

6   Business for Social Responsibility et al., 2017; International Centre for Trade and Sustainable Development, 2016; ILO, 2016a; IZA World of Labour, 2016.

7   Tariff escalation is the practice of imposing higher tariffs on finished and/or partially processed exports, giving rise to high rates of effective protection to processing industries in importing countries at the expense of those in countries of origin.

8   Garment exports from Haiti have duty-free access to the United States market under the Haitian Hemi-spheric Opportunity through Partnership Encouragement Act of 2008.

9   CUTS International, 2016; Economic Commission for Africa, 2014; OECD and World Bank Group, 2015; World Bank Group et al., 2017.

10 Postponable products are those which consumers may choose to defer purchases of to a later date, especially during economic downturns and times of uncertainty.

11 Fishing is part of the primary sector.

12 While agribusiness is widely associated with large-scale enterprise, the definition established by the Food and Agriculture Organization of the United Nations (FAO) also includes smaller farms, processors and so forth (FAO, 2013a). The agrifood industry is a subset of agro-industry centred on making, processing, preparing and packaging food products for human consumption.

13 Dihel et al., 2017; OECD, 2017c; OECD and FAO, 2017; UNCTAD, 2017i.

14 Government of Malawi et al., 2018; OECD, 2017a; Oya et al., 2017.

15 Keane, 2017; Minot and Ronchi, 2014; Nissanke, 2017.

16 Unlike the apparels segment, generally every step is mechanized in the modern textiles industry (weaving, spinning and processing industries). However, in some LDCs, such as Bangladesh, the textiles segment still uses traditional methods such as handlooms.

17 For example, preferences relating to the Everything But Arms initiative were recently extended to Jordan (European Commission, 2016).

18 Burundi, Kenya, Rwanda, South Sudan, United Republic of Tanzania and Uganda.

19 Hitt et al., 2001; ILO and World Trade Organization, 2011; Taglioni and Winkler, 2017; UNCTAD, 2016b.

20 A further complication is the susceptibility of the agricultural sector to entrenched perceptions whose validity may be questionable (Christiaensen and Demery, 2018), for example regarding the profitability of modern input use, the extent and nature of opportunities for rural non-farm enterprise, the assumed non-functioning of land markets in Africa and the assumed link from agricultural commercialization to improved nutrition.

21 The revealed comparative advantage index is used as an indicator of a country's relative advantage or disadvantage in producing certain goods or services based on its current trade flows, identifying sectors or activities where the revealed comparative advantage is highest as appropriate for specialization.

22 Benedictis, 2005; Platania, 2014; *The Economist*, 2012a.

23 International Organization for Migration, 2018; Kerr et al., 2016; UNCTAD, 2012d; World Bank, 2016b.

24 Similar effects may arise with regard to other occupations such as nursing, a skill targeted by countries such as the United Kingdom in a growing number of developing countries; however, there is a paucity of research in this area.

25 With the advent of globalization, the number of countries that now formally or informally allow citizens to hold dual citizenship has significantly increased.

PROACTIVE ROLE FOR THE STATE

ENTREPRENEURSHIP POLICIES

should go beyond market failure correction
and creation of an enabling business environment

OPPORTUNITIES

New areas of
entrepreneurship

Productivity gains at firm level

CHALLENGES

E-commerce
readiness for vendors
and customers

DIGITALIZATION

FOR ENTREPRENEURSHIP

Entrepreneurship in the least developed countries: Major constraints and current policy framework

CHAPTER 4

Entrepreneurship in the least developed countries: Major constraints and current policy frameworks

A. Introduction	**81**
B. Constraints to the emergence and growth of firms	**81**
1. Internal and external barriers	81
2. Insights from small and medium-sized enterprise competitiveness surveys	85
C. Key obstacles to enterprise	**86**
1. Entry regulations, formalization procedures and costs	86
2. Access to finance	89
3. Access to energy	90
4. Digital connectivity	91
5. Gender-based constraints	92
D. Current policy frameworks for entrepreneurship and structural transformation	**98**
1. National development plans	98
2. Industrial policies	99
3. Entrepreneurship and development policies for microenterprises and small and medium-sized enterprises	99
4. Institutional frameworks for enterprise policies	102
5. Recommended policy principles	102
Notes	**105**

A. Introduction

An important starting point for policies to promote structural transformation through entrepreneurship is to understand the major barriers to entrepreneurship growth. Such barriers may be viewed from two perspectives, namely at the firm level and at the national level.

It is also important to understand the direction of current and future policies in relation to entrepreneurship and structural transformation. An assessment of the effectiveness of development policies in LDCs for microenterprises and SMEs should be encouraged. The establishment of performance measurement systems for microenterprises and SMEs could also provide a means for Governments in LDCs to monitor the evolution of enterprises, improve their understanding of the nature and complexity of the constraints faced by enterprises of different types and sizes, and evaluate the impact of entrepreneurship policies on structural transformation.

This chapter is structured as follows. Section B provides an overview of barriers to competitiveness and performance in LDCs from the firm-level perspective, focusing primarily on external barriers. Section C addresses key constraints in LDCs at the national level, namely entry regulations, formalization procedures and costs; access to finance; access to energy; digital connectivity; and gender-based constraints. Section D provides an overview of existing policy frameworks for entrepreneurship in LDCs, concluding with a discussion of recommended areas for improvement.

Firms face both internal and external barriers to growth

B. Constraints to the emergence and growth of firms

1. Internal and external barriers

Firms face both internal and external barriers to growth (figure 4.1). High-growth firms are not exempt; a small proportion of such firms can create the majority of jobs and it is important to understand the obstacles to the success of both such firms and those firms with the potential to achieve high growth (Lee, 2012). For example, there is evidence that high-growth firms view internal barriers, which they can influence, as more binding than external barriers, although this may be more applicable in developed countries rather than in developing countries (Cooney, 2012; Lee, 2012). Further research is warranted in the context of LDCs.

Internal factors influencing firm growth may be divided into those related to the entrepreneur, to the firm and to strategy, as shown in table 4.1 (Storey, 1994). There is growing recognition in the literature that the most significant internal barriers to firm growth are psychological or motivational factors, such as the commitment of an entrepreneur to growth. Other widely cited factors include management capability, networking ability, funding level, sales and marketing

Figure 4.1

Barriers to firm growth

Source: UNCTAD secretariat, based on Cooney, 2012.

capacity, product and/or service offered and the level of orders. Recruiting suitable staff and skills shortages can also pose significant internal constraints (Lee, 2012). There is growing recognition of the importance of entrepreneurship education and training in overcoming internal barriers, including experiential learning to address motivational factors and learning from success and failure (Cooney, 2012).

It is often claimed in policy discourse that one important external barrier is the business climate, which can give rise to direct, indirect and hidden production costs; inhibit the adoption of new technologies; deter investment; weaken competitiveness and reduce market size (World Economic Forum et al., 2009). The relevance of the business climate has long been recognized in policy debates, notably through the work of institutions such as GEM, through its measurement of entrepreneurial framework conditions; the World Bank, through its Doing Business database; and the World Economic Forum, through its global competitiveness index and the associated report series. Disagreements on the scope of the concept and on related methodologies have been noted (Romer, 2018; *The Economist*, 2018b). UNCTAD has affirmed the need to optimize the regulatory environment and benchmark the national business climate, to create an institutional framework more supportive to start-ups (UNCTAD, 2012a), provided it is coherent with industrial policies and structural transformation strategies.

The business climate is conventionally encapsulated in the ease of doing business index of the World Bank, which ranks countries on the basis of the following

10 indicators: starting a business; dealing with construction permits; accessing electricity; registering property; securing credit; protecting minority investors; paying taxes; trading across borders; enforcing contracts; and resolving insolvency. Most LDCs rank low, with 32 of the 47 LDCs in the lowest quartile in 2018, out of 191 countries.

The business climate is largely shaped by government policies and legislation. Legislation affects the actual and perceived costs and benefits of entrepreneurial activity and the returns to investment for domestic firms. Legislation can also address existing barriers or create barriers for disadvantaged groups, including women (see section C.5), for example in accessing the inputs and resources needed to start and grow a business.

Competition policy and consumer protection laws are also of particular importance, as market structure and the intensity of competition in product markets affect industry and firm size, as well as the number of firms a product market segment can support, consistent with profitability. The absence or lack of enforcement of such laws can give rise to concentrated market structures that erode profitable entrepreneurial opportunities in certain economic activities and sectors, limiting new business formation and firm viability. Current entrepreneurs may also engage in unproductive or destructive entrepreneurship (Baumol, 1990) such as rent-seeking activities, for example the formation of cartels and other abusive behaviour by dominant firms, to prevent the entry of new entrepreneurs or limit their profitability. Competition policy therefore "has a bearing on the climate for entrepreneurship, as it is a

Table 4.1
Internal factors influencing growth in small firms

Entrepreneur level	Firm level	Strategy-related
Age	Age	Workforce training
Gender	Sector	Management training
Family history	Legal form	External equity
Social marginality	Location	Technology
Functional skills	Size	Market positioning
Education	Ownership	Market adjustments
Training		Planning
Management experience		New products
Motivation		Management recruitment
Prior unemployment		State support
Prior self-employment		Customer concentration
Prior sector experience		Competition
Prior firm size experience		Information and advice
Prior business failure		Exporting
Number of founders		

Source: UNCTAD secretariat, based on Cooney, 2012; Storey, 1994.

tool for challenging abusive and restrictive practices that stifle entrepreneurship" (Makhaya, 2012). This has led, for example, developing countries such as Singapore and South Africa to include provisions in competition laws to allow microenterprises and SMEs to participate equitably in the economy.

In addition, intellectual property provisions are needed to ensure an institutional environment that promotes and rewards innovation among entrepreneurs. There are important interactions between competition policy, intellectual property rights and entrepreneurship. For example, there is evidence that strengthened intellectual property rights protection adversely affects the entry of entrepreneurs adopting new technologies, but that this relationship can be weakened by the increased enforcement of competition policy, and that intellectual property rights and competition policy can have complementary effects on the rate of entrepreneurial innovation (Fu and Liu, 2013; Gans and Persson, 2013). In most LDCs, there is significant scope to build capacities in formulating, enforcing and revising competition laws and policies, to ensure a business environment that is conducive to entrepreneurship. UNCTAD has supported the establishment and strengthening of competition policy frameworks and institutions in the following LDCs: Ethiopia, Madagascar, Sierra Leone, the United Republic of Tanzania and Zambia.[1]

Beyond changes to legislation, improving the business climate requires, inter alia, investment in hard and soft infrastructure, including with regard to transport, energy, ICT and trade facilitation; the development of an efficient and high-quality services sector; and improved developmental governance, including regulatory and anti-corruption reforms.

Labour market conditions can also present an obstacle to firm growth. The absence of social safety nets or alternative income sources drives many of those unable to secure wage employment, in particular women and youth, to informal entrepreneurship in the form of own-account activities (see chapter 2). Unemployment rates in LDCs range from 0.2 per cent in Cambodia (men and women) to 23.1 per cent among men and 27.6 per cent among women in Lesotho (figure 4.2). This heterogeneity reflects a range of factors, which include the varied effectiveness of government policies, different rates of job creation associated with economic performance and different degrees of manufacturing development and rates of labour productivity growth (UNCTAD, 2013a). The rate of women's unemployment exceeds that of men's unemployment in 34 LDCs. Potential explanatory factors include gender-based inequality in accessing formal labour markets and productive

Lack of alternative income opportunities can give rise to survivalist entrepreneurs

inputs; a lack of State support for women with regard to childcare; and a greater concentration of women's labour in the rural agricultural sector (UNCTAD, 2015a). Unemployment among youth (15–24 years of age) is a particular challenge, especially in Haiti, Lesotho, Mozambique, the Sudan and Yemen, with rates exceeding 20 per cent among both men and women.

A lack of alternative formal income opportunities can give rise to survivalist entrepreneurs, who end up concentrated in sectors with low entry barriers. Because of the low value of alternative options, they are more likely to opt for entrepreneurship. This can result in sectors with low entry barriers becoming crowded with low-ability entrepreneurs, who cohabit with high-ability entrepreneurs, leading to depressed prices and profits, potentially endangering the viability of more dynamic enterprises. Unlike high-ability entrepreneurs, who are motivated by relatively high potential benefits from entrepreneurship, low-ability entrepreneurs are motivated primarily by low opportunity costs, reflecting their lack of alternative opportunities (Poschke, 2013). However, despite low productivity, such entrepreneurs are often persistent over time, lacking the potential for growth, but with a probability of exit no higher than that for larger enterprises in the medium term.[2] Such conditions can lead to a situation in which entrepreneurs of intermediate ability (with higher potential returns than low-ability entrepreneurs, but also greater opportunity costs) are crowded out, resulting in a polarization of entrepreneurship between those of high and low ability, which constrains the growth of the former. Selection into entrepreneurship from the high and low extremes of ability distribution explains the common empirical finding of greater variation in returns to entrepreneurship than in wages. This highlights the importance of absorbing necessity-driven and survivalist entrepreneurs into wage employment, and of targeting entrepreneurship support to entrepreneurs with greater ability and who are more dynamic (see chapter 5).

Another external barrier affecting firm growth is the level of access to markets, including export markets. Such access or a lack thereof has a direct effect on firm productivity, profitability, growth and survival. There is empirical evidence in LDCs and elsewhere that, controlling for other relevant factors, exporting firms have higher productivity levels, through learning

Figure 4.2

Unemployment rates in the least developed countries by age, 2018

(Percentage)

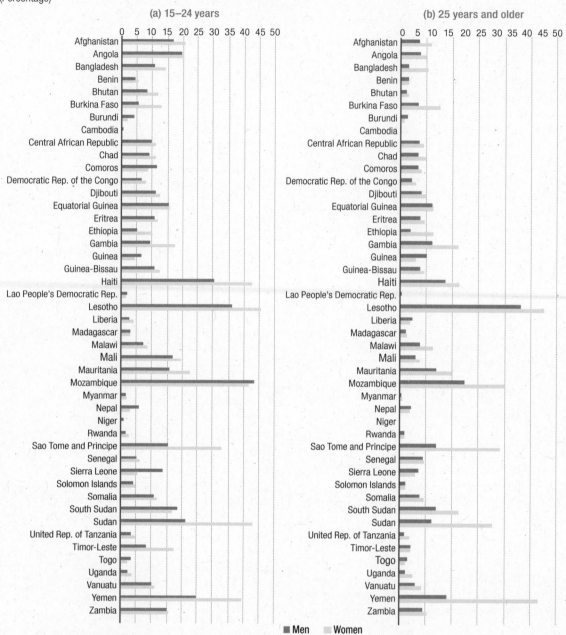

Source: UNCTAD secretariat calculations, based on ILO, 2018.
Note: Data not available for Kiribati.

by exporting, than non-exporters within the same industry (Fatou and Choi, 2015; Kamuganga, 2012; Siba and Gebreeyesus, 2014). Improvements in legal and institutional frameworks benefiting exporting firms can also have positive spillover effects on non-exporting firms (Chhair and Ung, 2014). Trade policies matter for entrepreneurship growth. There is a growing body of research that suggests that exporting leads to gains not only for larger firms but also smaller firms, allowing them to learn new skills, explore larger markets and raise the incomes of owners and their families (Atkin and Jinhange, 2017). This research

supports the case for designing policies that lower the costs for SMEs of finding foreign customers; increase their access to information on foreign markets, such as regulations on imported goods and services; and create a role for export promotion agencies that link local SMEs to foreign customers (Atkin and Jinhange, 2017).

Other important external factors affecting a firm's growth include the national level of economic development, which affects the range and depth of market opportunities available to firms; national economic performance, which affects both the composition and growth of demand and the availability and cost of capital; and the regional and global economic environment, which influences government policy and affects export opportunities. Macroeconomic variables such as exchange rates are also an important factor, affecting both the profitability of exports and import substitutes and the cost of imported inputs.

2. Insights from small and medium-sized enterprise competitiveness surveys

A more detailed picture of the constraints faced by firms in some LDCs is provided by the SME competitiveness surveys of the International Trade Centre. The ability of microenterprises and SMEs to compete in local and global markets is a key determinant of the probability of survival and the future growth trajectory. Understanding the determinants of competitiveness among SMEs in LDCs can inform policymakers in shaping entrepreneurship policies. The surveys assess the competitiveness of SMEs on the basis of the following three capacity pillars (International Trade Centre, 2017):

- Compete: static; centred on firm operations and efficiency in cost, time, quality and quantity.
- Change: dynamic; centred on firm response to or anticipation of market forces and innovation through investments in human and financial capital.
- Connect: links static and dynamic features of competitiveness; centred on the collection, processing and communication by firms of information and knowledge crucial for the digital economy and services.

Assessments are made at the following three levels of the economy: firm (including capabilities such as whether firms are managed according to best practices, need resources and have competencies to manage such resources); business ecosystem (whether business support institutions provide the resources and competences that enterprises need to be competitive); and national environment (macroeconomic and regulatory). The indicators characterizing the range of constraints that can affect the competitiveness of SMEs across the three capacity pillars and three economic levels are shown in table 4.2.

To date, surveys have been conducted in 11 LDCs, namely Bangladesh, Bhutan, Burkina Faso, Cambodia, Guinea, Madagascar, Malawi, Nepal, Rwanda, Senegal and the United Republic of

LDC firms' capabilities are weakest in their capacity to connect

Tanzania. The results provide insights on binding external constraints to a firm's performance and survival (figure 4.3).

A firm's capabilities tend to be weakest in the capacity to connect, except in Malawi and Rwanda, highlighting the need for greater investment by firms in ICT for production, management and marketing strategies. There is a particular need for improvement in the capacity to change in Burkina Faso and the United Republic of Tanzania within the business ecosystem, and in the capacity to connect in Guinea, and the capacity to change in Bangladesh within the national environment. In the 11 countries, large enterprises perform better than small enterprises in all three pillars. This is consistent with the findings showing faster productivity growth in large firms (see chapter 2) and is in line with one of the main messages of this report that support should be provided to firms not only at the initial stages of their life cycle but at all stages. In some LDCs in Africa, namely Guinea, Madagascar, Rwanda, Senegal and the United Republic of Tanzania, the gap between small and large firms is widest in the use of email and/or the operation of a business website. Elsewhere, there are considerable variations between small and large enterprises. For example, in Bangladesh and Burkina Faso, the widest gap is in the ownership of foreign technology licences; in Bhutan and Malawi, in the attainment of international quality certificates; in Cambodia, in having audited financial statements; and in Nepal, in having a bank account (International Trade Centre, 2017). In these 11 LDCs, some small firms underperform with regard to the following indicators:

- Having international quality certificates (for example in Bangladesh, Bhutan, Guinea and Malawi).
- Having bank accounts (Bangladesh, Cambodia, Rwanda and the United Republic of Tanzania).
- Investments financed by a bank (Cambodia, Madagascar and Senegal).
- Using email (Bangladesh, Burkina Faso, Nepal and the United Republic of Tanzania).
- Operating a website (Bangladesh, Bhutan, Burkina Faso, Guinea, Madagascar, Rwanda and the United Republic of Tanzania).
- Having audited financial statements (Bangladesh, Bhutan and Cambodia).

Table 4.2

Indicators for small and medium-sized enterprise competitiveness surveys

Firm capabilities	Business ecosystem	National environment
Compete		
International quality certification	Power reliability	Access to electricity
Bank account	Domestic shopping reliability	Ease of trading across borders
Capacity utilization	Dealing with regulations	Applied tariff, trade-weighted average
Managerial experience	Customs clearance efficiency	Prevalence of technical regulations
		Faced tariff, trade-weighted average
		Logistics performance index
		International Organization for Standardization 9001 on quality certificates
		International Organization for Standardization 14001 on environmental certificates
		Governance index
Connect		
Email	State of cluster development	ICT access
Website	Extent of marketing	ICT use
	Local supplier quality	Online government services
	University and industry collaboration in research and development	
Change		
Audited financial statement	Access to finance	Ease of getting credit
Investment financed by bank	Access to educated workforce	Interest rate spread
Formal training programme	Business licencing and permits	School life expectancy
Foreign technology licence		Ease of starting a business
		Patent applications
		Trademark registrations

Source: UNCTAD secretariat, based on International Trade Centre, 2017.

- Owning foreign technology licences (Bangladesh, Guinea and Nepal).
- Offering formal training programmes to employees (Bangladesh, Madagascar and Senegal).

At the national environment level, three of the four LDCs in Asia, namely Bangladesh, Cambodia and Nepal, score high under the trade policy indicator, along with two LDCs in Africa, namely Guinea and Malawi. Nepal and four LDCs in Africa, namely Burkina Faso, Madagascar, Senegal and the United Republic of Tanzania, score high under the prevalence of technical regulations indicator. In addition, Bangladesh scores high under the online government services and interest rate spread indicators; Bhutan, under the access to electricity and ease of trading across borders indicators; Burkina Faso, under the logistics performance index and ease of starting a business indicator; and Cambodia and Rwanda, under the ease of getting credit indicator. Such heterogeneity with regard to constraints highlights the need to tailor entrepreneurship strategies to each national context. Analysis based on the competitiveness surveys indicates the need for entrepreneurship policies

to rely on a range of interventions at various levels, including the firm, business ecosystem and national environment levels; and target the building of static and dynamic competitiveness between firms.

C. Key obstacles to enterprise

This section discusses a range of constraints to the emergence and growth of enterprises that are of particular relevance in LDCs, namely entry regulations, formalization procedures and costs; access to finance; access to energy; digital connectivity; and gender-based constraints.

1. Entry regulations, formalization procedures and costs

Entry regulations represent a key element in the incentive structure that affects the creation and formalization of new enterprises and the emergence of start-ups capable of competing with incumbent firms and challenging their business models (UNCTAD, 2012a). Some provisions and regulations are justified by economic, administrative, social or environmental

Figure 4.3

Small and medium-sized enterprise competitiveness by capacity pillar, selected least developed countries

(Percentage)

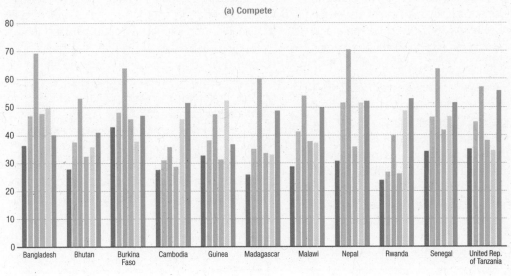

(a) Compete

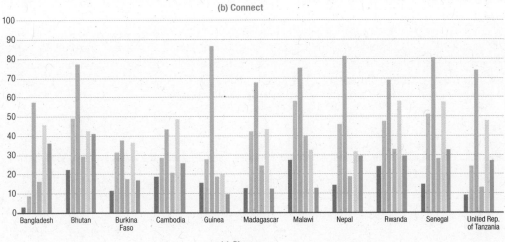

(b) Connect

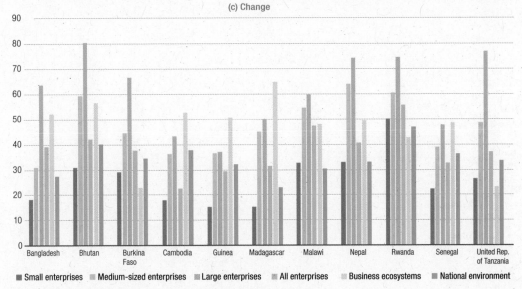

(c) Change

■ Small enterprises   ■ Medium-sized enterprises   ■ Large enterprises   ■ All enterprises   ■ Business ecosystems   ■ National environment

Source: UNCTAD secretariat calculations, based on International Trade Centre, 2017.

objectives, yet others unnecessarily tax potential entrepreneurs, involving costs that discourage start-ups and formalization. Disproportionate entry costs have long been identified as a potential hindrance to the establishment of firms in many developing countries (Djankov et al., 2002). Despite some signs of improvement, this remains the situation in many LDCs.

In 2015–2017, median start-up costs in LDCs were 40 per cent of per capita income, compared with a world average of 26 per cent, and 33 of the 46 LDCs for which data are available had start-up costs above the world average; the highest costs are in Chad, the Central African Republic, Somalia, Haiti and South Sudan (figure 4.4). The number of procedures required to start a business exceeded the world average in 21 LDCs, suggesting that time costs were also higher. In some LDCs (namely, Afghanistan, Benin, Guinea-Bissau, the Sudan and Yemen), women are subject to additional procedures with regard to starting a business, confirming the presence of additional constraints on women in engaging in entrepreneurship compared with men. For example, in some countries, women may have to seek permission from their husbands to apply for a loan or to sign business papers.

The high costs with regard to entry regulations can discourage the formalization of enterprises in LDCs, yet part of the decision on whether to formalize may be based on the need for time and resources for firms to explore and discover the range of profitable and sustainable entrepreneurial activities (see chapter 2). Such considerations highlight the limitations of conventional policy approaches focused on reducing administrative costs and strengthening penalties for non-registration and non-compliance with regulations. Greater administrative efficiency is important, yet there is also a need to enhance the benefits of registration, not least by promoting productivity increases among formal firms and improving access to finance (see chapter 5 for a discussion of policies on promoting the benefits of registration and formalization to firms).

In addition, the regulatory burden faced by firms can lower the impact of other interventions related to firm entry, performance and growth. Such a burden can affect the positive impact of trade on economic growth and, thereby, the rate of firm entry and survival prospects (Freund and Bolaky, 2008). The extent of regulation can also have considerable indirect effects that might influence firm entry. The positive effect associated with skills, such as educational attainment, diminishes considerably in countries

Figure 4.4

Costs and procedures to start a business in the least developed countries, compared with the world average, 2015–2017

(Percentage)

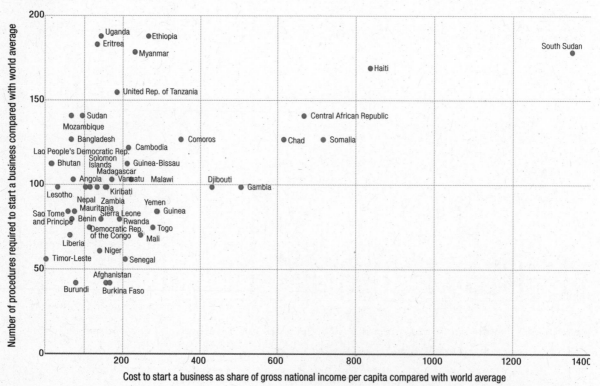

Source: UNCTAD secretariat calculations, based on data from World Bank Doing Business database.

with greater regulation, in particular for opportunity-based entrepreneurship (Ardagna and Lusardi, 2010). Some regulatory conditions, such as property rights protection or conditions related to human capital, can have idiosyncratic impacts on different types of entrepreneurship (Chowdhury et al., 2015).

2. Access to finance

Access to finance is a key pillar of entrepreneurship policies and a major constraint to enterprise (UNCTAD, 2012a). Informal firms, in particular, have limited access to finance from formal lenders, as shown in an analysis of the World Bank Enterprise Surveys of the informal sector (figure 4.5). In all of the LDCs for which data are available, internal funds are the predominant source of financing for day-to-day operations, typically followed by supplier credit and loans from friends or relatives. Financial actors, whether formal (such as banks and microfinance institutions) or informal (such as moneylenders), consistently play a limited role. Microfinance institutions, which might be expected to meet the needs of customers unable to access finance from banks, appear to be significant only in Nepal and to a limited extent in Burkina Faso, Madagascar and Rwanda. Allowing for some improvement in financial inclusion since the conduct of the surveys, the findings highlight the scale of credit rationing and the associated challenges for informal enterprises.

In LDCs, **internal funds** are by far the predominant **source of financing** in most firms

Limited access to finance may also present a binding constraint to productivity and enterprise survival, especially in rural areas, in which the availability of and access to credit is crucial to the success of both farm and non-farm enterprises (Alemu and Adesina, 2017; Gajigo, 2014; Osondu, 2014). In Uganda, for example, based on the living standards measurement study of the World Bank, the most important reasons that rural households report for enterprise exit involve economic factors, such as a lack of profitability and a lack of finance (Nagler and Naudé, 2017).

Figure 4.5

Sources of finance for day-to-day operations of informal firms, selected least developed countries

(Percentage)

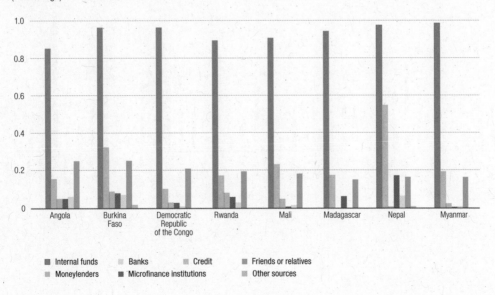

Source: UNCTAD secretariat calculations, based on data from World Bank Enterprise Surveys.

In principle, greater access to finance, in particular from the formal financial sector, is an important motivation to formalize. However, despite some signs of progressive financial deepening, such access remains limited in LDCs. The SME competitiveness surveys of the International Trade Centre highlight the limited access of firms in some LDCs to bank accounts and investment financing from banks. Domestic credit to the private sector relative to GDP increased in 36 of the 47 LDCs from 2004–2006 to 2014–2016 (figure 4.6), yet remained at 18 per cent of GDP in the median LDC, which is low by international standards and below the threshold beyond which the beneficial effects of financial depth on output growth begin to disappear.[3] Bolstering financial deepening, notably by fostering the emergence of a banking sector capable of adequately serving formal SMEs, therefore remains a crucial priority for LDCs, and this could also reinforce incentives for formalization.

3. Access to energy

Energy development is an important agenda item in many LDCs. For example, the national sustainable development plan of Myanmar recognizes the role of access to energy in facilitating the emergence of new and innovative SMEs and the development strategy of Senegal recognizes energy access as one of the most pressing issues.

In 2016, LDCs accounted for only 13 per cent of the world population, but 56 per cent of people without access to electricity globally. Lack of access to energy affects productive sectors as well as households; energy facilitates the entrepreneurship, innovation, technical change and productivity growth that drive the building of productive capacities and structural transformation, and unreliable power supplies can disrupt production, impair productivity and impose additional costs with regard to on-site generators,

Figure 4.6

Domestic credit to the private sector in the least developed countries as share of gross domestic product, 2004–2006 and 2014–2016

(Percentage)

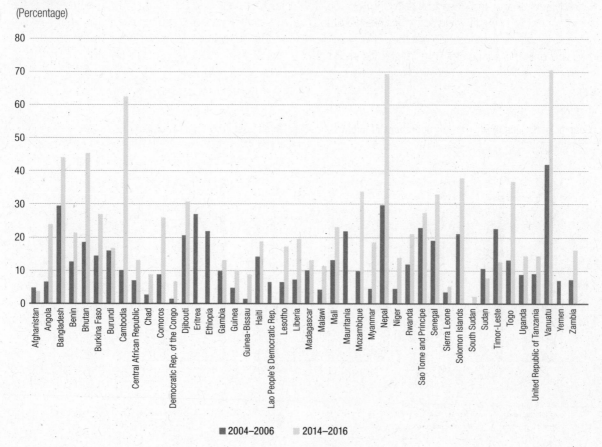

■ 2004–2006   ■ 2014–2016

Source: UNCTAD secretariat calculations, based on data from World Development Indicators database.

especially for microenterprises and small enterprises. Three quarters of firms in LDCs are affected by electrical outages. The reverse relationship is also critical, as access to energy helps to generate demand and create the markets that can help to lower electricity costs and lead to wider access. The nexus between energy access and structural transformation is critical to development in LDCs, but requires transformational energy access, meeting the needs of productive sectors as well as households (UNCTAD, 2017a).

Without access to modern, affordable, reliable and efficient energy, enterprises in LDCs can neither compete in global markets nor survive and expand in national markets, due to impaired productivity. For example, in sub-Saharan Africa, electrical supply interruptions equate to about three months of lost production time per year, resulting in the loss of about 6 per cent of turnover, and about half of all businesses use generators, leading to additional costs (Karekezi et al., 2012; World Bank, 2017). As shown in the World Bank Enterprise Surveys, for example, in 2013, power outages in the United Republic of Tanzania cost businesses around 15 per cent of annual sales (CDC Group, 2016).

In the median LDC, 42.2 per cent of the urban population lacks access to electricity and 89.3 per cent of the rural population lacks such access, rising to 94.9 per cent in LDCs in Africa and in Haiti (UNCTAD, 2017a). Rural entrepreneurship, whether in agricultural activities or involving non-farm activities, is severely constrained by unequal urban and rural access to energy in LDCs. The development of agribusiness and agro-value chains can unleash entrepreneurial opportunities in rural areas but requires improved access to energy and water. Limited access to energy also accentuates the lack of gender equality through effects on limits to the participation of women in entrepreneurial activities and structural transformation.

4. Digital connectivity

ICT, coupled with wider access to energy, has considerable transformative potential in LDCs. Increased access to and the effective utilization of ICT-based technologies can support both entrepreneurship and structural transformation in LDCs, for example through the use of mobile telephones to increase agricultural productivity and address specific challenges faced by farmers, such as lack of information and limited market access. For example, the Kisan Call Centres launched by the Ministry of Agriculture of Bangladesh in 2004 provide information via mobile telephone messages

The **gender gap in Internet use** in LDCs potentially **limits female** digital entrepreneurship

and real-time advice to farmers in local languages on livestock, prices and agricultural production via a toll-free number; the pink telephones project in Cambodia helps women using mobile technologies to exchange ideas and expertise and access agricultural resources; a women's cooperative for shea butter production in Mali, Coprokazan, uses ICT, including solar-powered computers, accounting software and digital videos and photographs, to deliver training, improve quality and increase sales; and a virtual agricultural platform in Senegal, Mlouma, provides real-time information on the price, location and availability of farm products via a website and mobile telephone messages. In addition, mobile telephone technology, such as M-Pesa, launched in 2007 in Kenya, can facilitate financial inclusion among those without access to banks and facilitate access to finance for entrepreneurs. M-Pesa is now available in the Democratic Republic of the Congo, Lesotho, Mozambique and the United Republic of Tanzania (International Telecommunication Union, 2008).

Despite recent advances in mobile telephone penetration, LDCs remain behind other developing countries in the provision of ICT infrastructure such as Internet access (International Telecommunication Union, 2008). In 2017, 17.5 per cent of the population in LDCs used the Internet, compared with 41.3 per cent in developing countries and 81.0 per cent in developed countries (figure 4.7 (a)). This gap is narrowing; in 2010–2016, the Internet penetration rate, that is, the proportion of the population with access to the Internet rose by a factor of 3 in LDCs, compared with 1.6 in the developed world, with the strongest increases in Cambodia, Ethiopia, Myanmar and Sierra Leone. However, this momentum needs to be consolidated. The gender gap in Internet use is wider in LDCs than in developing and developed countries, with 14.1 per cent of women using the Internet, compared with 21.0 per cent of men, representing a gender gap of 32.9 per cent (figure 4.7 (b)). This gap widened in LDCs from 2013 to 2017 (figure 4.7 (c)). Conversely, the digital gap between LDCs and developing countries is significantly narrower among youth (15–24 years); a significantly greater proportion of Internet users are in this age group in LDCs, at 35.1 per cent, than in developing countries, at 27.6 per cent, and developed countries, at 13.0 per cent (figure 4.7 (d)). Such patterns of Internet use have potentially important implications on the use of ICT to boost entrepreneurship and e-commerce among women and youth.

There is potential for e-commerce to provide growing entrepreneurial and development opportunities in LDCs, if greater numbers of producers and consumers can link to related platforms (UNCTAD, 2015d) and effective policies for building entrepreneurial and productive capacities are put in place. However, the related barriers need to be addressed. Common barriers to e-commerce development in LDCs include the insufficient development of telecommunications services, due to the lack of an independent regulator or licencing framework; the lack of a level playing field for operators or insufficient private sector participation; high costs for broadband and/or mobile Internet; deficits in energy and transport infrastructure; the lack of effective trade logistics and cross-border facilitation measures; insufficiently developed providers of local delivery services, including weak postal delivery services; an underdeveloped financial technology industry; weak legal and regulatory frameworks for online consumer protection; prevalent digital illiteracy and the lack of e-commerce skills development; financial constraints on e-commerce ventures and technology start-ups; and the lack of an overall national e-commerce strategy. To date, seven LDCs have undergone rapid eTrade readiness assessments supported by UNCTAD to identify such barriers: Bhutan, Cambodia, the Lao People's Democratic Republic, Liberia, Myanmar, Nepal and Senegal.[5]

The UNCTAD business-to-consumer e-commerce readiness index is a proxy for current levels of e-commerce development, reflecting the processes involved in an online shopping transaction. In 2017, the unweighted average score of LDCs, on a scale of 0 to 100, was 22.4, compared with 49.9 in other developing countries and 82.6 in developed countries. LDCs in Asia typically perform better than LDCs in Africa; the highest ranked are Uganda, the Lao People's Democratic Republic, Rwanda, Bhutan, Bangladesh and Nepal (figure 4.8).

5. Gender-based constraints

Women's entrepreneurship is widely recognized as contributing to poverty reduction and women's empowerment, and supporting women entrepreneurs is recognized as a strategy for promoting poverty alleviation and economic growth, as well as gender equality (Steel, 2017). However, some studies have questioned whether women's entrepreneurship necessarily reduces poverty or empowers women (Cornwall, 2007). Women's entrepreneurship may instead be viewed as a situational phenomenon, differing markedly between contexts, sectors and types of economic activity (Steel, 2017). Some women are positively motivated to start a business, while others are entrepreneurs by necessity or inheritors of a family business (Das, 2000). Some perform highly visible activities, such as selling in markets, while others are less evident, such as those operating as subcontractors for manufacturing companies (Steel, 2017).

In LDCs, gender-based constraints to women's participation in economic activities arise in large part from gender-related discrimination in laws, customs and practices (UNCTAD, 2015a). Such constraints inhibit women's access to inputs and resources, which can reduce both their disposition to engage in entrepreneurial activities and their chances of entrepreneurial success. There is evidence, for example, of differences between men and women entrepreneurs in the amount and composition of start-up capital; women face greater constraints than men (Brixiova and Kangoye, 2016; Malapit, 2012; Rouse and Jayawarna, 2006). In order to unleash the potential of women-owned enterprises, it is important to examine not only where gender-based constraints exist, but also to understand how such constraints interact with one another. For example, the lack of access to finance may be linked to weak property rights, since property is an important form of collateral. In some countries, women need their husbands' consent to start a business, which substantially reduces the proportion of women-owned microenterprises and SMEs in comparison with countries in which such a requirement does not exist (ILO, 2016b). In addition, many laws still prevent women from working in or running a business; 104 countries, including 32 LDCs, have laws that prevent women from working in specific jobs (box 4.1). Reforming such laws and regulations could improve the performance of women-owned firms (World Bank, 2018). LDCs without restrictions on women's employment are Burundi, Cambodia, the Comoros, Eritrea, the Gambia, Haiti, Kiribati, the Lao People's Democratic Republic, Liberia, Malawi, Rwanda,

Figure 4.7

Internet use by country group, age and gender

(Percentage)

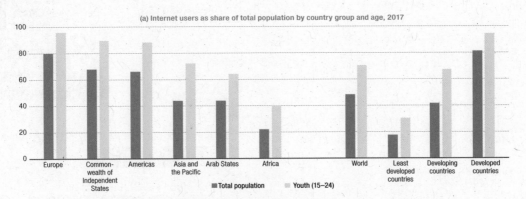

(a) Internet users as share of total population by country group and age, 2017

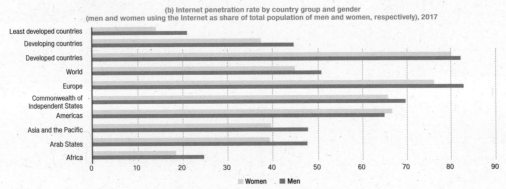

(b) Internet penetration rate by country group and gender
(men and women using the Internet as share of total population of men and women, respectively), 2017

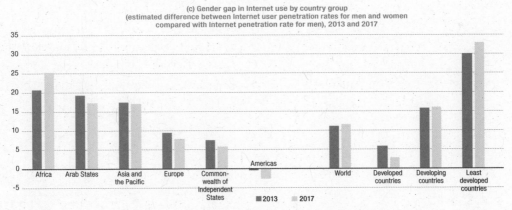

(c) Gender gap in Internet use by country group
(estimated difference between Internet user penetration rates for men and women
compared with Internet penetration rate for men), 2013 and 2017

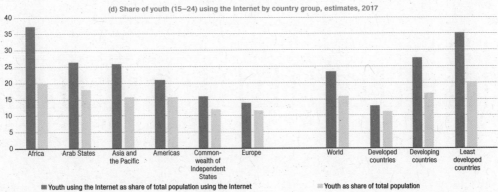

(d) Share of youth (15–24) using the Internet by country group, estimates, 2017

Source: UNCTAD secretariat, based on data from International Telecommunication Union.

Togo, Uganda, the United Republic of Tanzania and Zambia.

Case studies of women's entrepreneurship further highlight several common trends in gender-based constraints in LDCs, as follows (box 4.2):

- Access to finance is generally perceived as the most important constraint to the growth of women-owned enterprises.

- Family responsibilities and unpaid care work generally impose a major burden on women entrepreneurs, limiting the time they can devote to economic activities, compared with men entrepreneurs.

- The use of ICT by women entrepreneurs is limited by inadequate financial resources and training.

- Women have limited opportunities for formal and informal education and training.

- Women entrepreneurs are unable to take full advantage of their rights, business support or policy dialogue in some countries.

The e-commerce readiness index is low in LDCs

LDCs
22.4

Other developing countries
49.9

Developed countries
82.6

Figure 4.8

UNCTAD business-to-consumer electronic commerce readiness index score and rank, selected least developed countries, 2017

(Percentage)

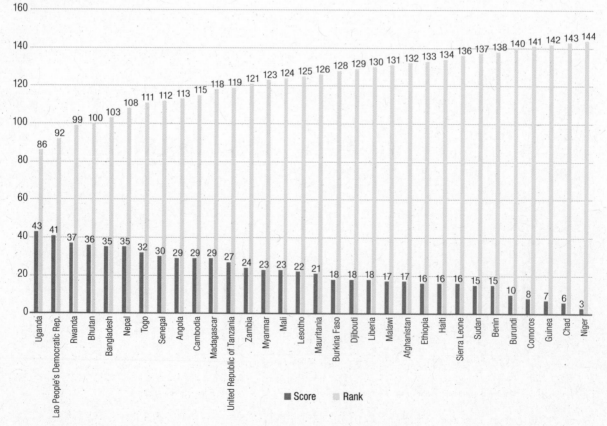

Source: UNCTAD business-to-consumer electronic commerce readiness index.

Notes: The index is composed of four indicators (percentage of population using the Internet, secure Internet servers per million inhabitants, share of population with a bank account and Universal Postal Union postal reliability score) and is normalized to range from 0 to 100 based on the lowest and highest value for each indicator in the country sample; data are available for 32 LDCs.

Box 4.1 **Women, business and the law**

The Women, Business and the Law project of the World Bank collects data on the legal obstacles to women's engagement in economic activity, using the following seven indicators based on 50 questions: protecting women from violence; building credit; going to court; providing incentives to work; getting a job; using property; and accessing institutions. On average in all 47 LDCs, protecting women from violence, building credit and providing incentives to work are the three areas in need of greater attention with regard to legal and regulatory reforms (box figure 4.1).

Box figure 4.1

Women, business and the law indicators: Average scores in the least developed countries

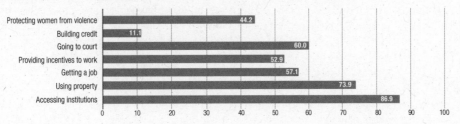

The least developed countries with scores of less than 50 on a scale of 0 to 100 are shown in box table 4.1.

Box table 4.1

Women, business and the law indicators: Least developed countries with scores of less than 50 on a scale of 0 to 100

Protecting women from violence	Angola, Burkina Faso, Democratic Republic of the Congo, Djibouti, Gambia, Guinea, Guinea-Bissau, Haiti, Kiribati, Lesotho, Liberia, Mali, Mauritania, Myanmar, Niger, Sierra Leone, Solomon Islands, South Sudan, Sudan, Timor-Leste, Vanuatu, Yemen
Building credit	All least developed countries except Cambodia, Djibouti, Guinea, Lesotho and Zambia
Going to court	Angola, Benin, Bhutan, Central African Republic, Eritrea, Lao People's Democratic Republic, Mauritania, Sao Tome and Principe, South Sudan and Yemen
Providing incentives to work	Bangladesh, Burundi, Democratic Republic of the Congo, Ethiopia, Guinea, Guinea-Bissau, Lao People's Democratic Republic, Lesotho, Madagascar, Myanmar, Nepal, Sao Tome and Principe, Solomon Islands, South Sudan, Togo, Vanuatu, Yemen
Getting a job	Afghanistan, Bangladesh, Central African Republic, Ethiopia, Guinea-Bissau, Mali, Nepal, Sierra Leone, Solomon Islands, South Sudan, Sudan and Yemen
Using property	Afghanistan, Bangladesh, Comoros, Djibouti, Mauritania, Senegal, Sudan, Uganda, Yemen
Accessing institutions	Sudan, Yemen

Source: UNCTAD secretariat, based on World Bank, 2018.

The women's entrepreneurship development assessment of ILO provides additional evidence on gender-based constraints in LDCs. The framework and methodology developed by ILO serves to assess national environments; identify country-specific policies and critical forms of support for women entrepreneurs; and assess the favourability of the policy environment to women's entrepreneurship on the basis of the following six conditions (Bushell, 2008; UNCTAD, 2014c):

- Gender-sensitivity of the legal and regulatory environment and its conduciveness to the economic empowerment of women.
- Effectiveness of policy leadership and coordination for the promotion of women's entrepreneurship development.

- Access to gender-sensitive financial services;
- Access to gender-sensitive business development support services.
- Access to markets and access, ownership and use of technology.
- Representation of women entrepreneurs and participation in policy dialogue.

A number of subconditions are identified under each of these as particularly relevant to women's entrepreneurship (figure 4.9). Among LDCs, women's entrepreneurship development assessments have been conducted in Lesotho, Malawi, Mali, Mozambique, Rwanda, Senegal, the United Republic of Tanzania and Uganda, and shown the existence of significant gender-based constraints on women's entrepreneurship.

Box 4.2 **Case studies of women's entrepreneurship in the least developed countries**

In the Gambia, a study on low-income women's home-based enterprises found that they were active in two sectors, namely food and domestic activities, suggesting that there is a form of segregation in place in line with women's perceived traditional roles. Gender-inequitable time burdens impose a range of direct and indirect constraints on women's ability to participate in economic activities. Their productive roles and family responsibilities are also impacted by deficiencies in public services, notably with regard to electricity and water supply.

In Nepal, family responsibilities are an important constraint on women's businesses. Women-owned enterprises are typically small and active in traditional manufacturing, small shops or informal vending with low turnovers, a low number of employees and no professional assistance. Access to capital and credit is a prominent issue; one study identified this as a major obstacle to enterprise growth. Women also have more limited education and training opportunities than men, with a gap of 20 percentage points in 2007 between literacy rates among men (80.6 per cent) and women (60.1 per cent). Limited education reduces women's ability to negotiate government and finance bureaucracies, and limits their voice. Most women-owned enterprises operate mainly among close connections and family members, with limited access to wider markets.

In Uganda, women-owned enterprises are concentrated in trading and are mostly informal. Women entrepreneurs are discouraged from formalization by the cost of social security charges and the geographical inaccessibility and cost of business registration procedures. Women-owned businesses are generally unable to engage in GVCs and their products are sold mainly in local markets, as their reputation for quality is insufficient for access to international and regional markets. Access to finance is an important obstacle, complicated by the requirement by banking institutions of a husband's consent and recommendations for loans, resulting in women often borrowing from family members or informal sources. ICT use is limited due to poor Internet access, especially in rural areas, lack of awareness of the potential benefits and inadequate training. Relatively few women entrepreneurs use mobile telephones and still fewer have access to computers for business activities. However, the presence of many women's organizations, which advocate for gender equality and economic empowerment, give women a strong advocacy voice.

In the United Republic of Tanzania, the time that businesswomen can dedicate to their ventures is limited by the need to fulfil traditional family and community obligations. The most important obstacle to their activities is access to credit, partly because women's limited property rights under customary law impair their ability to provide collateral. Limited access to ICT training is also an issue, as is the limited number of business associations dedicated to women, which means that their needs are not adequately represented.

Sources: Bushell, 2008; Chant, 2014; Cornwall, 2007; Das, 2000; Mori, 2014; Mugabi, 2014; Steel, 2017.

For example, in Senegal, the assessment showed that women entrepreneurs face almost identical constraints in the formal and informal sectors and in rural and urban environments, namely a lack of know-how, capital, technology and information; and discriminatory cultural and social values (ILO, 2011). In Burkina Faso, the national strategy for the promotion of women's entrepreneurship notes the range of factors inhibiting the participation of women entrepreneurs in economic activities, including the lack of guarantees for access to credit, lack of ownership of land, poor access to means of production, low incomes, illiteracy, limited educational attainment and qualifications, and sociocultural constraints, as well as, above all, the lack of coordination of interventions in the field of women's entrepreneurship. The removal of gender-based constraints to women's participation in entrepreneurial activities and structural transformation necessitates targeted public policy actions, as recommended, for example, in the national strategy of Burkina Faso (table 4.3). It is too early to evaluate the effectiveness of these policy actions.

Research by ILO under the women's entrepreneurship development programme sheds light on the types of interventions that have proven effective in strengthening women's entrepreneurship in beneficiary countries. There is little rigorous evidence that either access to finance or business training alone lead to sustained business growth among microenterprises headed by women. Rather, interventions that combine finance, especially grants, and business training appear to be more effective. There is also evidence that business training combined with follow-up technical assistance and business grants together with business training may be effective (ILO, 2018). In addition, interventions need to be part of a package of multiple measures that address several constraints at the same time by bundling services or combining interventions (ILO, 2018). Other important factors include addressing systemic barriers such as the lack of electricity or land rights, combining access and incentives to incite behavioural change and designing interventions that take into account women's mobility constraints. For example, evidence suggests that programmes that hold business training sessions in locations that are close to the homes or places of work of participants and that offer subsidized or free-of-charge transport and/or childcare are more effective in retaining participants (ILO, 2018).

Figure 4.9

Women's entrepreneurship development assessment framework conditions and subconditions

 Gender-sensitive legal and regulatory system that advances women's economic empowerment

(a) Labour laws and regulations
(b) Business registration and licencing regulations and procedures
(c) Property and inheritance rights

 Effective policy leadership and coordination for the promotion of women's entrepreneurship development

(a) Women's entrepreneurship development as national policy priority
(b) Presence of government focal point for promotion and coordination of women's entrepreneurship development and support actions

 Access to gender-sensitive financial services

(a) Participation by women entrepreneurs in generic financing programmes
(b) Financing programmes specifically targeted to women-owned enterprises

 Access to gender-sensitive business development support services

(a) Women's access to mainstream business development support services
(b) Mainstream business development support services respond to needs of women entrepreneurs
(c) Presence of women-focused business development support services

 Access to markets and technology

(a) Export promotion of women entrepreneurs
(b) Government procurement programmes actively target women's enterprises
(c) Supply chains and linkages integrate women-owned enterprises
(d) Information and communication technology and other technology access by women entrepreneurs

 Representation of women entrepreneurs and participation in policy dialogue

(a) Representation and voice of women in business sector and membership associations
(b) Presence of women entrepreneurs' associations and networks
(c) Participation of women entrepreneurs in public–private sector policy dialogue and influence on outcomes

Source: UNCTAD, 2014c.

Table 4.3

Burkina Faso: Main pillars and objectives of national strategy for promotion of women's entrepreneurship

Pillar	Objectives	
1. Improve legal and institutional framework supporting women's entrepreneurship	(a)	Improve texts and laws in favour of women's entrepreneurship
	(b)	Strengthen institutional framework for promoting women's entrepreneurship
	(c)	Strengthen steering and monitoring and evaluation of national strategy
2. Promote access of women and girls to means of production	(a)	Improve access of women and girls to land and technologies for production, processing and conservation
	(b)	Facilitate access of women and girls to finance
3. Develop opportunities to create employment and self-employment for women and girls	(a)	Strengthen technical and vocational training of women
	(b)	Encourage business creation by women and girls
4. Promote commercialization of women's and girls' products and viability of their businesses	(a)	Increase turnover of women's and girls' businesses
	(b)	Increase viability of enterprises headed by women and girls

Source: Burkina Faso, 2015.

D. Current policy frameworks for entrepreneurship and structural transformation

This section summarizes the major goals of development strategies and policies in LDCs and the role they ascribe to entrepreneurship. The analysis is based on a comprehensive mapping of current national development plans, industrial policies and development policies for microenterprises and SMEs (that is, either for SMEs or for microenterprises and SMEs) in the 44 LDCs which have such plans (Eritrea, Somalia and South Sudan are not included in the analysis). The strategies and plans described represent the stated intentions of the Governments rather than policy outcomes. An assessment of the effectiveness and implementation of development policies for microenterprises and SMEs in LDCs is beyond the scope of this report, but should be a priority for future research. Policies may not be fully supported by all stakeholders and may be subject to significant revisions, for example due to changes in the Government or modifications by incumbent government officials. The analysis serves to indicate the state of government policy on entrepreneurship and on structural transformation in LDCs.

1. National development plans

All LDCs have either a national development framework or plan or a poverty reduction strategic framework that is generally intended to operationalize a strategic long-term vision. In most instances, the national development plan or poverty reduction strategic framework states the broad development objective and/or vision of the country, along with a description of what should be the main pillars (that is, strategic or development priorities) in achieving the objective or vision. Sustained and inclusive economic growth, poverty reduction, economic diversification and improved competitiveness are often cited as priorities, together with strengthening governance, improving access to basic social services, developing infrastructure, developing the private sector, ensuring peace and security, developing human capital and protecting the environment and addressing climate change.

Structural transformation is explicitly identified as a pillar in the plans of relatively few LDCs (namely, Benin, Burundi, Ethiopia, the Gambia, Guinea, Liberia, Mozambique and Senegal), yet the development plans of many LDCs encompass policies aimed at achieving aspects of such transformation, namely raising productivity, moving up value chains and transforming economic sectors such as manufacturing and agriculture in pursuit of strong and sustained economic growth.

The development plans of all LDCs contain multiple references to the need to support entrepreneurship and many include clearly defined policies for this purpose, generally under the objectives of economic growth and private sector development. Areas of intervention relate mainly to improving the business climate and access to finance and facilitating training and business advisory services.

In at least one third of LDCs (namely Afghanistan, Bhutan, Burundi, Cambodia, the Comoros, the Democratic Republic of the Congo, Djibouti, Haiti, Kiribati, Lesotho, Liberia, Mali, Mauritania and Zambia), microenterprises and SMEs are viewed as potential engines of economic growth and sources of employment and income to reduce poverty. Fewer LDCs (including Angola, Ethiopia, Cambodia, Guinea, the Lao People's Democratic Republic and Myanmar) envisage support measures for large enterprises, generally as part of large-scale interventions for structural transformation, strategies to foster national champions or value chain programmes aimed at building linkages between smaller and larger enterprises.

Most references to enterprises occur under the economic pillar, yet reference to entrepreneurship is also made under the social pillar, which relates to education, human resource development and social protection. This is indicative of a potential disconnect within existing plans between addressing entrepreneurship and addressing broader enterprise development for economic objectives.

The term entrepreneurship appears in 36 of the 44 national development plans and poverty reduction strategic frameworks reviewed, yet specific policy actions to promote entrepreneurship or enhance an entrepreneurial culture are generally limited and sometimes vague. Such actions mainly take the form of integrating entrepreneurship into curricula in schools and universities and into technical and vocational education and training (such as in Angola, Burundi, Lesotho, Malawi, Sao Tome and Principe, Sierra Leone, Solomon Islands and Timor-Leste); establishing business incubators (such as in Angola and Benin); and/or promoting entrepreneurship among women and youth (such as in Burundi, the Central African Republic, the Comoros, Djibouti, the Gambia, Guinea, Haiti and Uganda). In a few LDCs (such as Bangladesh), plans mention the potential of harnessing ICT to promote entrepreneurship within e-commerce strategies or harnessing the diaspora to promote entrepreneurship.

Several LDCs include cluster and spatial development zones in national development plans, industrial policies and development policies for microenterprises and SMEs (such as Burundi, Cambodia, Ethiopia, the Lao People's Democratic Republic, Mali, Mauritania, Myanmar, Senegal and Uganda) and several have plans for business incubators (such as Liberia, Mozambique and Senegal).

Notable gaps in plans include the elaboration of policies on the clustering of enterprises (except in Angola and Cambodia) and discussions on the interface between policies on industry, trade, investment, regional integration and entrepreneurship. For example, only the plans of Afghanistan, Angola, Cambodia and the Lao People's Democratic Republic refer to either strategic trade or regional integration.

2. Industrial policies

The interface between entrepreneurship and structural transformation is generally articulated more clearly in national industrial policies than in development plans. However, while at least 20 LDCs have a national industrial policy, another 20 LDCs have yet to formulate such a policy. In addition, while all of the industrial policies reviewed contain explicit measures with regard to entrepreneurship, including microenterprises and SMEs, and 19 of the 20 explicitly refer to entrepreneurship, much less attention is devoted to the determinants of entrepreneurship. As well as increasing competitiveness through measures directed at improving the business climate and financing, industrial policies seek to place enterprises at the core of industrial development by, inter alia, the following:

- Developing and modernizing microenterprises and SMEs, including through explicit development policies and/or the creation of development agencies.

- Creating market linkages within and outside the country.

- Attracting FDI to create larger enterprises and value chains linking microenterprises and SMEs to larger companies.

- Establishing local content policies to stimulate linkages between the extractive sector and indigenous enterprises.

- Improving the governance of State-owned enterprises.

- Establishing protectionist trade measures to promote local industrial production through import substitution, along with competition policies to guard against monopolistic practices.

Most LDC industrial policies refer to entrepreneurship, but do not address its determinants

---

- Developing spatial development initiatives, including the establishment of special economic zones, economic poles and industrial clusters.

- Establishing science, technology and innovation policies encompassing technology transfer.

- Establishing measures to enhance cooperation between the private sector and academic institutions and research centres.

- Including special provisions for women and young entrepreneurs, as part of initiatives for rural industrialization, gender mainstreaming and formalization, among others.

Following Lall (1996) and Lall and Teubal (1998), UNCTAD work on industrial policy has emphasized the distinction between vertical, horizontal and functional industrial policies (UNCTAD, 2014d; UNCTAD and UNIDO, 2011). Horizontal policies aim to promote activities that benefit all sectors, such as capacity-building in science, technology and innovation; vertical policies target support to specific firms, industries or sectors; and functional policies aim to improve the operation of markets, in particular factor markets, without favouring specific activities, such as interventions to prevent collusion and facilitate market entry by entrepreneurs.

All of the countries reviewed embrace a mix of all three types of policies, yet in most LDCs, the distinction between the policies is often insufficiently clear, the discourse on the synergies between the policies is relatively weak and the different types of enterprises to be promoted are insufficiently articulated, for example, with regard to the role of the establishment and growth of enterprises of opportunity-driven entrepreneurs in achieving the goals of vertical policies and of other types of enterprises in the implementation of horizontal policies. A clearer distinction between horizontal, vertical and functional industrial policies could improve policy design and targeting.

3. Entrepreneurship and development policies for microenterprises and small and medium-sized enterprises

As with industrial policies, about half of all LDCs have adopted a development policy for microenterprises and SMEs or, for example in Benin, the Democratic

Republic of the Congo and Togo, a charter for SMEs; and the other half have yet to formulate an entrepreneurship development policy. As yet, only three LDCs have formulated a national entrepreneurship policy, namely Burkina Faso and, with technical assistance from UNCTAD, the Gambia and the United Republic of Tanzania. Burkina Faso also has a national entrepreneurship strategy for women, in place since 2015 (table 4.3).

Around half of the LDCs with national industrial policies also have a development policy for microenterprises and SMEs, including Bangladesh, Cambodia, Ethiopia, Lesotho, Liberia, Mozambique, Myanmar, Rwanda, Sierra Leone, Uganda and Zambia. However, the periods covered by the different strategies — that is, national development plans, poverty reduction strategic frameworks, industrial policies and development policies for microenterprises and SMEs — do not always coincide, indicating the need for better alignment of the respective cycles of preparation, revision and updating, to strengthen policy coherence and consistency.

The development policies for microenterprises and SMEs vary widely in their goals. In some countries, the overarching goal is employment creation and poverty reduction, in particular for vulnerable groups such as women, youth and rural populations, rather than structural transformation or economic diversification. Other objectives include export promotion and import substitution (for example in Afghanistan), industrial diversification and technology adoption (Cambodia), formalization (Democratic Republic of the Congo), reduced income inequality through increased economic opportunities for underserved groups (Liberia), empowered local populations (Malawi), more effective participation in regional integration (Myanmar), strong and sustained economic growth (Senegal) and increased value addition in the exploitation of local raw materials (Zambia).

In many LDCs, microenterprises and SMEs, rather than large enterprises, are seen as the key engines of economic growth and as the main source of employment creation, although definitions of microenterprises, SMEs and large enterprises vary between countries. This view is stated explicitly in the development policies for microenterprises and SMEs in, for example, Bangladesh, Bhutan, Myanmar, Solomon Islands and Uganda. However, some countries, such as Cambodia, Guinea, the Lao People's Democratic Republic, Malawi, Mozambique, Myanmar and Zambia, also explicitly recognize the importance of promoting linkages between SMEs and larger enterprises, including FDI-driven

transnational companies, as a means of addressing the lack of medium-sized firms, that is, the missing-middle phenomenon.

The primary focus of policy interventions is on improving access to finance and providing a business-enabling environment by improving legal, regulatory, institutional and policy frameworks (figure 4.10). In some LDCs, for example Afghanistan, Lesotho and Rwanda, the role of the Government is limited to facilitation and ensuring an enabling environment, possibly reflecting a donor-driven agenda. Such an approach does not encompass a broader developmental role for the State and rules out the development or strengthening of State-owned enterprises in particular sectors as an instrument of vertical industrial policy and the use of public investment to catalyse private investment in certain stages of enterprise or sector development. It thereby limits the scope for exploiting synergies between public and private investment to address developmental failures (UNCTAD, 2014e). In other countries, a wide array of policy areas is identified for action, including fiscal and other incentives; the provision of supportive infrastructure, including business advisory services and training; acceleration of the formalization of informal enterprises; and special measures targeted at women, youth and/or other vulnerable and disadvantaged groups. Science, technology and innovation and skills development through technical and vocational education and training also receive attention in the majority of LDCs.

Fewer LDCs (for example Bangladesh, Rwanda and Togo) have policy frameworks that explicitly mention the necessity of harnessing ICT to improve competitiveness or identify new niche sectors. Specific references to developing an entrepreneurship culture also seldom appear prominently in policy documents on microenterprises and SMEs. There is thus scope for more LDCs to explore the potential of digitalization in supporting the start-up and growth of microenterprises and SMEs, especially given the rise of e-commerce and the digital economy, as well as to define policy elements to nurture an entrepreneurship culture. For example, Rwanda has identified ICT as a sector that can enable entrepreneurship development and knowledge-based structural transformation, and the Government has committed to developing a superior Internet and mobile telecommunications infrastructure and prepared five-year national policy plans on ICT infrastructure aimed at establishing the country as an ICT hub in the East African Community. The Smart Rwanda Master Plan 2015–2020 aims to power the socioeconomic transformation of Rwanda towards a knowledge economy.

Figure 4.10

Thematic coverage in development policies for microenterprises and small and medium-sized enterprises: Share of least developed countries with thematic element in policy

(Percentage)

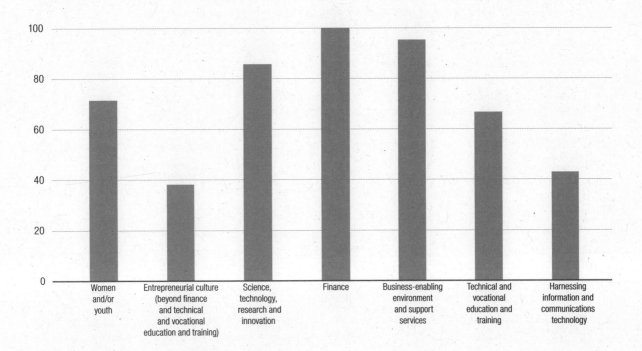

Source: UNCTAD secretariat calculations, based on publicly available information.

Note: Policies are publicly available for 21 LDCs, namely Bangladesh, Benin, Bhutan, Cambodia, the Democratic Republic of the Congo, Ethiopia, the Gambia, the Lao People's Democratic Republic, Lesotho, Liberia, Malawi, Mozambique, Myanmar, Rwanda, Senegal, Solomon Islands, Togo, Uganda, the United Republic of Tanzania, Yemen and Zambia.

Aside from measures aimed at vulnerable or disadvantaged groups, most LDCs have a blanket approach to supporting entrepreneurship. None of the national industrial policies or development policies for microenterprises and SMEs distinguish, for policy purposes, between different types of enterprises, that is enterprises of necessity- or opportunity-driven entrepreneurs, transformational enterprises, social enterprises or cooperatives, among others. Only a few policies (such as in Myanmar, Rwanda, Senegal and the United Republic of Tanzania) include measures targeted at rural non-farm enterprises or aimed at building linkages between rural and urban enterprises. Similarly, with the exception of those in Ethiopia (box 4.3) and Senegal, few policies recognize the importance of tailoring support to enterprises according to their stage of development, that is, start-up, growth, expansion and maturity. Neither eligibility criteria for enterprises to qualify for policy measures and incentives nor sunset clauses for enterprise termination are generally clearly defined or even discussed.

Development policies for microenterprises and SMEs do not generally recognize the need for supportive

policies in other areas or for coherence across policy areas and effective intersectoral coordination. There are some exceptions, such as in Rwanda, the United Republic of Tanzania and Zambia.

As with national development plans and industrial policies, there are few LDCs in which development policies for microenterprises and SMEs include an integrated monitoring and evaluation framework, reflecting in part the absence of a monitoring and evaluation culture in most LDCs. Exceptions include Rwanda and Uganda. The policy in Rwanda enumerates a set of factors for success, based on lessons from other countries, including time-bound support and incentives for new activities, clear benchmarks to measure success over time and active monitoring and evaluation, as well as sustained dialogue with the private sector, high-level political oversight and ownership of policy implementation. The policy in Uganda includes specific, measurable, attainable, realistic and time-bound objectives, with a five-year timeline for review.

In over 70 per cent of LDCs, development policies for microenterprises and SMEs include specific measures

Box 4.3: **Ethiopia microenterprise and small enterprise development policy and strategy: Stages of enterprise development**

The microenterprise and small enterprise development policy and strategy distinguishes between the transition of enterprises between size categories, from microenterprises to small enterprises and from small to medium-sized enterprises, and the process of maintaining and strengthening competitiveness within each category, recognizing the need for government support to take into account these distinct processes. The strategy cites the example of Malaysia, which identifies four stages of enterprise growth and the related objectives of support:

- Start-up, when the objectives are to enhance access to skilled labour, facilitate the supply of raw materials and access to infrastructure and build marketing skills.
- Growth, when the objectives are to obtain certificates of competence, achieve product and service standards, benefit from tax relief and obtain technical support.
- Expansion, when the objectives are to build technological capacity; increase managerial competence; develop trademarks, marketing networks and information and communications services; and access venture capital and outsourcing opportunities.
- Maturity, when the objectives are to develop product design capacity, promote trademarks and access external financing.

The strategy also cites the example of Japan, which distinguishes the following three stages of growth and the related objectives of support:

- Launch, when the aim is to enable enterprises to withstand start-up challenges.
- Strengthening, when the focus is on professional support to build management competence.
- Maturity, when the aim is primarily preventive and involves enabling enterprises to withstand current and future risks.

Source: Ethiopia, 2016.

to promote entrepreneurship among women and/or youth (figure 4.10). However, such policies are often oriented towards improving livelihoods, lifting women and youth out of poverty, empowering women and other social goals, rather than towards promoting structural transformation, innovation and productivity growth through the emergence of women and youth as high-impact, high-growth and innovative entrepreneurs. For example, the main objective of the national strategy for the promotion of women's entrepreneurship in Burkina Faso is to contribute to women's empowerment. In the Gambia, the national entrepreneurship policy is aimed at improving conditions for enterprise creation and growth, with an emphasis on "women and youth, including groups prone to migration, who represent the main drivers of new enterprise development" and a youth empowerment project aims to address the "the root causes of the high levels of irregular migration from the Gambia, particularly by young people leaving the country" (Mulligan, 2017; UNCTAD, 2017g).

4. Institutional frameworks for enterprise policies

Institutional arrangements for microenterprise and SME policies vary widely across LDCs (table 4.4). In eight LDCs, the title of the ministry responsible for the enterprise sector includes the words SMEs, small businesses or entrepreneurship, a possible indicator of the significance attached to SMEs and enterprise development; in 14 LDCs, there is a directorate or

department within a particular ministry specifically oriented towards SMEs or entrepreneurship; and eight LDCs have a dedicated State-led institution not within a ministry dedicated to microenterprises and SMEs. The remaining 14 LDCs (excluding Eritrea, Somalia and South Sudan) do not have a ministry or other institution specifically focused on microenterprises and SMEs or enterprise or entrepreneurship development issues, although a few have a development policy for microenterprises and SMEs or a national entrepreneurship policy, such as Burkina Faso and the Gambia. In these 14 countries, such policies are typically the responsibility of a directorate for industry within the ministry of trade and industry. The creation of a dedicated agency focused on supporting the development of enterprises, working in close coordination with ministries and relevant agencies, could help facilitate intersectoral coordination and improve the effectiveness of entrepreneurship policies.

5. Recommended policy principles

The mapping of policy frameworks in LDCs in this section highlights the need for the greater prioritization of structural transformation in the strategic development plans and visions of LDCs and stronger alignment between development plans, industrial policies and entrepreneurship development policies towards this goal. The mapping also underlines the importance of policies that extend beyond providing a business-enabling environment; harnessing

Table 4.4

Mapping of government institutions in the least developed countries in charge of enterprise development

Countries in which SMEs, small businesses and/or entrepreneurship are specified in the title of the ministry	Countries in which the ministry has a directorate for SMEs and/or entrepreneurship	Countries that do not fall under the previous two categories, in which the Government has established a State institution dedicated to SMEs, entrepreneurship and/or enterprises	All other countries
Benin	Afghanistan	Angola (Instituto de Fomento Empresarial)	Burkina Faso
Central African Republic	Bhutan	Bangladesh (SME Foundation)	Burundi
Democratic Republic of the Congo	Cambodia	Ethiopia (Federal Small and Medium Manufacturing Industries Development Agency)	Chad
Djibouti	Haiti	Mozambique (Institute for the Promotion of SMEs)	Comoros
Guinea	Lao People's Democratic Republic	Sierra Leone (SMEs Development Agency)	Gambia
Lesotho	Madagascar	Timor Leste (Instituto de Apoio ao Desenvolvimiento Empresarial)	Guinea-Bissau
Niger	Malawi	Togo (National Agency for Promoting and Guaranteeing SME and Small and Medium-sized Industry Financing)	Kiribati
Senegal	Myanmar	Zambia (Small Industries Development Organization)	Liberia
	Nepal		Mali
	Rwanda		Mauritania
	Uganda		Sao Tome and Principe
	United Republic of Tanzania		Solomon Islands
	Vanuatu		Sudan
	Yemen		Tuvalu

Source: UNCTAD secretariat, based on publicly available information.
Note: Data not available for Eritrea, Somalia and South Sudan.

entrepreneurship for structural transformation requires entrepreneurship policies and vertical, horizontal and functional industrial policies, as well as a range of supportive complementary policies.

A clearer distinction is needed between entrepreneurship policies and general enterprise development policies, along with a more effective articulation of each type. More LDCs could benefit from formulating a national entrepreneurship strategy centred on structural transformation, to foster entrepreneurial talent and sustain enterprise development across the life cycles of enterprises. Similarly, vertical, horizontal and functional industrial policies should be more clearly distinguished, to allow for improved design and targeting towards enterprises with the potential to drive structural transformation.

The design of a national entrepreneurship strategy needs to be tailored to the particular historical, institutional, political and cultural context in the country. Policy priorities will vary over the course of structural transformation, with some forms of support declining in importance as the private sector gains strength and others becoming more important as the needs of enterprises evolve.

An important priority is to nurture an entrepreneurial culture with an appropriate understanding of the microlevel determinants of entrepreneurial talent and capabilities. Experiences in other developing countries demonstrate that entrepreneurship skills, but not necessarily entrepreneurial mindsets, are teachable and can be fostered by appropriate policies at the microlevel, mesolevel and macrolevel. However, the policies needed to promote a transformational entrepreneurial culture depend, inter alia, on initial conditions in the private sector, the historical context, the quality of institutions, State–private sector relations, public sector capabilities, cultural attitudes towards risk and failure, the openness of the economy and the extent of regional integration.

There is a need for clear differentiation between types of enterprises by size, nature and motivation, with policy incentives tailored to their respective roles in structural transformation. This implies placing a greater emphasis on large enterprises; distinguishing between necessity-driven entrepreneurs and high-potential and low-potential opportunity-driven entrepreneurs; recognizing the catalytic role of State-owned enterprises in key sectors in which the private sector is absent or weak; and making efforts to build linkages between SMEs and large enterprises, to promote the development of national and regional value chains.

Public policies to scale up businesses

are **as important** as fostering **start-ups**

As in other areas, entrepreneurship development policies in LDCs should include a monitoring and evaluation framework that assesses results against performance indicators and allows lessons to be learned from successes and failures and integrated into policies. The time frames of different policies should be harmonized, to allow for more effective monitoring and evaluation.

Public support should also be steady throughout the life cycles of enterprises, recognizing that sustaining and scaling up businesses are as important as starting them. Public support should be sustained for long enough to allow enterprises to grow and withstand market cycle fluctuations, while reflecting variations in business needs throughout the life cycle. The fiscal burden of support can be mitigated by the establishment of cost-sharing mechanisms between the public and private sectors.

Entrepreneurship depends on many interdependent factors and therefore requires supportive policies in many different sectors under different government entities, as well as direct policy support. A coordinated approach is needed to ensure coherence within a wider strategic framework, with mandates, competencies and responsibilities clearly defined and agreed between all institutional partners and responsibility for implementing entrepreneurship strategies vested in a single entity (UNCTAD, 2012a). Such a coordination mechanism could be initiated by establishing a public–private working group or advisory council and later take the form of a fully institutionalized agency.

Notes

1   See http://unctad.org/en /Pages/DITC/Competition Law /Competition-Law-and-Policy.aspx.

2   Persistence may be explained by models of occupational choice between wage employment and entrepreneurship in which agents face uncertainty about productivity and are heterogenous in their abilities and start-ups differ with regard to productivity.

3   In 2014–2016, domestic credit to the private sector was 130 per cent of GDP globally, although this figure may be inflated by hyperfinancialization (UNCTAD, 2017b). The effect of financial depth on output growth at the national level becomes negative when this ratio reaches 100 per cent (Arcand et al., 2015).

4   See   http://unctad.org/en/Pages/Publications/E-Trade-Readiness-Assessment.aspx.

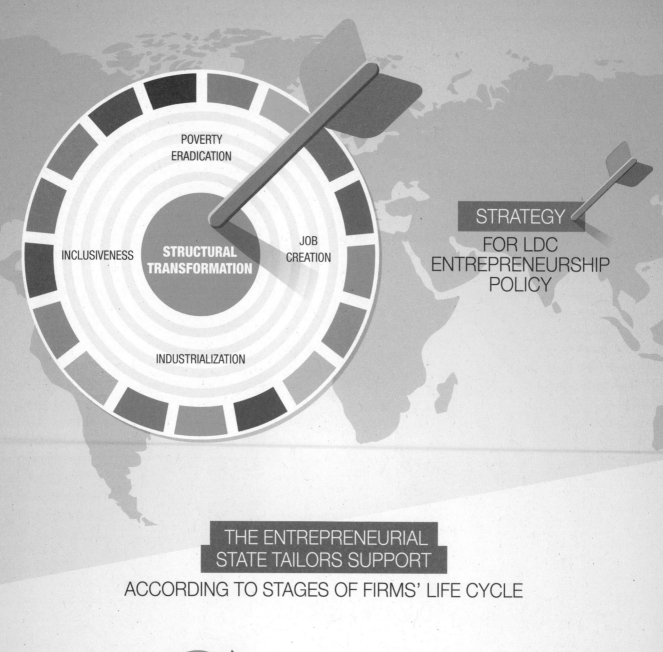

POVERTY
ERADICATION

INCLUSIVENESS

STRUCTURAL
TRANSFORMATION

JOB
CREATION

INDUSTRIALIZATION

STRATEGY
FOR LDC
ENTREPRENEURSHIP
POLICY

THE ENTREPRENEURIAL
STATE TAILORS SUPPORT

ACCORDING TO STAGES OF FIRMS' LIFE CYCLE

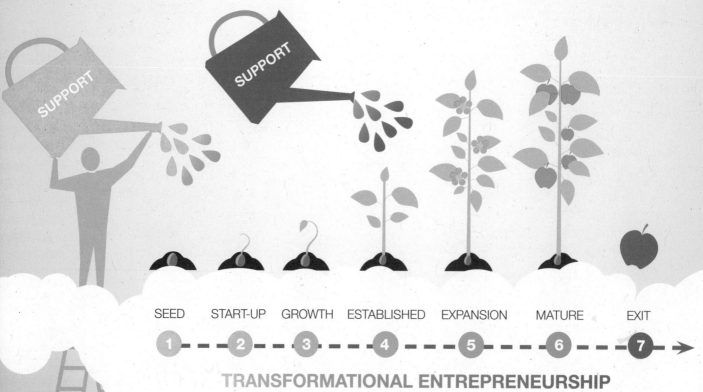

SUPPORT

SUPPORT

SEED	START-UP	GROWTH	ESTABLISHED	EXPANSION	MATURE	EXIT
1	2	3	4	5	6	7

TRANSFORMATIONAL ENTREPRENEURSHIP

Policies for
transformational entrepreneurship

CHAPTER 5
Policies for
transformational entrepreneurship

A. Introduction	**109**
B. Policy principles	**109**
1. Policy coherence: A whole-of-government approach	109
2. Entrepreneurship policy principles and main features	109
3. Framework of national-level policy options	115
C. Entrepreneurship policies	**116**
1. Microenterprises and small enterprises	118
2. Medium-sized and large enterprises	116
3. Promoting formalization	119
4. Support across the enterprise life cycle	120
5. Repositioning female and youth entrepreneurship	121
D. Entrepreneurship within general economic policies	**123**
1. Provision of finance	123
2. Building technological capabilities	126
3. Digitalization and e-commerce readiness	128
4. Entrepreneurship education and skills development	138
E. Entrepreneurship and the developmental State	**129**
1. The entrepreneurial role of the State	129
2. Public investment and infrastructure	131
3. The role of State-owned enterprises	132
4. Strengthening public–private sector dialogue	132
F. Summary and conclusions	**134**
Notes	**136**

A. Introduction

Entrepreneurship, by nature complex and multifaceted, has the potential to drive structural transformation and sustainable development. Yet not all types of enterprises contribute equally (or always positively) to structural transformation. Harnessing entrepreneurship for these related purposes thus requires policies, not to promote enterprise creation for its own sake, but rather to support and sustain the high-growth and innovative enterprises central to economic structural transformation. In addition to entrepreneurial talent and capabilities, this requires effective entrepreneurship policies, institutions and reward structures to influence firms' trajectories over time, support their sustainability and maximize their contribution to both structural transformation and sustainable development.

This chapter suggests policies to strengthen entrepreneurship's contribution to structural transformation in LDCs. Section B begins with a discussion of the overall principles which should guide the formulation and implementation of entrepreneurship policies in LDCs. Section C explains the priority areas for entrepreneurship policy. Section D analyses the facets of overall economic policies that are especially pertinent to entrepreneurship development. Section E presents the concept of the entrepreneurial State and its role in entrepreneurship development in LDCs. The last section summarizes and outlines the chapter's conclusions.

B. Policy principles

1. Policy coherence: A whole-of-government approach

Enterprises are affected, directly and indirectly and to varying degrees, by most areas of government policy. They are also major players in the delivery of many development goals and in strategies for agricultural and rural development; and they depend on the success of development strategies for the expansion of markets, availability of human resources, access to finance, infrastructure and public services.

Entrepreneurship policy thus needs to be an integral part of a wider set of strategies and policies for structural transformation and sustainable development. The policy suggestions provided in this chapter should therefore be considered in conjunction with those of previous editions of *The Least Developed Countries Report*, as summarized by UNCTAD (2018a) in *Achieving the Sustainable Development Goals in the Least Developed Countries: A Compendium of Policy Options*.

> **LDCs are advised to focus their entrepreneurship policies on the objective of structural transformation**

Coordination and coherence are essential to exploit the synergies between entrepreneurship policy and broader economic development policies and maximize their economic and social benefits. This requires a whole-of-government – that is, a systemic and holistic – approach, with strong commitment at the highest level and coordination across ministries and in partnership with the private sector and civil society stakeholders, including academia, non-governmental organizations and community organizations. One institution or ministry should be given the lead responsibility for implementing and revising the entrepreneurship strategy and coordinating functions across the different ministries and agencies involved, as well as engaging in the development of strategies in other policy areas to ensure consistency and coherence (UNCTAD, 2012a).

2. Entrepreneurship policy principles and main features

Formulation of entrepreneurship policies in LDCs should be guided by the fact that entrepreneurship is fundamental to structural transformation, which is, in turn, required for achieving sustainable development (as shown in chapter 1). For entrepreneurship to reach its optimal socially desirable outcome, LDCs are advised therefore to focus their entrepreneurship policies on the objective of structural transformation of their economy. The main goal of such policies should not be entrepreneurship per se or even the positive side-effects of entrepreneurship, such as job creation, inclusiveness, industrialization or poverty eradication. Rather, by successfully targeting structural transformation, national policies will also achieve these other socially desirable targets.

As already argued in this report, not all types of enterprises contribute equally to structural transformation. On the contrary, it is typically high-growth entrepreneurship that has the highest impact. A review of the experience of countries that have successfully fostered development of high-growth entrepreneurship can thus yield useful lessons and principles for LDCs on formulating entrepreneurship policies. As there is scant research and literature on the effectiveness in LDCs and Africa of high-growth entrepreneurship development programmes (which excludes cooperative models and social enterprises),

Entrepreneurship programmes based on selectivity can help build credibility

this section presents cases studies conducted in four very successful countries: Finland, the Republic of Korea, Chile and India (boxes 5.1 to 5.4). While the levels of development of these other developing and developed countries differ from that of LDCs, their experiences can nonetheless provide valuable pragmatic and actionable insights into the principles that should govern the design, formulation and implementation of entrepreneurship development programmes.

The four case studies demonstrate the potential role of government-led initiatives, and political sponsoring, backed by effective communication strategies, in shaping entrepreneurial culture, stimulating entrepreneurship and encouraging investment in innovative start-ups. Government-certified entrepreneurship programmes based on selectivity that establishes milestones to be achieved at each stage of development and links rewards to performance can also help to build international credibility and branding, helping to attract FDI by building a reputation for quality investments.

The experiences of Finland and the Republic of Korea, in particular, highlight the benefits of broad-based, holistic and diverse entrepreneurship development programmes that bring together stakeholders from Government, the private sector, academia, civil society and the international community, to exploit synergies and complementarities among multiple actors. All four case studies underline the need for entrepreneurship development to be rooted in a systemic approach underpinned by public–private sector dialogue and collaboration. The Government of the Republic of Korea, for example, gathered a wide range of opinions and suggestions from the private sector in preparing the creative economy action plan and established a creative economy joint task force, including representatives of venture companies, SMEs and large companies, to institutionalize private sector participation (UNCTAD, 2013d). In an LDC context, consultative mechanisms can be fostered and matched by public-sector governance reforms that emphasize transparency, information sharing and accountability.

In Finland, the Young Innovative Company and Vigo Accelerator programmes highlight the need for complementarity between programmes, to ensure financing for enterprises at different stages of development. For instance, a first programme may target linking entrepreneurs with venture capitalists to mobilize seed capital so as to translate ideas into businesses, while at a later stage a different programme links up growing firms with capitalists in order to expand into new markets. In the cases of both Finland and the Republic of Korea, there were complementarities across initiatives, and efforts stressed linking venture capitalists with new entrepreneurs and new entrepreneurs with older experienced entrepreneurs (business angels) who could mentor and coach them.

Complementarity is also needed between entrepreneurship development programmes that promote commercialization of ideas and inventions into products and trade policies that provide market opportunities. For example, the Make in India initiative aims at developing market outlets for start-ups in India, complementing the role of the Start-up India initiative in nurturing innovation. Rwanda operates a Made in Rwanda trade policy with the objective of promoting domestic market development and support national economic transformation. In particular, the goal of the Made in Rwanda is to increase the competitiveness of the country's economy and improve the trade balance by both recapturing parts of the Rwandan market from imports and improving the ability of Rwandan producers to compete in export markets in order to create productive jobs in dynamic and resilient firms (Rwanda, 2017).

The case of Chile illustrates the importance of maintaining the continuity of programmes in the face of domestic political change, but also of flexibility when flaws in programme design become apparent. The Start-up Chile programme kept its mission unchanged and received sustained increases in budget, despite changes in Government. Likewise, the Scale programme under Start-up Chile was established to address the low retention rate among graduating entrepreneurs. Vesting responsibility in a single autonomous agency with a clear mandate can help to ensure independence from political interference. Independence, transparency and accountability are important to avoid capture by vested interests: decisions on the selection of firms and their continuation in support programmes should be objective and impartial to the extent possible, for example, through use of external panels, as in Finland, or strengthening of governance mechanisms for development.

Research and development plays an important role at all stages of a firm's life cyle. In addition to the radical innovations that lead to new start-ups, incremental innovations are important to help existing firms to grow and survive. Clusters of learning, innovation

Box 5.1 Finland: A history of high-growth entrepreneurship policy

Experiences from Finland in designing high growth-entrepreneurship policy indicate that policy can have an impact on new firm growth if it is correctly designed. In addition, they indicate that policy initiatives that are highly selective based on growth motivation, that stage support according to the achievement of milestones and that solicit active public–private collaboration can be effective in facilitating the growth of new ventures.

Economic development, including structural transformation, relies on dynamism in firms, and dynamism implies innovation. Since not all new firms contribute equally to the economy, there should be a focus on new and innovative firms. Yet gaps in finance and skills, including difficulties in acquiring finance and operational resources, constrain the growth of such firms. In Finland, for example, insufficient numbers of experienced professionals opt for entrepreneurship. Policies in Finland have been effective in addressing gaps in finance and skills in the entrepreneurial system and thereby assisting new and innovative firms to grow more quickly.

Entrepreneurship policies in Finland are distinct from others as they have a strong systemic approach, that is, policy programmes are not designed and implemented in isolation, but rather to support and complement each other. In addition, policy planning and implementation are carried out with close coordination between government officials, the venture capital industry and entrepreneurs. There are two key programmes, namely the Young Innovative Company programme of the Finnish Funding Agency for Technology and Innovation and the Vigo Accelerator programme of the Ministry of Employment and Economy, in operation since 2007 and 2009, respectively. The two programmes complement each other.

The Young Innovative Company programme provides a combination of capacity-boosting for growth and bridging services. It offers financial support for contracting expert services for business planning, developing growth strategy and strengthening managerial competencies. It facilitates networking between participants and links with domestic and international venture capitalists, in addition to promoting the exchange of experiences and good practices. The programme acts as a branding mechanism that provides participants with credibility. Selection into the programme is done by the Finnish Funding Agency for Technology and Innovation upon the recommendation of an external panel made up of new venture experts and venture capitalists. Upon selection, the Finnish Funding Agency for Technology and Innovation sets customized milestones for each participant and continuity in the programme is conditional upon these milestones being met. In the first phase, participants must demonstrate an ability to compete in international markets and, at the end of the phase, participants must present their progress to an evaluation panel made up of venture capital investors, business angels and company directors. In subsequent phases, participants must be able to attract external funding and engineer and sustain rapid growth. By emphasizing selectiveness, growth motivation, capacity-building, hands-on support, networking, public–private collaboration and the use of performance milestones, the Young Innovative Company programme exhibits all of the essential characteristics of a high-growth entrepreneurship policy initiative.

The focus of the Vigo Accelerator programme is on supporting a high-growth talent pool of new entrepreneurs through a pool of venture capital teams, from which actors participate in the projects of new entrepreneurs. Sufficient funds must be forthcoming from both the public and private sectors. The system is supported by research institutions, large firms and educational institutions that provide a flow of technological and other innovations, and performs well, reaping social and economic returns and resulting in the creation of new high-growth firms if all of the constituents are in alignment.

The Vigo Accelerator programme is closely connected to the Young Innovative Company programme. Vigo Accelerators are private firms that invest in and help manage high-potential growth ventures, providing experience, expertise and hands-on managerial support to their portfolio of firms. They invest their own funds by taking equity stakes in their portfolio firms and are expected to help raise additional equity financing from other investors. There are dedicated public sector agencies to provide coordination services and favour Vigo Accelerators in their search for public support, such as support under the Young Innovative Company programme. Similar to the latter, the Vigo Accelerator programme was designed and is implemented with continuous public–private sector dialogue. By connecting new entrepreneurs with experienced entrepreneurship professionals, the Vigo Accelerator programme encourages the development of portfolio firms and elicits increased interest from investors. Empirical analysis supports the hypothesis that participants in the Young Innovative Company programme achieve superior performance because they participated in the programme and not simply because the right firms selected themselves into the programme. The superior performance can be ascribed to a self-confidence effect and to certification.

Finland has also actively promoted technical and vocational education and training and the concept of lifelong learning. Entrepreneurship education has also been integrated at all levels of schooling. Denmark, Finland, Norway and Sweden have established a model in entrepreneurship education that may be distinguished from those of other countries and includes the following common features: cross-ministerial cooperation; a key role for junior achievement and young enterprise organizations; the full autonomy of educational institutions in implementing entrepreneurship education, provided they are compliant with the national qualification framework or steering documents; intensive engagement with business; entrepreneurship education embedded at all levels and types of education; and the role of teachers as facilitators.

Sources: Clement et al., 2016; Rannikko and Autio, 2015.

Venture capitalists are major actors in the entrepreneurship development framework

---

and creativity involving universities, schools, research and vocational institutes and experimental laboratories can help to sustain a flow of new ideas into firms throughout their life cycle. All four countries considered have networks of stakeholders that support entrepreneurship development. Clusters can usefully be nurtured for economic sectors identified as priorities in national development plans and industrial policies, as in the case of the Creative Economy Valley in Pangyo, south of Seoul (UNCTAD, 2013a).

All case studies make it clear that venture capitalists are major actors in the entrepreneurship development framework. In an LDC context, this calls for a clear resource mobilization strategy that identifies sources of seed capital from the public and private sectors, including measures to attract domestic, regional and international venture capital, anchored within an overall financial development strategy.

Entrepreneurship development programmes should also include an exit strategy for start-ups and enterprises that fail. In the Republic of Korea, the creative economy plan, led by the Small and Medium Business Administration, is based on creating a virtuous cycle of "starting, growing, investment recovery and restarting". The third plank of the programme is to improve systems to increase leniency towards failure and easing restart. The Small and Medium Business Administration is intended to reform systems that have blocked entrepreneurs' attempts at restarting (UNCTAD, 2013a).

The approach of Chile, though it has limitations, is noteworthy for seeking to attract entrepreneurial talent internationally (chapter 3). The country's success reveals that national entrepreneurial capacities can be strengthened by harnessing the expertise and creativity of foreign entrepreneurs who can transfer knowledge, skills and expertise to locals. Start-up Chile has a social impact component that aims at changing and improving Chilean entrepreneurial culture. Foreign beneficiaries of Start-up Chile are required to engage with the local business ecosystem by conducting activities that generate social impact. The return value agenda, an innovative scoring

---

Box 5.2 **Republic of Korea: Revitalizing the economy through small and medium-sized enterprises**

In the Republic of Korea, the limitations of an economic development model heavily based on large industrial groups started to become apparent in the 1990s. Since then, the Government has paid increasing attention to the role that SMEs can play in industrial and technological policies and as part of developing new engines of growth in the Republic of Korea, emphasizing the creation of start-ups and the strengthening of existing SMEs.

The Government has institutionalized a system for certifying and promoting venture firms. The Special Law to Promote Venture Capital Companies was enacted in 1997 and a rule for certifying venture firms was set up by the Small and Medium Business Administration, defining certified venture firms on the basis of investment criteria, research and development expenditure and business assessment. In addition, the Government designates and supports innovative firms that have been active for at least three years and assessed as innovative, according to criteria based on the Oslo Manual of OECD and Eurostat and including capabilities in technology innovation, commercialization and managing innovation, as well as innovation performance. Such firms are eligible for a range of policy support packages. This government-endorsed system of certifying venture and innovative firms achieves the following three major goals as part of policies to support SMEs: policy support is effectively targeted towards firms that are eligible, willing and able to follow policy guidance; support serves as a signalling and advertising mechanism with regard to the direction of government policy; and the system provides a set of incentives for firms to voluntarily develop into the type of enterprises the Government wishes to support in order to implement its industrial and technological vision.

The Small and Medium Business Administration has a central role in supporting SMEs and start-ups, and is supported in the delivery of its functions by the following ministries: Ministry of Culture, Sports and Tourism; Ministry of Education; Ministry of Employment and Labour; Ministry of Science, ICT and Future Planning; Ministry of Strategy and Finance; and Ministry of Trade, Industry and Energy. In the Republic of Korea, support policies for start-ups cover the life cycle of a business and consist of two parts, namely research and development and commercialization. Six stages are identified in the process, from identifying to commercializing ideas, namely business ideas, concept development, research and development planning, research and development, commercialization and marketing. The first four stages, given the requirement for research and development support, are coordinated by the Ministry of Science, ICT and Future Planning; the final two stages are coordinated by the Ministry of Strategy and Finance. The Small and Medium Business Administration is involved in diverse areas, including direct funding programmes for start-up research and development, business model development, financial support for operations, indirect support policies to improve the business environment and infrastructure for start-ups. Support policies of the Ministry of Science, ICT and Future Planning are centred on promoting and commercializing ICT-based innovations, enhancing infrastructure for nurturing ideas and facilitating commercialization; other ministries focus on more specific areas

Box 5.2 (continued)

related to start-ups and ventures that fall under their substantive mandates. For example, the Ministry of Trade, Industry and Energy supports start-ups in the area of energy.

In 2013, the Republic of Korea established a creative economy initiative, Action Plan for Creative Economy, and measures to establish a creative economic ecosystem, based on the following six strategies: properly compensate for creativity and create an ecosystem that promotes the creation of start-ups; strengthen the role of ventures and SMEs in the creative economy and their ability to enter global markets; create growth engines to pioneer new markets and new industries; foster global creative talent that has the spirit to rise to challenges and pursue dreams; strengthen the innovation capacity of science, technology and ICT, which form the foundation of a creative economy; and promote a creative economic culture together with the population. The initiative led to three programme initiatives, namely the online Creative Economy Town, Centres for Creative Economy and Innovation and the Idea Innovation Six Months Challenge Platform. The latter was designed to accelerate the start-up process over a full cycle in six months in 2015, to facilitate 100 start-ups, selected from 1,000 ideas submitted by citizens and aspiring entrepreneurs, through the Creative Economy Town and the Centres for Creative Economy and Innovation. The platform aimed to provide intensified support by start-up specialists over a six-month period in the areas of business model development, application and registration of intellectual property rights and preparation of business plans. Specialists were also employed by the Centres for Creative Economy and Innovation and a dedicated firm to provide support for the commercialization of ideas. Once the ideas were identified, the platform accelerated the commercialization process by providing systematic support through networking by critical stakeholders in the process of establishing a new business, namely government ministries, public research institutes, universities, private holding companies, special districts for research and development and other individual firms, all with clearly defined roles.

Sources: Chiang, 2016; Jung and Kim, 2017; OECD and Eurostat, 2005; UNCTAD, 2013d.

Box 5.3 **Chile: Harnessing immigration for entrepreneurship**

Start-Up Chile was launched by the Government in 2010 as an initiative to "change the nation's culture towards entrepreneurship and to position Chile as the hub of innovation for Latin America" (see www.startupchile.org/economic-impact/). The Production Development Corporation, which developed the Start-Up Chile initiative, was established in 1939; its main objective is to anticipate and plan the next stage of development in Chile.

In each round, 100 start-ups are chosen from worldwide applications for the six-month programme. The chosen start-ups each receive $40,000 in equity-free funding, a one-year temporary visa, office space and opportunities for mentoring and coaching. Chile has one of the fastest business registration processes globally. The start-ups must then earn 4,000 social capital points, by hosting workshops, mentoring local entrepreneurs, teaching classes and organizing hackathons. More than 1,200 start-ups from 72 countries have graduated from the Start-up Chile programme and participants have raised over $100 million and created more than 1,500 jobs. In addition, over 200,000 nationals of Chile have benefited from community outreach activities organized by the start-ups. However, it has been difficult to find local venture capitalists and to retain programme participants in Chile. To address these issues, the Government has developed the Scale programme, which initially offered about $100,000 in new financing to three out of 30 graduates upon completion of a three-month programme. The funding is equity free, but recipients must incorporate in Chile and operate a business there. Since then, 50 countries have emulated the example of Chile and set up similar programmes.

Since 2016, the new goals of Start-Up Chile have been to ensure that Chile remains a world hub for technological innovation and known as a driver of technological enterprises that have positive impacts on the domestic economy. Chile has three distinct accelerator programmes, as follows: S Factory is a pre-accelerator for start-ups led by women entrepreneurs, providing two groups of 20–30 companies per group each year with four months of training and about $15,000 in funding; Seed is an acceleration programme for companies with a functional product and early validation; and follow-on funds are destined for leading performance companies incorporated in Chile seeking to expand in Latin America and globally.

In 2016, Start-Up Chile conducted a survey to measure the economic impact of the programme. Based on a response rate of 71 per cent, the survey indicated that 51.1 per cent of start-ups accelerated by the programme were still active in 2016. Of the 51.1 per cent of surviving start-ups, 55.4 per cent were Chilean. The retention rate was 34 per cent, that is, after participation in the programme, start-ups remained in Chile to run operations. Start-ups had collectively raised $30.5 million in capital, 29 per cent of which was from public funds and 71 per cent, private sources. An estimated 5,162 job positions had been created worldwide, with 30 per cent in Chile; average monthly salaries ranged from $1,216 to $2,280 (see www.startupchile.org/). Chile was ranked third in the Global Accelerator Report 2016 of Gust in terms of the value of investments generated from start-ups, behind the United States and the United Kingdom, and sixth in terms of the number of start-ups accelerated, behind the United States, the United Kingdom, France, Israel, Mexico and Brazil.

Sources: Egusa and O'Shee, 2016; Gust, 2016; The Economist, 2012b; West and Karsten, 2015.

LDCs can do **more** to attract high-skilled diaspora entrepreneurs

system, was set up to measure the social impact that entrepreneurs generate, in organizing keynotes, workshops, mentorships and events related to entrepreneurship and innovation, when they approach the local community.

Some countries, including India, have earmarked FDI as a pillar of their entrepreneurship programmes, while Ireland runs a global diaspora policy. Among LDCs, Bangladesh and Ethiopia recognized their diasporas as assets to be harnessed in their entrepreneurship development agendas. Examples of measures to attract the diaspora (chapter 3) include allowing for dual citizenship, operating diaspora support programmes, allowing the diaspora to have local bank accounts in foreign currency and actions to reduce fees on remittances.

Box 5.4 India: In search of creative disturbers to foster a culture of entrepreneurship and innovation

India provides an example of the launch of a broad and diverse set of initiatives to nurture innovation across a number of sectors, engaging with academia, industry, investors, small and large entrepreneurships, non-governmental organizations and the most underserved sections of society, with a particular focus on women. The Government seeks to bring women to the forefront of the national entrepreneurial system by providing access to loans, networks, markets and training. According to the Global Accelerator Report 2016 of Gust, India ranked tenth in terms of the value of investments generated from start-ups and of the number of start-ups accelerated. Four national initiatives are described in this box.

Start-up India

This initiative was launched in 2016, and aims to promote entrepreneurship by mentoring, nurturing and facilitating start-ups throughout their life cycles. An action plan published by the Government describes the three component pillars, namely simplification and handholding; funding support and incentives; and industry–academia partnerships and incubation. The initiative is based on a 360-degree approach to enable start-ups and includes a free four-week online learning programme. Nationwide research parks, incubators and start-up centres have been set up through a network of industry and academic bodies. In addition, a fund of funds has been created to help start-ups gain access to funding. Mechanisms to accompany the initiative include online recognition of start-ups, a learning programme, facilitated patent filing, easier compliance norms, relaxed norms of public procurement for start-ups, incubator support, innovation-focused programmes for students, funding support, tax benefits and the addressing of regulatory issues. The action plan includes a set of promotional slogans intended to flag the key advantages of the initiative to investors, such as "ecosystem without the trappings of the system"; "no tunnel – only light"; "disturbers wanted"; and "incubators available".

Make in India

This initiative was launched in 2014, and aims to promote the transformation of India into a global design and manufacturing hub. There are four component policies, as follows: promoting national manufacturing; attracting foreign direct investment; stimulating the generation and commercialization of intellectual property rights; and stimulating new initiatives, including the creation of industrial corridors and 21 new nodal cities. Among other measures, the initiative ensures the replacement of obsolete and obstructive frameworks with transparent and user-friendly systems, to facilitate the procurement of investments. The Government aims to harness local public procurement policies to promote the manufacturing and utilization of locally made goods and services in its manufacturing development.

Atal Innovation Mission

This initiative is designed to promote a culture of innovation and entrepreneurship and to serve as a platform for the promotion of world-class innovation hubs, grand challenges, start-up businesses and other self-employment activities, in particular in technology-driven areas. Atal tinkering labs have been created across the country, serving as workspaces in which students can use tools and equipment to gain hands-on training in the concepts of science, technology, engineering and mathematics. In addition, Atal incubation centres have been created to build innovative start-up businesses as scaleable and sustainable enterprises. The nationwide centres provide incubation facilities with appropriate physical infrastructure, including capital equipment and operating facilities, as well as access to sectoral experts, business planning support, seed capital, industry partners and training, to encourage innovative start-ups.

Box 5.4 (continued)

Digital India

This initiative aims to modernize the economy of India to make all government services available electronically; to transform India into a digitally empowered society and knowledge economy, with universal access to goods and services; and to enable the country to harness the benefits of digitalization for its transformation. There are nine component pillars, including building broadband highways, ensuring universal access to mobile connectivity, electronic governance, electronics manufacturing and the electronic delivery of services.

Sources: Global Entrepreneurship Summit, 2017; Gust, 2016.

Digitalization and local public procurement can be harnessed to sustain entrepreneurship development. Both India and the Republic of Korea have identified the ICT sector as having the potential to stimulate entrepreneurship in new economic sectors. LDCs must position themselves to increasingly benefit from the business opportunities enabled by ICT, either to support structural transformation in economic sectors such as agriculture and manufacturing, or as a stand-alone economic sector (UNCTAD, 2017a). Local public procurement programmes can also stimulate demand for SME products and services, but must be matched by proper procurement laws and regulations to avoid political capture.

An international review of best practices commissioned by the Ministry of Trade and Industry of Finland (Autio et al., 2007) identified a number of key principles for policies towards high-growth SMEs:

- A high level of selectivity, particularly at the later stages of venture development.
- Requirement of strong growth motivation on the part of participants.
- Proactivity in identifying prospective growth firms.
- Consistency in addressing managerial motivation and skills.
- Close collaboration with private sector service providers.
- An image of professionalism and competence and a degree of exclusivity.

- Sustained and focused development efforts.
- Tailored management development activities that encompass experience sharing and interactivity.
- Linking participation and grants to growth aspirations and achievement of milestones.
- Acceptance of casualties.
- Involvement of seasoned managers with experience in rapid growth.

3. Framework of national-level policy options

Policies aimed at establishing, nurturing or strengthening entrepreneurship for structural transformation in LDCs need to be a combination of vertical and horizontal policies. Vertical policies are targeted towards specific sectors, activities or (types of) enterprises that contribute significantly to structural transformation and form the core of entrepreneurship policies (as defined strictly), which are discussed in section C of this chapter. Horizontal policies potentially affect all sectors, economic activities and firms. Section D focuses on entrepreneurship in horizontal policies, rather than on an overall discussion of horizontal policies. These different types of policies, strategies and programmes need to be designed and put in place by a developmental State which incorporates the specific features of an entrepreneurial State. Table 5.1 sets out a framework of national-level policies that promote transformational entrepreneurship in LDCs. The framework is consistent with the UNCTAD Entrepreneurship Policy Framework.

Table 5.1

Framework of policy options for transformational entrepreneurship in the least developed countries

Entrepreneurship policy	Entrepreneurship dimension of general economic policies	Entrepreneurial State
• Absorbing survivalist entrepreneurs into wage employment	• Providing finance	• Providing public investment and infrastructure
• Supporting enterprise growth	• Building technological capabilities	• Establishing a role for State-owned enterprises
• Promoting formalization and formal–informal linkages	• Enhancing digitalization and e-commerce	• Ensuring public–private dialogue
• Supporting enterprises throughout their life cycles	• Enhancing education and skills development	
• Repositioning women's and youth entrepreneurship		

Source: UNCTAD secretariat.

Note: Policies can be at the macrolevel, mesolevel or microlevel and mesolevel policies can build on the UNCTAD Entrepreneurship Policy Framework (annex 3).

> **The expansion of dynamic firms plays a critical role in structural transformation**

The UNCTAD Entrepreneurship Policy Framework was itself formulated to support the design of initiatives, measures and institutions that promote entrepreneurship, particularly the emergence of new entrepreneurs and establishment of start-up businesses, in the context of overall economic and entrepreneurship development policies.[1]

C. Entrepreneurship policies

Policies for entrepreneurship development are not about unwavering support for the creation of new enterprises, which is not automatically beneficial. Economic contributions depend on the nature of the enterprises created. Nor is enterprise creation the only, or the most important, means through which entrepreneurship can contribute to structural transformation – expansion of existing enterprises is also critical. Structural transformation is thus best served by a balanced mix of interlinked enterprises of different sizes, rather than the indiscriminate proliferation of microenterprises and small enterprises. This requires policymakers to differentiate between the various types, sizes and stages of the life cycle of enterprises and to devise and implement programmes and measures tailored to their varied characteristics and distinct contributions to the process of structural transformation.

Entrepreneurship policies should also incorporate the following elements:

- Selection of firms to receive support made on the basis of independent, transparent and accountable criteria, to the degree possible, and free from vested interests and political interference;
- Adoption of time-bound rewards, advantages and incentives, linked to performance and clearly communicated to stakeholders.

1. Microenterprises and small enterprises

As discussed in chapter 2, a large proportion of enterprises in LDCs are microenterprises driven by necessity rather than choice, and a large portion operates in the informal sector. Some entrepreneurs in this situation may discover a talent for entrepreneurship by opportunity and go on to develop enterprises that will contribute positively to structural transformation. However, "many informal entrepreneurs would gladly close their businesses to work as employees in the formal sector if offered the chance, even if wages in the formal sector are taxed while income in the informal sector is not. Few of them have this opportunity" (La Porta and Shleifer, 2014).

Far from promoting structural transformation, low-potential, necessity-driven enterprises tend to act as a brake on the process. Rather than devoting scarce resources to supporting survivalist entrepreneurs with low potential, policies should be oriented towards either nudging them towards opportunity-driven ventures or absorbing them into other, more productive, economic activities, through employment creation by more dynamic and transformational enterprises.

Creation of decent jobs is thus an important objective of entrepreneurship policies. Labour-intensive public sector works programmes as part of large-scale infrastructure development programmes can also play an important role in employment creation, especially in rural areas, helping to kick-start a virtuous circle of increasing incomes, rising demand and economic diversification as part of a wider programme of rural economic transformation (UNCTAD, 2013a; UNCTAD, 2015a) and agricultural modernization. Other relevant policies to absorb labour include promoting the development of labour-intensive services such as tourism and use of local content policies, such as local content in goods and personnel, as well as accelerating the implementation of a national employment policy that includes developing early apprenticeship schemes to improve skills development among youth, enforcing bans on child labour, improving information on labour market employment opportunities and enacting government-sponsored employment migration programmes for a variety of skills with countries that are short on labour.

Differentiation among opportunity-driven microenterprises and small enterprises is also important. As discussed in chapter 2, many are me-too enterprises, operating in existing economic activities with existing business models and technologies. While such enterprises can be useful in providing employment opportunities, their contribution to structural transformation is limited. Priority in the allocation of scarce public resources should instead be given to more dynamic and innovative enterprises that create spillover effects that benefit less dynamic enterprises, while also offering quality employment as a viable option to unsuccessful microentrepreneurs. The expansion of dynamic enterprises plays a critical role in structural transformation, both directly and through its contribution to the employment creation needed to absorb survivalist entrepreneurs. Empirical evidence (mainly from developed countries) shows that most net job creation comes from a few rapidly growing firms. In general, half to three-quarters of new jobs are generated by high-growth firms, representing just 4–6 per cent of all enterprises (OECD, 2013a).

2. Medium-sized and large enterprises

While entrepreneurship policies are often preoccupied with enterprise creation and microenterprises and small enterprises, enterprise expansion and larger enterprises are also critical to structural transformation. In addition to their direct contribution, through increasing productivity and shifting production patterns, and their contribution to employment creation, larger firms play a key role in fostering entrepreneurial skills and innovation capabilities through "intrapreneurship" – the ability of managers to act entrepreneurially within the firm. Policies should therefore aim at establishing a balanced enterprise ecosystem that includes firms of all sizes and types. Furthermore, larger enterprises, as well as microenterprises and SMEs should be supported across their life cycle. This is true also for State-owned enterprises with the potential to catalyse structural transformation.

Linkages. Linkages between microenterprises and SMEs and larger enterprises should also be promoted, to foster national and regional value chains, strengthen domestic supply capacities and open up opportunities for upgrading and growth of microenterprises and SMEs (chapter 3). The UNCTAD Empretec business linkages programme has assisted LDCs such as Uganda and Zambia in creating these types of linkages. In addition, fiscal, consumption and productive linkages are central to industrialization and economic development (Böhme and Thiele, 2012).

Policy measures to foster linkages between microenterprises and SMEs and larger enterprises include the promotion of business clusters through spatial development initiatives and clustering and through networking and alliances, as well as use of strategic local content policies in the extractive sector to build linkages between large multinationals and domestic enterprises, including to support new and nascent local supply chains to boost domestic economic complexity (chapter 3).

Clustering. The establishment of special economic zones and industrial parks offers a means for Governments to relieve limitations on firms' productivity, by addressing multiple soft and hard infrastructure resource constraints holistically (African Development Bank et al., 2017) but, as discussed in chapter 3, they are not a panacea. If tailored to

Policies should aim at a balanced enterprise ecosystem

the key supply-side bottlenecks faced by producers, and geared to promoting both continued innovation and emergence of business clusters, these tools can generate positive spillover effects, especially in countries with significant infrastructural gaps. They help to develop business clusters, which are a physical concentration of firms producing similar or complementary products or requiring similar skills, technologies or inputs, including suppliers of specialized inputs and infrastructure. Such positive spillover effects hinge, however, on the gradual establishment of a dense network of linkages among businesses and between businesses and supportive institutions, in terms of upstream/downstream activities and of know-how and knowledge diffusion. This explains the importance of connecting special economic zones and industrial parks with governmental and other institutions (e.g. universities, standard-setting agencies, think tanks, vocational training providers and trade associations) that provide specialized training, education, information, research and technical support (Porter, 1998), and with the wider economy outside of economic zones and industrial parks.

Business clusters promote coordination, cooperation and competition among participating firms, facilitating exchanges of information and technology, recruitment of specialized personnel, sharing of overhead costs and joint funding of facilities. By helping to build mutual trust and reputation, they also favour local sourcing of inputs and help to lower transaction costs. There is some evidence that such effects can increase firms' productivity, efficiency and flexibility and promote continuing innovation, allowing firms to survive and grow.

Other potential benefits of business clusters include lowering the perceived risks of entry and exit for firms, enhancing their voice in seeking improved services and quasi-public goods and enabling them to access larger markets and exploit division of labour to operate at a larger scale. Successful clusters tend to attract entrepreneurial talent and attention from Governments, investors and the private sector (UNIDO, 2013b).

Support for revitalization of business clusters to LDCs from the UNIDO (2013b) cluster development programme includes:

Networks under South–South cooperation can boost LDC firms' growth

- Building trust, to enable cluster stakeholders with different or conflicting interests to work together.

- Improving cluster governance to improve sustainability, by instilling norms and values that facilitate joint actions and sustain collaboration over time.

- Promoting business networks among entrepreneurs with shared commercial interests and objectives, horizontally (among similar enterprises) and vertically (through buying and selling relationships).

- Institutional capacity-building, to strengthen the capacity of supporting institutions to provide efficient and effective services and enhance their dialogue and collaboration with entrepreneurs.

Networking and alliances. Alliances between local SMEs and large multinationals can offer opportunities for growth and expansion to local SMEs. An alliance is formed by firms coming together under some contractual arrangement. Well-known types of contractual arrangements include: (a) subcontracting, which involves buying supplies from another firm and working closely on detailed specifications for a complex product; (b) licensing, which includes permission to manufacture a product under licence, distribute a product and include a product in another design; (c) joint venture, which involves the creation of a third firm to manufacture or market a product, with equity usually shared by the partners; (d) strategic alliance, which is essentially a joint venture without the creation of a third firm and with no equity involved; and (e) consortium, which is usually a group of firms joining together to purchase components or equipment that they will share (Hussain, 2000). Bangladesh and Uganda (box 5.5) are two LDCs that have used licensing arrangements and joint ventures with foreign multinationals to develop a local pharmaceuticals industry of medium-sized to large enterprises.

The formation of networks among firms under South–South cooperation arrangements and firms sharing a regional economic community could offer possibilities for growth and expansion of LDC firms, as an alternative policy option to global value chains (chapter 3).

Local content policies in the extractive sector can also boost entrepreneurship and structural transformation, as in Angola, by increasing value added in the sector and building linkages between transnational corporations and domestic enterprises. The use of local content policies in the natural resources sector is far from new: 90 per cent of resource-rich

---

Box 5.5   Bangladesh and Uganda: Pharmaceuticals industry in the least developed countries

Bangladesh has succeeded in building a technological base for pharmaceutical production, namely the production and sale of generic medications. Two large pharmaceutical companies in Bangladesh, BPL and Square, are examples of companies that have succeeded in both the domestic and export markets. Both of these private sector initiatives built their capacity at the early stage through technical collaboration with multinational corporations operating in Bangladesh and, in some instances, by gaining expertise from India, and followed up such capacity-building under licencing arrangements, as well as marketing and contract manufacturing, to branch off on their own.

Uganda has had a measure of success in building technological capacities in the domestic manufacturing production of pharmaceuticals. For example, Quality Chemicals, a local pharmaceutical company, has been producing drugs for the treatment of HIV/AIDS and malaria since 2009. As a result of its joint venture with Cipla Pharmaceuticals in India, Quality Chemicals transformed from a local distributor of imported drugs to the largest local producer of drugs of importance to public health, providing an example of South–South technology transfer. The firm also exports to other countries in the region. The Government of Uganda played a key role in facilitating the joint venture, not only by adopting a variety of incentives to attract the initial investment, but also through an agreement to invest a 23 per cent stake as part of Quality Chemical's local equity to allow the plant to be completed as intended in 2008. The most significant feature of the joint venture was the focus on the tacit know-how and skills training that Cipla Pharmaceuticals was expected to provide, which was central to ensure the sustainability of the venture and to promote the entrepreneurial base of Uganda. The joint venture envisaged not only training for scientists, chemists and other management personnel, but also training in organizational issues. The Government of Uganda provided the salaries for experts from Cipla Pharmaceuticals to conduct this skills transfer over 3 to 5 years.

These examples may not be replicable in the short to medium term in all LDCs, depending on national human capital and technological bases. However, they demonstrate how the coupling of entrepreneurship policy with industrial policy and policies for science, technology and innovation can lead to the establishment and development of new sectors and to entrepreneurship development in LDCs.

Source: UNCTAD, 2011a.

countries employ some form of local content policies, and many are reviewing or revising mining and investment codes and contracts to enhance mining's contribution to economic development. However, there are cautionary tales as well as success stories. Political patronage and politicization can derail the success of local content policies (Hansen et al., 2014). Key ingredients for success include clear alignment of local content policy objectives with entrepreneurship development and structural transformation objectives; careful identification of opportunities, gaps and weaknesses; close attention from the start to feasibility and the capacity-building required to widen the scope for local procurement over time; and independent monitoring and evaluation mechanisms to ensure the accountability of public institutions and other stakeholders (Intergovernmental Forum on Mining, Minerals, Metals and Sustainable Development, 2018). Local content policies' effectiveness may be enhanced by the establishment of specialized institutions, funded by the State and/or transnational corporations, to provide technical and financial support to capacity-building by SMEs.

3. Promoting formalization

An element of entrepreneurship policy is promoting formalization of informal enterprises. In many LDCs, there are linkages between the formal and informal sectors, for example in urban West Africa (Böhme and Thiele, 2012). Such linkages can benefit the formal sector, for instance by reducing the cost of certain inputs. The informal sector can also be a seed-bed for creativity, promoting innovation and new ventures (Williams and Gurtoo, 2017). Moreover, as discussed in chapter 2, the informal sector can provide a testing ground for new business models.

A gradualist approach to formalization, informed by each economy's specific conditions, may therefore be appropriate, aiming at maximizing the contribution of enterprises currently in the informal sector to structural transformation. This means encouraging and easing transition of these enterprises into the formal sector, so as to facilitate public support where appropriate, improve their access to finance and business services and thus increase their productivity and contribution to structural transformation.

This requires ensuring that informal entrepreneurs understand the formalization process, and that they find it easy and desirable (UNCTAD, 2014f). Lack of awareness of the rules and procedures involved, and fear that they will be too onerous, can be major deterrents to formalization. Clear and easily understandable information should therefore

---

90 per cent of resource-rich countries have local content policies

---

be made available to entrepreneurs on registration procedures and the advantages and disadvantages of alternative legal regimes, including step-by-step guides. Microfinance institutions, non-governmental organizations, small trader associations, churches, schools and colleges and other community institutions can provide useful channels to deliver such information (UNCTAD, 2014f).

Formalization procedures should be made as simple and inexpensive as possible, for example by creating a one-stop-shop or using e-government tools. Accessible and strategically located physical one-stop-shops, with manual information processing, can greatly facilitate formalization. An increasing number of countries have special schemes for individual entrepreneurs. Small business schemes usually include a single tax system, combining the income tax, value added tax and social contributions, and a forfait payment.[2] Small-taxpayer units can be created in areas where business is conducted, such as the Bloc Management System[3] introduced by the Rwanda Revenue Authority in 2009 (UNCTAD, 2014f).

Another key part of promoting formalization is publicizing the benefits, such as improved access to credit and investment, greater opportunities to sell to other formal businesses and public entities, opportunities for international trade, the ability to rent or buy premises and so forth. Benefits can also be reinforced, for example by linking social protection (health care, retirement benefits, unemployment protection, etc.) with formalization or extending it to non-wage operators and their families, where this is not already the case (UNCTAD, 2014f).

In addition to understanding, ease and desirability of the process, formalization depends on informal firms attaining an adequate level of productivity for survival in the formal sector. Public provision of managerial training, entrepreneurship education and skills development programmes for informal entrepreneurs, coupled with business support services, may help to address the issue: there is evidence that the most important determinant of low productivity among informal firms is limited human capital of their managers (La Porta and Shleifer, 2008),[4] which may even be the most important constraint to formalization at the enterprise level (La Porta and Shleifer, 2014).

Informality can hamper the development of the formal enterprise sector

A vicious circle often operates in LDCs. Large segments of poor, uneducated, vulnerable people work in the informal sector, which produces cheap, low-quality goods (or in some cases deals with cheap, inferior imports) and has low productivity and wages that consequently keep demand for such goods high and depress demand for the higher-priced, higher-quality products manufactured by the domestic formal sector, endangering the viability of formal sector firms. These are standard predictions arising out of demand-driven dualism theories (La Porta and Shleifer, 2014). This vicious circle highlights the role that macro-level policies should play on the informality–formality issue in LDCs (e.g. demographic policies to slow down population growth, trade policies to limit cheap, poor quality imports and create export outlets for goods manufactured in the formal sector, and urban and rural development policies).

Pending operationalization of such macrolevel policies, specific measures to foster formal–informal linkages and raise productivity and wages in the informal sector could contribute towards enhancing the survival and viability of formal firms. Raising productivity and wages in the informal sector for a period of time can stimulate demand for the goods produced by formal firms and help sustain survival and growth in the formal entrepreneurship sector for a while (African Development Bank et al., 2017). These measures are, however, of secondary importance to the central objective of fostering transformational entrepreneurship, especially in the formal sector.

4. Support across the enterprise life cycle

Support to enterprises comprises several forms and instruments, including technical assistance, credit, development of technological capabilities, skills development, regulatory change, etc., as analysed throughout this chapter. It should reflect the life cycle of a firm – starting, sustaining and scaling up businesses and managing their end. Patterns of resource use and risk–return profiles differ between the start-up and maturity stages of a business, giving rise to differences in the scope, magnitude and duration of the support needed. Support should be sufficiently sustained to allow enterprises to grow and withstand market cycles and fluctuations, with clear performance-related criteria for an enterprise's entitlement to support as well as for eventual removal of that support.

Promoting the creation of start-up businesses can make a major contribution to structural transformation and inclusive and sustainable development, if the outcome leads to the establishment of high-growth, innovative and dynamic enterprises. This requires an effective entrepreneurship strategy. A valuable starting point for LDCs in formulating such a strategy is the UNCTAD Entrepreneurship Policy Framework, the basis of the long-standing role of UNCTAD in advising developing countries on policymaking in this area. The Framework is aimed at supporting the design of initiatives, measures and institutions to promote entrepreneurship, particularly the emergence of new entrepreneurs and establishment of start-up businesses, within the context of overall economic and entrepreneurship development policies (table 5.1). Among LDCs, this has involved UNCTAD technical assistance to Ethiopia, the Gambia and the United Republic of Tanzania in the preparation of their respective national entrepreneurship strategies.

Policies are thus also needed to ensure that start-ups survive and mature, particularly by addressing the many obstacles firms in LDCs face, including a weak business climate, insufficient financing, skills, deficient infrastructure (e.g. energy and ICT) and gender biases, as well as specific constraints that rural enterprises face (chapter 4).

In some respects, the end of the life cycle can be as informative as its beginning for the rest of the economy. Entrepreneurial failures can contribute to structural transformation as well as successes, by providing information about what does and does not work in the local economic and social context. Thus, successful entrepreneurship development strategies are those that maximize learning from such failure by promoting informational spillovers and supporting a process of entrepreneurial discovery, rather than those that do not consider enterprise failure. High rates of entry and exit of enterprises are often associated with economic vibrancy, while failed first-movers can sometimes lead to the emergence of an entirely new set of industries (Aldrich and Fiol, 1994). Entrepreneurs who persist in the face of failures may develop knowledge that enhances their abilities (Forbes, 2017).

Thus, rather than denying the possibility of failure, entrepreneurship development programmes should include an exit strategy for enterprises that fail to minimize costs and maximize benefits. Particularly where cultural attitudes towards failure impede entrepreneurial creativity, entrepreneurship education in schools could promote experiential learning that emphasizes the role of learning from failure in fostering subsequent success.

5. Repositioning female and youth entrepreneurship

As noted in chapter 4, microenterprise and SME development policies in many LDCs have special measures for women and youth. Such policies may be beneficial, but their purpose needs to be carefully considered.

Special measures to promote women's and youth entrepreneurship are often directed towards social goals such as poverty reduction and empowerment of youth and women, without a clear link to the goal of structural transformation. From an economic development perspective, however, such approaches are likely to be suboptimal: it may be preferable to address instead barriers that young people and women face in accessing waged employment, that is, to promote the labour market's absorption of the survivalist entrepreneurs among them. While support to women's and youth entrepreneurship may also be motivated by a perception that they are intrinsically more successful as entrepreneurs than other population groups, the empirical evidence for this view is unclear. The observation that views of entrepreneurship become progressively more favourable as one moves from evidence-based analysis to public policy (Nightingale and Coad, 2014) applies equally to women's and youth entrepreneurship. If the premise is incorrect, this raises questions about the long-term impacts of youth and women's entrepreneurship strategies, not only on the optimality of such uses of public resources, but also on the effects on youth and women's welfare.

Special measures for women and young entrepreneurs are more appropriate to address the particular barriers they face in accessing the inputs and resources required for successful entrepreneurship, such as gender-based constraints to inputs and resources that arise from discriminatory laws, customs and practices (UNCTAD, 2015a). There are gender-based differences in factors that motivate engagement in entrepreneurial activity, and influence its outcomes, and in linkages between entrepreneurial outcomes and economic growth, innovation and employment (Hafer, 2017; Minniti and Naudé, 2010). There is also evidence that young people are constrained in entrepreneurial activities by more limited human, social and financial capital, despite higher rates of latent entrepreneurship (OECD, 2013b).

Entrepreneurship strategies can usefully address such constraints directly when aligned to the goal of structural transformation, ensuring that policies to foster high-impact, high-growth, innovative entrepreneurship take into account the particular barriers faced by women and youth.

By targeting structural transformation, **entrepreneurship policies address** the challenges of **women's and youth** empowerment more sustainably

Appropriate measures in this context may include:

- Entrepreneurial skills programmes tailored to the specific barriers women face and delivered to women-only groups of beneficiaries.

- Support to the formation of women-focused venture capital investments (e.g. offering matching funds for investment in women-owned or women-led start-ups, early-stage and expansion-stage ventures) (OECD and European Union, 2017).

- Reforming laws that discriminate against women in their access to collateral, such as land and other resources, and designating a lead agency to enforce compliance with the laws.

- Ensuring equal access to quality education, including entrepreneurship education, between males and females.

- Providing subsidized child care to allow women more time to engage in entrepreneurial activities.

- Granting women entrepreneurs preferential access to credit in economic sectors vital to structural transformation (e.g. as a mandated requirement imposed on commercial banks by a central bank).

- Women-only credit guarantee schemes and incubator and accelerator programmes (as in the case of the S factory in Chile —see box 5.3) .

- Establishing platforms for dialogue between women entrepreneurs, civil society and Government, to allow women to express their concerns and seek consensual solutions.

- Creating and sponsoring business networks and support groups for women entrepreneurs.

Sociocultural constraints to female entrepreneurship require a change in mindset, and will take longer to address. One potential policy instrument is use of media-based and education campaigns on women's

Constraints to women's entrepreneurship hamper rural transformation

rights both in urban and rural areas. Multi-faceted interventions may also be needed. A pilot programme in Uganda sought to overcome the social obstacles impeding female entrepreneurs by combining the hard skills of vocational training with education on marriage and reproductive health. After two years, programme participants were 72 per cent more likely to engage in income-generating activities, including self-employment, while rates of marriage and childbearing at a young age fell considerably (Siba, 2016).

Constraints to women's entrepreneurship are a particular obstacle to the transformation of rural economies in LDCs (UNCTAD, 2015a). Promoting the role of women in non-farm rural activities could help to create a new female entrepreneurial class, adding to the dynamism and diversification of rural economies. Since 2014, UNCTAD has proposed the establishment of female rural entrepreneurship for economic diversification as an international support measure, aimed at supporting the development and consolidation of women's non-agricultural enterprises in rural areas. While gender-related constraints to rural women's entrepreneurship vary considerably between local contexts, appropriate support activities include: funding for the initiation and expansion of individual and collective enterprises led by women in rural areas; training in enterprise management and production skills, particularly in traditionally male occupations (taking account of low female literacy rates where appropriate); promoting and facilitating the consolidation of existing microenterprises run by women and the establishment of women's

cooperatives and collectives; promoting networking and collaboration among new and existing rural women's enterprises and facilitating mutual learning and sharing of experiences; and developing and/or disseminating appropriate mobile phone applications and other technologies (e.g. production methods and equipment) to meet the needs of rural enterprises and supporting their local adaptation and use.

Similarly, youth entrepreneurship in high-growth and transformative economic sectors and activities can be promoted through public policy measures tailored to address the specific challenges young entrepreneurs face (OECD, 2017b). Evidence-based needs assessments are needed to inform policy and programme design. Screening mechanisms, such as entrepreneurship contests, within a coherent programme for structural transformation can help to identify young people with entrepreneurial potential (section D.2). Entrepreneurship education, coaching and mentoring programmes are important, but should clearly communicate the risks of entrepreneurship, as well as confer the necessary skills. Continued public support should be clearly linked to performance benchmarks and their impact on structural transformation.

Digitalization is of particular relevance to youth entrepreneurship in LDCs, given the greater use of the Internet among young people (chapter 4). Youth entrepreneurship programmes should therefore include measures to help young people harness ICT for high-growth entrepreneurship, such as integrating digital entrepreneurship courses in school and university curricula. Conversely, the gender gap in Internet use in LDCs indicates a need for policies to increase the ability of women to exploit opportunities for digital-based entrepreneurship, including adult education courses for women on ICT and awareness-raising campaigns on its benefits.

Box 5.6 **Rwanda: Finance for business development, innovation and research**

In March 2018, the Government of Rwanda and the African Development Bank signed an agreement for a $30 million loan to finance the establishment of the Rwanda Innovation Fund. The objective of the fund is to stimulate structural transformation through research and development in innovative market-oriented products and processes in all economic sectors, by providing equity financing for technology-enabled SMEs; training technology-oriented entrepreneurs in business planning and management; and increasing awareness of and sensitization to intellectual property rights. The aim of the fund is to provide patient institutional growth capital and deep business support to invest in and develop world-class innovative businesses in Rwanda and East Africa. The fund is expected to support more than 150 companies and invest in about 20 opportunities at the early-growth stage, as well as to create more than 2,000 direct jobs and 6,000 indirect jobs over its 10-year life cycle. A national research and innovation fund is also being developed, to support joint research and development projects between private businesses and public entities.

Source: African Development Bank, 2018.

D. Entrepreneurship within general economic policies

1. Provision of finance

The UNCTAD Entrepreneurship Policy Framework recommends a set of actions to address access to finance (annex 3), aimed at improving the availability of financial services on appropriate terms, promoting funding for innovation, building the capacity of the financial sector to serve start-ups and encouraging responsible borrowing and lending, as well as improving financial literacy among entrepreneurs.

National development banks, with their long history and widely recognized role in development, are an important instrument for financing structural transformation. The Addis Ababa Action Agenda states that "national development banks... can play a vital role in providing access to financial services. We encourage both international and domestic development banks to promote finance for micro, small and medium-sized enterprises, including in industrial transformation, through the creation of credit lines targeting those enterprises, as well as technical assistance" (United Nations, 2015b).

National development banks can support the entrepreneurial State (section E) by providing equity and loan financing to public–private ventures and for the establishment of State-owned enterprises to catalyse the creation of new economic sectors; providing long-term financing for infrastructure development; providing preferential credit to SMEs in priority sectors; and facilitating SMEs' access to long-term finance through guarantee mechanisms. National development banks should be involved in financial inclusion strategies to address the obstacles to enterprises' access to finance.

There have been failures as well as successes among national development banks, which are affected by some of the concerns surrounding State-owned enterprises, such as political patronage and interference (section E), as well as lack of prudential regulation and supervision and insufficient capital. Identifying lessons learned, best practices, regulatory and governance frameworks are important.

The State can play a useful role as a co-provider (with the private sector) of venture capital to entrepreneurs for research and development and innovative activities in designated sectors, and by providing guarantees against risks in the early stages of innovative activity. The Rwanda Innovation Fund is a recent example (box 5.6). Public venture capital can also be targeted more broadly towards higher-productivity, higher

The State together with the private sector can provide venture capital

value added activities, as in the case of the Venture Capital Trust Fund of Ghana, established in 2004. This revolving fund provides funding to enterprises in priority sectors such as agriculture, pharmaceuticals, ICT, tourism and energy, through tax-exempt intermediary institutions established in partnership with private and public sector institutions (Sackey, 2013).

Such financing by an entrepreneurial State (section E) should set the direction and route of change, by shaping and creating markets, and focus on the sectors and entrepreneurs expected to generate the greatest value added and productivity growth. Capital should be patient and provided over a sufficiently long enough period for enterprises to build capabilities and become profitable.

Financial risks can be limited by a portfolio approach, spreading investment across a range of firms in different sectors (Mazzucato, 2013). Since public venture capital funding can be undermined if decision-making is marred by factors such as political affiliation (Afful-Dadzie et al., 2015), selection criteria must be objective, enforced by an independent panel, and performance should be properly monitored and evaluated, with exit strategies in case of failures.

Public support can also be targeted towards entrepreneurship, microenterprises and SMEs and larger enterprises through specialized State-owned agencies, funded by cost-sharing between the domestic and international private sector and the State. A few LDCs propose the creation of such enterprise support agencies in their microenterprise and SME development policies or national industrial policies. Such agencies should be given clear mandates and well-defined roles, matched by sufficient funding and human resources, with clear and time-bound goals (chapter 4).

Sovereign wealth funds can also be an important source of sustained, long-term financing for industrialization and entrepreneurship development programmes. More LDCs earning substantial natural resource rents should aspire to create a sovereign wealth fund to channel the revenues generated into supporting entrepreneurship for structural transformation. The sovereign wealth fund of Timor-Leste, for example, was among the six best performing in 2017, as measured by the resource governance index of the Natural Resource Governance Institute. However, in some cases opacity in transactions and absence of appropriate mechanisms for transparency and accountability can lead to mismanagement. A clear separation is also needed between the Government as a promoter of investments and as owner of the sovereign wealth fund. Moreover, capacity-building is needed to allow the sovereign wealth fund to operate as an expert professional investor and appraise prospective investment opportunities independently (Sharma, 2017).

Well-managed sovereign wealth funds can also serve to attract additional long-term private investments in sectors that are strategic for entrepreneurship and structural transformation, such as infrastructure (section E and chapter 3). Consideration could be

given to policies to attract investment from international sovereign wealth funds and other sources, such as establishment of a sovereign development fund or strategic investment fund to channel funding into strategic economic sectors. The National Investment and Infrastructure Fund in India provides an example (Sharma, 2017). Senegal has set up a strategic investment fund to attract international institutional investors to develop sectors such as energy. Clear investor protection clauses and dispute settlement mechanisms can help to increase the confidence of private investors (Hove, 2016).

The financial sustainability of public support to businesses is an important consideration. The fiscal burden on LDC Governments could be eased

Figure 5.1

Official development assistance disbursements to the least developed countries, by sector, 2007 to 2016

(Millions of dollars; constant 2016 prices)

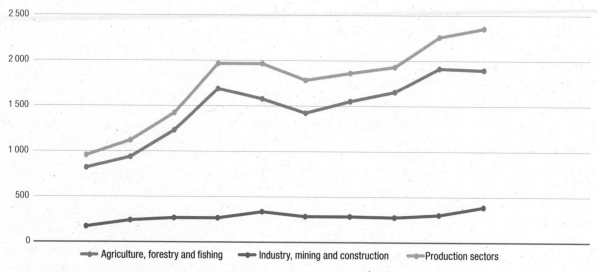

Source: UNCTAD secretariat calculations, based on OECD Development Assistance Committee database.
Note: Data availability by country varies by year.

Figure 5.2

Official development assistance disbursements to the least developed countries, 2016

(Millions of dollars; constant 2016 prices)

Source: UNCTAD secretariat calculations, based on OECD Development Assistance Committee database.

through mechanisms for cost-sharing between the State and the private sector. Other possible funding sources include domestic resource mobilization, official development assistance, loans from regional and international development banks, South–South development finance, capital market development and innovative sources of finance, such as diaspora finance, crowdfunding and impact financing (United Nations, 2017b).

Apart from domestic resources, entrepreneurship development in LDCs can potentially also benefit from external public financing. Official development assistance allocations to productive sectors (in terms of disbursements), such as industry and agriculture, have increased in real terms since 2007 in LDCs (figure 5.1). Total official development assistance to LDCs grew on average 4.8 per cent per year over the period 2007 to 2016, while growth in the productive sectors of agriculture and industry averaged more than 10 per cent per year. The share of official development assistance allocated to productive sectors in LDCs continues to remain low, at only 5.1 per cent in 2016, with the lion's share (about 80 per cent) allocated to agriculture, forestry and fishing (figure 5.2 (a)). A greater allocation of official development assistance towards both productive sectors and industrial development could benefit entrepreneurship development.

SME development accounts for 42 per cent of total official development assistance for industry, while agro-industry receives 16 per cent (figure 5.2 (b)). There is a case for an increase in official development assistance allocations to industrial development, and particularly to fostering linkages between microenterprises and SMEs and large enterprises and to agro-industrial development.

In broader terms and in the medium term, reducing dependence on official development assistance through improved domestic resource mobilization can help LDCs achieve a less donor-driven approach towards entrepreneurship and development in general (UNCTAD, 2009; UNCTAD, 2018a).

Beyond national borders, developmental regionalism could support entrepreneurship for structural transformation in LDCs in Africa (UNCTAD, 2013e) and Asia, through spatial development initiatives such as regional business clusters, regional development projects and infrastructure corridors, thereby increasing market opportunities for enterprises by facilitating participation in regional value chains (as an alternative to GVCs) and improving competitiveness. Landlocked LDCs, in particular, should engage in regional transport and transit facilitation projects with their coastal neighbours to expand market opportunities for their firms. The Ethiopia–Djibouti

Greater allocation of official development assistance to productive sectors could benefit entrepreneurship

corridor is one example. UNCTAD is currently assisting these two LDCs to improve the corridor's governance and logistical performance through the Diagnostic Trade Integration Study process under the Enhanced Integrated Framework.

The Belt and Road Initiative in Asia is an example of developmental regionalism in practice, within the context of South–South cooperation, with the potential to increase the connectivity of Asian LDC enterprises globally. Developmental regionalism can be supported through involvement of the private sector in regional integration initiatives, including communication on trade and regional integration to enterprises and establishment of consultative mechanisms with the private sector to identify bottlenecks to accessing regional markets (UNCTAD, 2010).

South–South cooperation helps enterprises in LDCs to access the skills, knowledge, technology and finance they need to strengthen their competitiveness. South–South development finance can be mobilized to fund the implementation of the national entrepreneurship strategies, while South–South technical assistance can support the strengthening of implementation capacities in entrepreneurship and niche exporting development strategies. South–South trade can help LDCs reduce their export dependence on competitive developed markets and on North-led GVCs. Cooperation agreements on intellectual property rights and technology transfer can enable indigenous enterprises in LDCs to build technological capabilities and access the patents needed to produce certain goods locally, while agreements on dumping and counterfeit goods can shield local enterprises from unfair competition from development partners in the South. In addition, South–South cooperation can be harnessed to build capacities of LDCs to comply with export non-tariff measures to developed markets. As noted in chapter 4, failure to meet international quality standards is a constraint to SME competitiveness in some LDCs.

In international trade and investment negotiations, LDCs must remain vigilant to maintain their policy space (both at the World Trade Organization and in regional and bilateral trade agreements) in order to be able to industrialize through use of infant industry provisions, public procurement measures and local content requirements; remain watchful

LDCs can strengthen domestic and regional value chains to foster entrepreneurship

of restrictive rules of origin and non-tariff measures on their niche exports (UNCTAD, 2018a), especially in agro-processing, as seen in chapter 3; and build capabilities to develop their own standards with which importers should comply, so as to avoid unfair imported competition from undermining national development. In e-commerce, LDCs are advised to seek to negotiate with one voice on the imposition of tariffs on digitally traded imports, to prevent such imports from harming their local industrial and entrepreneurship development (UNCTAD, 2017h).

As discussed in chapter 3, integration into GVCs should not be at the expense of development of national supply chains and generation of opportunities for local entrepreneurial activities. On the one hand, policies are needed for ensuring that GVCs do not weaken or undermine local entrepreneurship while on the other hand, policies should continue to support the development of niche local productive capacities both in the tradable and non-tradables sectors, including high-value services in tourism, and the fostering of intersectoral linkages. Examples of such policies include: applying selective incentives to diversify FDI away from commodity extraction and towards commodity-based industrialization; extending entrepreneurship development support programmes to rural areas that focus on agro-processing and local value added activities; strategically using rules of origin in regional integration agreements to support development of regional value chains (as an alternate or stepping stone to GVCs, matched by expansion of domestic supply chains); incentives to support intraregional FDI (such as easing restrictions on movement of capital, goods, labour and services in regional trade protocols to support regional value chains); greater use of local content requirements in FDI (regional and global) to promote local entrepreneurship; and building linkages between the extractive sector and the rest of the local economy.

2. Building technological capabilities

In order to survive, upgrade along value chains (chapter 3) and seize opportunities from advances in ICT, firms need to build their technological capabilities through acquisition, local adaptation and deployment of foreign technologies (which requires technology absorptive capacity) and through indigenous innovation nurtured by national innovation ecosystems.

Specific policy instruments to foster such technological capabilities include incentives for firm-level innovation (e.g. grants, loans and tax credits for research and development) and government procurement policies, which have met with much success in other developing countries such as Thailand; government-funded training for SMEs on harnessing new technologies; provision of technology-related information, e.g. through mobile applications; sponsoring participation of firms in technology fairs; and establishing public research centres within universities to support innovation in particular sectors (UNCTAD, 2015e).

Public support to research and development can help promote the elaboration and deployment of locally appropriate technologies in areas such as renewable energy and off-grid solutions for rural areas, to ease constraints to rural entrepreneurship (UNCTAD, 2017a). Such support may include grants to universities and research centres and the establishment of training centres (UNCTAD, 2011b), as well as provision of equity capital for rural and community-based energy start-ups involved in the development and application of such technologies.

Technological capability-building must be accompanied by support to translate technologies into business ideas and support for their commercialization. The UNCTAD Entrepreneurship Policy Framework recommends approaches such as public innovation awards to promote the commercialization of high-technology ideas by early-stage enterprises. A few countries, including LDCs such as Togo, organize entrepreneurship tournaments to identify and reward the entrepreneurs with the greatest potential.

Many developing countries seek to kick-start high-growth entrepreneurship through accelerator programmes, business incubators, science parks and technology research hubs, to provide a range of core support services and infrastructure, targeted business development programmes, mentoring and advice on access to finance and intellectual property, in order to promote survival among technologically intensive firms. Such support programmes are often situated close to universities and research institutes, to facilitate access to technological advice

(UNCTAD, 2012a). In LDCs, accelerator programmes and business incubators can target start-ups, and/or firms that provide services such as ICT to other firms, in priority economic sectors. Ideally, these support programmes should be implemented as part of a coherent entrepreneurship programme targeting structural transformation in LDCs. This would help to enhance their effectiveness and contribution to development.

Promoting technological progress also requires coherence and coordination between industrial policy and science, technology and innovation policies. Policy inconsistencies and incoherence can arise from slow or ineffective policy transitions, institutional resistance and inertia, and insufficient policy competence and foresight. Measures to improve coherence include improving alignment of policy frameworks in these areas; linking new policies to existing initiatives and agency mandates; identifying and eliminating duplication; ensuring that policy changes are appropriately funded, with transparent budgets, and adequately staffed; jointly establishing schedules and milestones for policies in both areas; establishing monitoring and evaluation frameworks; and ensuring an appropriate balance of funding between capital and recurrent expenses (UNCTAD, 2015e).

Intellectual property rights policy should ensure that patent rights reward risk-bearing inventors and innovators, while clearly defining the conditions for such patents, to be transferred to encourage further innovative activity. Incentives to move technology from the laboratory to commercialization can also be strengthened by giving researchers and innovators preferential access to cost-effective patent information and protection (UNCTAD, 2012a). However, a pro-competitive innovation system depends on intellectual property right policies interfacing with competition policies (chapter 4).

LDCs such as Madagascar have a vast potential to tap into medicinal plants to kick-start pharmaceutical,

Governments can foster technological learning through policy directives and regulation

cosmetics and fragrance industries. Processing medicinal plants can be a profitable opportunity for SMEs, as this does not require enormous investments in terms of capital or machinery and can also be environmentally friendly (Gurib-Fakim, 2011). In order to commercialize biodiversity and harness its potential for entrepreneurship and creation of value added, a series of obstacles need to be lifted. These barriers include lack of publicly supported research and development and indigenous innovation, ignorance of the patenting mechanisms and skills and financing gaps to translate research from academia into marketable products (Rasoanaivo, 2011). Public funding (including venture capital) to support research and development and innovation in nascent firms can contribute to overcoming some barriers.

LDC Governments can also foster technological capacity-building through non-market mechanisms such as policy directives, regulatory requirements and South–South cooperation mechanisms. Bangladesh is an example of a country that made use of regulatory requirements and policy directives (e.g. the National Drug Policy of 1982), in addition to technology transfer at early stages to support development of its local pharmaceuticals industry (Amin and Sonobe, 2013). The exemption that allows LDCs to delay patent protection for pharmaceutical products under the Agreement on Trade-Related Aspects of Intellectual Property Rights of the World Trade Organization until 2033 can provide an opportunity to develop manufacturing of generic versions of drugs that are patent-protected elsewhere (UNCTAD, 2011a), but this requires adequate investments in domestic technological capabilities. UNCTAD had been supporting LDCs since 2005 to establish domestic intellectual property regimes that facilitate

Box 5.7 UNCTAD eTrade for all initiative

The eTrade for all initiative, launched in 2016, seeks to raise awareness, enhance synergies and increase the scale of existing and new efforts by the development community to strengthen the ability of developing countries, particularly LDCs, to engage in and benefit from e-commerce, by addressing the following seven policy areas: e-commerce readiness assessment and strategy formulation; ICT infrastructure and services; trade logistics and trade facilitation; payment solutions; legal and regulatory frameworks; e-commerce skills development; and access to financing. Demand-driven assessments are carried out to provide a basic analysis of the current e-commerce situation and identify opportunities and barriers. In addition to assisting LDCs in identifying areas in which they could benefit from assistance by development partners, the reports prepared under the initiative are a valuable input to the involvement of countries in discussions related to e-commerce and digital trade, such as at sessions of the Intergovernmental Group of Experts on E-Commerce and the Digital Economy, as well as under the work programme on e-commerce of the World Trade Organization.

Source: UNCTAD secretariat.

LDCs should participate in global e-commerce as producers

---

increased access to affordable medicines and, where feasible, support the creation of local or regional pharmaceutical production and supply capacities, including in cooperation with investors.

3. Digitalization and e-commerce readiness

As noted in chapter 4, LDCs need to position themselves to benefit from the increasing business opportunities afforded by ICT, both as a catalyst for structural transformation and as a sector in its own right. Digital entrepreneurship is a key part of the twenty-first century landscape, with the global e-commerce market amounting to $22 trillion (UNCTAD, 2017e). Nevertheless, few LDCs currently identify ICT as a policy priority in their microenterprise and SME development policies (chapter 4).

While digitalization can transform the way enterprises operate, there is a widening gap between developed and developing countries in the use of digitalization to enhance manufacturing competitiveness (UNCTAD, 2017h), and digitalization in developed markets poses a direct threat to the sustainability of industrialization in developing countries, including LDCs (Banga and te Velde, 2018). Bridging this digital gap is essential for LDCs to avoid further marginalization in the global economy. However, significant additional investment is needed to increase its deployment and contribution to transformative development.

Supporting digitalization, by helping enterprises to harness ICT and engage in the global digital and knowledge-based economy, thus merits much greater policy support. The State has a leading role in this process, as a co-investor in innovative forms of investment partnerships. At the same time, a broad range of other investors should also be present, e.g. angel investors, venture capitalists, capital markets and private equity (UNCTAD, 2017g). In light of the high rates in business failure characteristic of the ICT sector, equity finance has advantages over debt financing in funding ICT start-ups and scaling-up, as it provides incentives for investors to provide other forms of support, such as entrepreneurial coaching and assistance in economic networking and discovery.

As discussed in chapter 4, LDCs are advised to put in place e-readiness policies to enable domestic firms to access national, regional and global e-commerce

markets, and leverage the market opportunities to improve their competitiveness, viability and profitability. E-readiness policies for entrepreneurship and structural transformation in LDCs can be mainstreamed into the Action Matrix of Diagnostic Trade Integration Studies, to facilitate resource mobilization from the international community. The UNCTAD eTrade for all initiative offers technical assistance to LDCs to formulate e-readiness policies and improve their ability to use and benefit from e-commerce (box 5.7).

E-readiness policy actions include developing a national e-commerce strategy aligned with other strategies; conducting a market assessment for the national ICT industry; strengthening the capacity of national customs authorities and postal services to clear and deliver parcels more efficiently; developing secure online payments services, e-commerce and consumer protection laws, as well as regulations for the ICT sector and e-commerce awareness programmes for firms; designing training programmes for firms on e-commerce and use of ICT tools, including e-commerce in trade-promotion activities; reducing Internet tariffs for firms; supporting education and training of ICT professionals at universities; and promoting and facilitating access to finance for e-commerce start-ups.[5] Establishing and enforcing taxation of e-commerce transactions can also generate fiscal revenues to fund structural transformation and the attendant projects of the entrepreneurial State (section E). Entrepreneurship development and building productive capacities are central to ensuring that LDCs participate in the global e-commerce market as producers, not merely as consumers. Development of local e-commerce platforms, including rural e-commerce can help to counter restrictions imposed by global e-commerce companies on participation of local vendors on their platforms. In Bangladesh, several e-commerce sites (e.g. clickbd.com) are targeting the domestic market (UNCTAD, 2015d).

4. Entrepreneurship education and skills development

Entrepreneurship education policies focus on developing transferable skills that can contribute to firms' survival and growth, aiming both to strengthen individuals' desire and capacity to become entrepreneurs and to develop and foster an entrepreneurial culture (UNCTAD, 2012a). This includes soft skills (attitudes), such as persistence, networking and self-confidence, as well as hard skills, such as business planning, financial literacy and managerial skills.[6]

The impact of traditional approaches to business training, focusing on hard skills, is limited, according to a number of studies (Campos et al., 2017; Cooney, 2012; Gibb, 1987). UNCTAD provides technical assistance in development of soft skills through its Empretec training workshops, emphasizing 10 personal entrepreneurial competencies (opportunity-seeking and initiative, persistence, commitment, demand for efficiency and quality, taking calculated risks, goal-setting, information-seeking, systematic planning and monitoring, persuasion and networking and independence and self-confidence). A study based on a randomized control trial, with a sample of 1,500 microentrepreneurs in Lomé, suggests that psychology-based entrepreneurial training may be more effective in helping entrepreneurs to remain profitable than traditional approaches and may be particularly effective among women: profits among female-owned businesses receiving personal initiative training increased by 40 per cent, compared with only 5 per cent for those receiving traditional business training (Campos et al., 2017).

Entrepreneurial skill development could benefit from a shift in emphasis on memorization and rote-learning towards experiential learning, problem-solving, team-building, risk-taking, critical thinking and student involvement in community activities. Such reforms are already taking place in a few LDCs. Since 2016, Rwanda has made a major shift towards more interactive, student-centred learning. All secondary school students are required to take an entrepreneurship course encompassing: active, hands-on "scripted learning activities", emphasizing entrepreneurship skills; a "skills lab pedagogy", with class time structured in a laboratory format; and "student business clubs" that start and run school-based businesses.[7] However, such changes further increase the need for expanded education budgets, to reduce class sizes, develop tailored materials and train teachers.

Further mechanisms to improve entrepreneurial education include:

- Scholarships for potential entrepreneurs (e.g. selected from accelerator programmes or entrepreneurship contests) to pursue university training in entrepreneurship abroad, followed by internships in the countries of study.

- Apprenticeships for local entrepreneurs in foreign start-ups and for foreign entrepreneurs in local start-ups, taking advantage of the LDC services waiver under the General Agreement on Trade in Services of the World trade Organization.

Structural transformation rests on building a developmental State with entrepreneurial approach

---

- Mentoring programmes between experienced entrepreneurs (business angels) and new entrepreneurs.

- Promotion of greater uptake of science, technology, engineering and mathematics among secondary and tertiary students, particularly girls and women.

- Greater use of local languages and local context in content design to improve learning effectiveness.

- Development of tailored online content based on digitalization.

E. Entrepreneurship and the developmental State

1. The entrepreneurial role of the State

Structural transformation in LDCs rests on the building of a developmental State and the promotion of development governance, oriented to solving common national development problems, creating new national development opportunities and achieving common national development goals (UNCTAD, 2009). A developmental State is a "State that puts economic development as the top priority of government policy and seeks to design policies and institutions to promote this goal" (Mkandawire, 2001).

The four major functions of successful developmental States are to provide a vision; support the development of institutional and organizational capabilities to implement the vision; coordinate economic activities to ensure co-evolution of different sectors and different parts of the economic system; and manage conflicts (UNCTAD, 2009). In this context, the extent to which a developmental State assumes its entrepreneurial functions is particularly critical to support the process of innovation and technological upgrading which support structural transformation, in line with national industrial and entrepreneurship policies.

An entrepreneurial State is entrepreneurial in its approach to development, rather than simply engaging in entrepreneurship. It may be defined in terms of ambition in approach and ability and willingness to:

In LDCs capabilities required for a developmental and entrepreneurial State can be acquired gradually

---

- Envision and guide the direction of change across public agencies and departments as well as nationally.

- Undertake mission-oriented public investments and actions that create and shape markets rather than merely "fixing" them.

- Make long-term investments, including in capital-intensive areas characterized by high risk or extreme uncertainty, which the private sector tends to avoid.

- Provide patient, long-term capital when needed to support sectors and technologies with long lead-times (Mazzucato and Perez, 2014).

In an LDC context, the private sector is weakened by the lack of institutional support and by information and coordination failures, seriously impairing its ability to provide the innovation required for structural transformation, in the absence of a proactive developmental State. The entrepreneurial State approach is thus particularly pertinent in LDCs. The role of Governments needs to extend beyond correcting market failures and ensuring a business-enabling environment, given that, as recognized by the international community, "structural constraints, particularly infrastructural bottlenecks, and institutional constraints have limited the growth of the private sector in least developed countries". This is consistent with the Istanbul Progamme of Action's advocacy of "a dialogue between the private sector and government and strengthen[ing of] public–private partnerships with a view to ensuring that policies address key constraints" (United Nations, 2011).

While public sector capabilities are limited in many LDCs, the capabilities required for a developmental and entrepreneurial State can be acquired gradually. This requires reform of public sector governance and strengthening the institutional framework to ensure transparency, accountability and independence of public sector institutions. A pragmatic, strategic, incrementalist and evolutionary approach is called for, undertaking a limited number of institutional reforms depending on the context, building on islands of excellence, promoting policy learning and nurturing political coalitions for change. The Governments of East Asian countries, for example, had limited technical capacities when they embarked on their industrialization and development processes, but built them over time as the process unfolded. Their strategy was to focus on building a few strategically important agencies, rather than seeking to improve government effectiveness across the board (UNCTAD, 2009).

Thus, LDC Governments need to increase public sector capabilities in parallel with progressively increasing engagement in entrepreneurial State activities aimed at fostering innovation and technological capabilities in the enterprise sector and supporting high-growth, high-productivity activities in economic sectors considered vital to structural transformation. This is in line with the incrementalist approach advocated by UNCTAD for building developmental States in LDCs (UNCTAD, 2009).

The role of the entrepreneurial State includes, but extends far beyond, improvements to regulatory regimes. Within the regulatory sphere, start-ups can be facilitated by simplifying procedures and lowering costs for registration (e.g. through online access and one-stop-shops) and improving regimes for licensing, labour market regulation, property registration, credit regulation, corporate governance, tax administration, trade and investment, contract enforcement, dispute settlement, production and environment standards, competition, public procurement and governance (Economic Research Institute for ASEAN (Association of Southeast Asian Nations) and East Asia, 2014).

Regulatory review and regulatory impact analysis can help to ensure that existing and new legislation and regulations are not unduly burdensome, but allow enterprises to thrive, for example by establishing clear property rights, reducing the cost of dispute resolution, increasing the predictability of economic interactions and providing parties to contracts with certainty and protection from abuse. LDC Governments could create an entity to assess, monitor and revise business regulations on a regular basis, in consultation with the private sector, similar to the Accounting and Corporate Regulatory Authority of Singapore (Economic Research Institute for ASEAN and East Asia, 2014). The UNCTAD e-regulations and e-registration programme has helped LDCs to clarify, publicize and simplify business registration procedures. In the United Republic of Tanzania, for instance, the e-regulations system is an "online database that provides investors and entrepreneurs with full transparency on investment-related procedures in [the United Republic of] Tanzania: at each step, the system tells where to go, who to see, what to bring, what to pay, what to get, what is the legal justification and who to complain [to] in case there is a problem".[8]

Beyond this, however, enhancing the effectiveness of enterprises as agents of structural change requires a range of policies at the macrolevel, mesolevel and microlevel, together with entrepreneurship development programmes based on incentives and well-defined selection, exit and performance criteria, designed to stimulate transformational entrepreneurship. In addition to measures to improve access to finance, promote technological capabilities among firms, enable firms to exploit opportunities for digitalization and promote entrepreneurial skills development within education systems, as previously discussed, policies should also address the infrastructure constraints entrepreneurs face in LDCs, e.g. through public investment, an area where the entrepreneurial State has a critical role to play.

2. Public investment and infrastructure

A key role of the entrepreneurial State in an LDC context is to undertake public investments oriented towards structural transformation. This is particularly important in LDCs, where critical shortcomings in infrastructure require complementary and interdependent investments in multiple sectors to relieve binding constraints to entrepreneurship. Energy and ICT, in particular, are critical to development, while also offering important entrepreneurial opportunities (UNCTAD, 2017a). Transport and trade facilitation infrastructure also need to be improved, especially in rural areas.

Considerable public investment is needed in the energy sector in LDCs, to boost enterprises' access to quality energy services through both grid-based national electrification programmes and decentralized energy solutions. In many LDCs, the potential of energy renewables, especially in non-hydropower, remains largely unexploited and could be harnessed through public investments. This is a clear case of transformative, mission-oriented public investment, as private investment in energy supply is deterred by a combination of irreversibility associated with large sunk and fixed costs,[9] substantial front-loading, long lead times and high risks (UNCTAD, 2017a).

The LDC entrepreneurial state undertakes public investment for structural transformation

However, the scale of energy requirements in LDCs means that public investment, even if supported by official development assistance, needs to be complemented by private financing (UNCTAD, 2017a). This is likely to require innovative public–private finance mechanisms, including cooperation partnerships between the State, domestic and international private sectors and the donor community. A key objective is to exploit the complementarities between public and private investment, to ensure that public investment catalyses additional private investment in areas that would otherwise be underfinanced (UNCTAD, 2014e).

Although LDCs have made impressive strides in ICT access as discussed in chapter 4, significant additional public and private investments are needed in order to broaden deployment of ICT-based technologies further and boost their effective utilization by enterprises for transformative development purposes. The State has a lead role to play in the process and should act as a co-investor in innovative forms of investment partnerships.

Rwanda is an LDC that has earmarked ICT, both as an enabler of entrepreneurship development and knowledge-based structural transformation and as a sector which can boost entrepreneurship on its own. Rwanda displays many characteristics of an entrepreneurial State in harnessing the ICT sector for entrepreneurship and structural transformation. As discussed in chapter 4, Rwanda has committed to developing a world-class Internet and mobile telecommunications infrastructure and prepares five-year National Information Communication Infrastructure policy plans. The aim is to become an ICT hub for the East African Community. The country has also been successful in mobilizing public–private partnerships to improve its ICT infrastructure, acting

Box 5.8 Rwanda: Public–private partnerships in the information and communications technology sector

In 2014, the Government of Rwanda and [Republic of] Korea Telecom established a joint venture company within a public–private partnership to deploy a high-speed broadband network that aimed to cover 95 per cent of the population in three years. As principal shareholders, Korea Telecom aimed to provide expertise and funding of around $140 million; the equity investment of the Government of Rwanda included the assignment of its national fibre-optic network assets (over 3,000 km), spectrum and a wholesale-only operator licence. The public–private partnership model was used to address the aim of the Government to rapidly deploy high-speed mobile broadband across the country. Korea Telecom built the network and acted as a wholesaler, selling capacity to existing mobile operators and Internet service providers. In 2015, the unique fourth generation approach won a global award for innovation in business models.

Sources: International Telecommunication Union, 2018; Tumbewaze, 2013.

State-owned enterprises contribute to transformational entrepreneurship

as a co-investor (box 5.8). Execution of the Smart Rwanda Master Plan 2015–2020 relies on use of public–private partnerships, with the Government involved by "providing support through regulation and policy, strategy and arbitration management, setting guidelines and providing seed capital" (Rwanda, 2015).

3. The role of State-owned enterprises

State-owned enterprises[10] also have a role to play in boosting entrepreneurship for structural transformation in LDCs. Motivations for establishing and running State-owned enterprises include increasing access to public services; providing public and merit goods; generating public funds; limiting private and/or foreign control of the economy; and promoting industrialization and economic development by sustaining priority sectors, launching new industries or controlling the decline of sunset industries (OECD, 2005; Price Waterhouse Cooper, 2015). State-owned enterprises in network industries such as energy and water supply, ICT services and transportation, in particular, can enhance efficiency and affordability of such services to enterprises and thus support competitiveness. At the same time, development-oriented State-owned enterprises such as national development banks (see section D) can be an important means of supporting industrial, entrepreneurship and innovation policies. State-owned enterprises also play a particularly important role in the extractive sector.

State-owned enterprises have been used successfully to create new economic activities, e.g. to promote economic diversification in Chile (UNCTAD, 2006b; UNCTAD, 2014e) and industrialization in Singapore (Price Waterhouse Cooper, 2015). According to the OECD (2015b):

> If the Government of a low-income country embarks on a strategy of catch-up industrialization, a case can certainly be made for establishing [State-owned enterprises] to carry out key functions: very likely, there is no domestic entrepreneurship available to fill the void, and unless the country in question is particularly large, the interest of foreign investors to participate may be limited. In addition, if the Government's ambition is to follow a development path already trod by

numerous comparable nations, it is relatively easy to hammer out a strategy and provide the [State-owned enterprises] with company-specific objectives toward the fulfillment of the strategy. Experience also shows, however, that some crucial conditions generally need to be met for such [State-owned enterprise]-based strategies to be successful.

Specifically, these conditions are:

- A competent bureaucracy empowered to exercise the ownership function effectively, reward success and punish failure, without condoning impunity among managers who are politically connected.
- Clearly defined developmental objectives, separate from social objectives.
- Insulation from political interference.
- Engagement in areas free of concentrations of commercial, financial and other market powers, to avoid elite capture.
- Dismantling or divestiture of the State from State-owned enterprises when their usefulness diminishes, as the country approaches middle-income level (OECD, 2015b).[11]

According to Price Waterhouse Cooper (2015), "[State-owned enterprises] are likely to remain an important instrument in any Government's toolbox for societal and public value creation given the right context", but only if they satisfy "four Cs": clarity (a clear understanding of their purpose, objectives and roles); capacity (time and resources to fulfil this role); capability (the necessary expertise and experience for management); and commitment to integrity (serving the purpose of societal or public value creation). Fulfilment of these conditions can be supported by State-owned enterprise governance frameworks underpinned by performance and learning feedback mechanisms, monitoring and evaluation frameworks and sunset clauses or exit plans.

4. Strengthening public–private sector dialogue

Among the lessons learned from the experiences of Chile, Finland and the Republic of Korea (section B) on successful entrepreneurship development programmes are the importance of collaboration, consultation and dialogue between the public and private sectors. Beyond use of public–private partnerships in infrastructure development (section 2 above), this means revitalizing the relationship between the public sector (including subnational authorities in decentralized systems) and the private sector, cultivating a culture of public–private dialogue and establishing mechanisms for dialogue, consultation, debate, information-sharing and trust-building. Public–private dialogue comes in many forms. It can be structured or ad hoc, formal or informal, wide-ranging or focused on specific issues. Tangible benefits include the policy reforms it can precipitate, improvement in the investment climate and building of an atmosphere of mutual trust and understanding between the public and private sectors (Herzberg and Wright, 2013).

Regular working meetings between the State and the private sector, backed by work plans encompassing agreed areas of negotiations and milestones for progress, could help to foster a culture of public–private dialogue. Formation of one or more coordinating bodies representing private enterprises, meeting regularly to adopt common positions on key issues, could contribute to the success of such meetings, while ad hoc participation of civil society and academia may also be beneficial.

Examples of successful consultative public–private mechanisms include Barbados and Mauritius. Business Mauritius (a coordinating body founded by the private sector in 1970 as the Joint Economic Council) meets regularly with the Government to express its views on the development strategy and to defend the interests and current demands of the private sector, allowing bottlenecks in programme implementation to be identified and resolved. Barbados has had a public–private sector alliance and dialogue mechanism in place since the 1990s (Economic Commission for Latin America and the Caribbean, 2010). The country's Social Compact is a tripartite mechanism for consultation, negotiation and agreement on a common shared development vision, social protocols and policy between the State, employers' organizations and trade unions.

What constitutes effective State–business relations when it comes to successfully implementing industrial policies (for entrepreneurship and structural transformation) and what factors are driving it are not well known (Economic Commission for Latin America and the Caribbean, 2010; te Velde, 2013b). However, it has been argued that effective State–business relations can address market, coordination and government failures and can reduce policy uncertainty (te Velde, 2010). A large survey of firms in some sub-Saharan African countries (Qureshi and te Velde, 2013) indicates that firms derive growth benefits from being a member of a business association, consistent with the fact that business associations lobby on their behalf (in addition to direct lobbying) and provide relevant information (te Velde, 2013b). There is emerging evidence that

Entrepreneurship development programmes should be underpinned by

Dialogue

Collaboration

between the public and private sectors

effective State–business relations can raise firm-level productivity, both in the formal and informal sectors and that strategic coordination with the private sector can provide a "helping hand" to Government, by identifying concrete public actions to foster more rapid enterprise growth and provide feedback on what works and what does not (Lemma and te Velde, 2017). Strategic interactions with the private sector can also guide Governments in identifying new areas of comparative advantage, new sectors of economic activity and future strategic direction. For instance, the flower industry's potential in Ethiopia was revealed by the private sector (Gebreeyesus, 2017).

The successful practice of industrial policy requires new approaches towards government–business coordination, according to recent research (Page and Tarp, 2017). Such new approaches involve strengthening coordination within the public sector itself as well as between the public and private sectors, while emphasizing commitment (to the coordination agenda), focus (on addressing constraints to firms' performance and by creating localized enabling environments), experimentation and feedback. Designating a champion within Government to promote industrial policy (and entrepreneurship), minimizing donor-driven influences on national institutional settings, setting clear and transparent rules to guide private–public sector interactions, and keeping public–private dialogue open to new entrants should be part of the new approach in State–business relations (Page and Tarp, 2017).

Reinvigorating public–private collaboration in LDCs and improving on developmental governance require strengthening the capabilities of both the public and private sectors. Ideally, strengthening and building up institutional, managerial, technological and policy capacity in the public and private sectors should take place in parallel, through a process of continuous learning (UNCTAD, 2009).

F. Summary and conclusions

This chapter has put forward the main elements that an LDC developmental State with an entrepreneurial role can implement in order to foster transformational entrepreneurship, which contributes to leading these countries towards sustainable development. Policy analysis is clustered around three axes, as summarized below.

First, entrepreneurship policy:

- Entrepreneurship policies are most effective if focused on the central goal of structural transformation and need to be consistent with other components of government development strategies and policies (e.g. industrial policy, science, technology and innovation policy, macroeconomic policy, etc.).

- Public support to firms should target transformational entrepreneurship (high-growth, high-impact and innovative enterprises), which contributes most to structural transformation. It needs to be sustained throughout a firm's life cycle and tailored to the changing needs and characteristics of firms along their growth trajectory.

- Survivalist entrepreneurship is best absorbed into waged employment.

- Entrepreneurship policies should incorporate the following elements:

  > Selection of firms for support based on independent, transparent and accountable criteria.

  > Adoption of time-bound rewards, advantages and incentives, linked to performance and clearly communicated to stakeholders.

  > Establishment of a balanced enterprise ecosystem which includes firms of all sizes and types.

- Gradual formalization of dynamic informal enterprises can be promoted by launching multichannel formalization campaigns that publicize the benefits of formalization and by reinforcing these benefits.

- Entrepreneurship policies need to foster linkages between firms of different sizes, stages of maturity and sectors, inter alia, by means of business clusters, networking and alliances. Greater attention needs to be given to the development of domestic supply chains in both the tradables and non-tradables sectors, within an intersectoral linkages approach.

- The best developmental contribution of youth and women's entrepreneurship is achieved by directing them towards promoting structural transformation, rather than towards reducing poverty and empowerment. Special barriers faced by women and youth entrepreneurs need to be addressed through targeted measures, rather than entrepreneurship policies.

Second, entrepreneurship dimensions of general economic policies:

- Deficiencies in financing of firms can best be addressed through national development banks, innovation funds, sovereign wealth funds, official development assistance and South–South cooperation.

- Creating clusters of learning, innovation and creativity involving universities, schools, research and vocational institutes and experimental laboratories allows sustaining a flow of new ideas into firms throughout their life cycle and enables the growth of transformational firms.

- The growing digital economy offers opportunities for entrepreneurship development which should be harnessed by policy, including ICTs as an economic sector per se, as an instrument of the productive transformation of other sectors and as an enabler of producers' access to wider markets through e-commerce.

- Entrepreneurship education and skills development should be introduced in both mainstream and specialized education programmes.

Third, the entrepreneurial State:

- The entrepreneurial State has an entrepreneurial approach to development, which envisions and guides the direction of economic change, and undertakes mission-oriented public investments and actions that create and shape markets. It goes beyond "fixing" markets and ensuring a business-enabling environment. It is particularly pertinent to fostering entrepreneurship in LDCs.

- Public investment in infrastructure plays a key role in addressing bottlenecks to entrepreneurship development. It can be boosted through the strategic and judicious use of public–private partnerships.

- Development-oriented State-owned enterprises can be an instrument of implementation of national industrial policies and national entrepreneurship strategies, by providing public and merit goods, generating public funds, promoting industrialization, sustaining priority sectors and launching new industries.

- Entrepreneurship development programmes can best be underpinned by dialogue and collaboration between the public and private sectors, which allows for identification of obstacles to entrepreneurship development and discussion of actions to eliminate or attenuate them.

Notes

1 The main features of the UNCTAD Entrepreneurship Policy Framework are outlined in annex 3.

2 Under a forfait system, tax assessment can be negotiated between the taxpayer and the tax authority. Typically the tax authority first specifies the tax amount based on available information such as the taxpayer's gross receipts, number of employees and the like. The taxpayer can accept or challenge the tax assessment and if the assessment is challenged, the tax payer has to provide means of verification (Taube and Tadesse, 1996).

3 See http://www.rra.gov.rw/fileadmin/user_upload/block_management.pdf.

4 Similar findings have been reported among formal firms globally (Gennaioli et al., 2013).

5 See, for example, Bhutan and Nepal, available at http://unctad.org/en/Pages/Publications/ETrade-

6 Readiness-Assessment.aspx, and Rwanda (UNCTAD, 2017g).

7 Financial literacy can be defined as "the ability to use knowledge and skills to manage one's financial resources effectively for lifetime financial security. As operationalized in the academic literature, financial literacy has taken on a variety of meanings; it has been used to refer to knowledge of financial products, knowledge of financial concepts, having the mathematical skills or numeracy necessary for effective financial decision-making and being engaged in certain activities such as financial planning" (Hastings et al., 2013).

8 See https://www.povertyactionlab.org/ (accessed June 2018).

See http://tanzania.eregulations.org/ (accessed June 2018).

9 Sunk costs are costs that have already been incurred and cannot be recovered, while fixed costs are costs that do not vary according to production levels.

10 There are various definitions of State-owned enterprises. This report adopts the OECD (2005) definition of entities in which the Government is a shareholder with at least a significant minority stake (at least 10 per cent).

11 Similarly, privatization of State-owned enterprises should also be carefully handled to avoid political capture and rent seeking (Gonzalez et al., 2018).

Annexes

Annex 1

Country and year coverage in Global Entrepreneurship Monitor data

Least developed countries	Year	Other developing countries and territories	Year	Developed and transition economies	Year
Angola	2015	Algeria	2014	Australia	2017
Bangladesh	2011	Argentina	2017	Austria	2016
Burkina Faso	2016	Barbados	2015	Belgium	2015
Ethiopia	2012	Belize	2016	Bosnia and Herzegovina	2017
Madagascar	2017	Bolivia (Plurinational State of)	2014	Bulgaria	2017
Malawi	2013	Botswana	2015	Canada	2017
Senegal	2015	Brazil	2017	Croatia	2017
Uganda	2014	Cameroon	2016	Cyprus	2017
Vanuatu	2010	Chile	2017	Czechia	2013
Yemen	2009	China	2017	Denmark	2014
Zambia	2013	Hong Kong	2016	Estonia	2017
		Taiwan Province of China	2017	Finland	2016
		Colombia	2017	France	2017
		Costa Rica	2014	Georgia	2016
		Dominican Republic	2009	Germany	2017
		Ecuador	2017	Greece	2017
		Egypt	2017	Hungary	2016
		El Salvador	2016	Iceland	2010
		Ghana	2013	Ireland	2017
		Guatemala	2017	Israel	2017
		India	2017	Italy	2017
		Indonesia	2017	Japan	2017
		Iran (Islamic Republic of)	2017	Kazakhstan	2017
		Jamaica	2016	Latvia	2017
		Jordan	2016	Lithuania	2014
		Lebanon	2017	Luxembourg	2017
		Libya	2013	Netherlands	2017
		Malaysia	2017	New Zealand	2005
		Mexico	2017	Norway	2015
		Montenegro	2010	Poland	2017
		Morocco	2017	Portugal	2016
		Namibia	2013	Romania	2015
		Nigeria	2013	Russian Federation	2016
		Pakistan	2012	Serbia	2009
		Panama	2017	Slovakia	2017
		Peru	2017	Slovenia	2017
		Philippines	2015	Spain	2017
		Qatar	2017	Sweden	2017
		Republic of Korea	2017	Switzerland	2017
		Saudi Arabia	2017	the former Yugoslav Republic of Macedonia	2016
		Singapore	2014	United Kingdom	2017
		South Africa	2017	United States	2017
		Suriname	2014	Kosovo*	2014
		Syrian Arab Republic	2009		
		Thailand	2017		
		Tonga	2009		
		Trinidad and Tobago	2014		
		Tunisia	2015		
		Turkey	2016		
		United Arab Emirates	2017		
		Uruguay	2017		
		Venezuela (Bolivarian Republic of)	2011		
		Viet Nam	2017		
		State of Palestine	2012		
		Puerto Rico	2017		

* United Nations Administrative Region, Security Council resolution 1244 (1999)

Source: GEM database.

Note: In figures for which the source is a full national data set, coverage is based on the latest available data set (full data sets are released by GEM three years after data collection); data coverage includes full national data sets as shown, except for the following: Angola, 2014; Burkina Faso, 2014; Madagascar, unavailable as survey was conducted in 2017; and Senegal, unavailable as survey was conducted in 2015.

Annex 2

Country and year coverage in World Bank Enterprise Surveys

Country	Year	Country	Year	Country	Year
Afghanistan	2014	Ethiopia	2015	Rwanda	2011
Angola	2010	Guinea	2016	Senegal	2014
Bangladesh	2013	Lao People's Democratic Republic	2016	Sierra Leone	2017
Benin	2016	Lesotho	2016	Solomon Islands	2015
Bhutan	2015	Liberia	2017	South Sudan	2014
Burkina Faso	2009	Madagascar	2013	Sudan	2014
Burundi	2014	Malawi	2014	United Republic of Tanzania	2013
Cambodia	2016	Mali	2016	Timor-Leste	2015
Central African Republic	2011	Mauritania	2014	Togo	2016
Chad	2009	Mozambique	2007	Uganda	2013
Democratic Republic of the Congo	2013	Myanmar	2016	Vanuatu	2009
Djibouti	2013	Nepal	2013	Yemen	2013
Eritrea	2009	Niger	2017	Zambia	2013

Source: World Bank Enterprise Surveys.

Annex 3

Set of recommended actions in the *Entrepreneurship Policy Framework and Implementation Guidance*

Policy objectives	Recommended actions
1. Formulating a national entrepreneurship strategy	
(a) Identify country-specific challenges	Map current national status of entrepreneurship
	Identify country-specific entrepreneurship opportunities and challenges
(b) Specify goals and set priorities	Define strategies to achieve specific goals and reach specific target groups
	Develop and prioritize actions
(c) Ensure coherence of entrepreneurship strategy with other national policies	Align entrepreneurship strategy with overall development strategy and other private sector development strategies
	Manage interaction and create policy synergies
(d) Strengthen institutional framework	Designate lead institution
	Set up effective inter-agency coordination mechanism and clarify mandates
	Engage with private sector and other stakeholders
	Ensure business-like service delivery
(e) Measure results and ensure policy learning	Define clear performance indicators and monitor impacts
	Set up independent monitoring and evaluation routines
	Incorporate feedback from lessons learned
2. Optimizing the regulatory environment	
(a) Examine regulatory requirements for start-ups	Benchmark time and cost of starting a business
	Benchmark sector- and region-specific regulations
	Set up public–private dialogue on regulatory costs and benefits
	Balance regulations and standards with sustainable development objectives
(b) Minimize regulatory hurdles for start-ups where appropriate	Review and, where appropriate, reduce regulatory requirements (such as licences, procedures and administrative fees)
	Introduce transparent information and fast-track mechanisms and one-stop shops to bundle procedures
	Enhance ICT-based procedures for business registration and reporting
(c) Build entrepreneur confidence in regulatory environment	Ensure good governance
	Make contract enforcement easier and faster
	Establish alternative conflict resolution mechanisms
	Guarantee property protection
	Reduce stigma of bankruptcy and facilitate starting anew
(d) Guide entrepreneurs through start-up administrative process and enhance benefits of formalization	Carry out information campaigns on regulatory requirements
	Make explicit the link between regulatory requirements and public services, including business support services
	Assist start-ups in meeting regulatory requirements
3. Enhancing entrepreneurship education and skills development	
(a) Embed entrepreneurship in formal and informal education	Mainstream development of entrepreneurship awareness and entrepreneurial behaviours starting at primary school level, such as risk-taking and teamwork
	Promote entrepreneurship through electives, extracurricular activities, career awareness seminars and visits to businesses at secondary school level
	Support entrepreneurship courses, programmes and chairs at higher education institutions and universities
	Promote vocational training and apprenticeship programmes
	Promote and link up with entrepreneurship training centres
(b) Develop effective entrepreneurship curricula	Prepare educational material on basic entrepreneurial skills
	Encourage tailored local material, case studies and role models
	Foster interactive and online tools
	Promote experiential and learning-by-doing methodologies
(c) Train teachers	Ensure that teachers engage with private sector and entrepreneurs and support initiatives that bring entrepreneurs to educational establishments
	Encourage entrepreneurship training for teachers
	Promote entrepreneurship educator networks
(d) Partner with private sector	Encourage private sector sponsorship for entrepreneurship training and skills development
	Link up businesses with entrepreneurship education networks
	Develop mentoring programmes
4. Facilitating technology exchange and innovation	
(a) Support greater dissemination of ICT in private sector	Launch awareness and capacity-building campaigns on ICT use
	Stimulate introduction of ICT into businesses
	Support development of online and mobile market information platforms
	Provide training on ICT to target groups such as women and rural entrepreneurs
(b) Promote interfirm networks that help spread technology and innovation	Promote horizontal linkages through cluster development
	Provide assistance for standardization and quality certification to networks of local enterprises, including social and environmental standards
	Promote business linkages through supplier development
(c) Build bridges between public bodies, research institutions, universities and private sector	Identify joint research activities with clearly designated participants and beneficiaries
	Promote public–private partnerships and mixed public and private structures to disseminate innovation
	Develop market-friendly university and industry collaboration
	Promote sectoral-level institutional synergies
(d) Support high-technology start-ups	Establish high-technology business incubators, knowledge hubs and science parks
	Facilitate start-ups that commercialize innovation
	Build networks in knowledge-intensive sectors with leading scientific experts and academics worldwide
	Give researchers and innovators streamlined access to cost-effective patent protection

Annex 3 (continued)

Policy objectives	Recommended actions
5. Improving access to finance	
(a) Improve access to relevant financial services on appropriate terms	Develop public credit guarantee schemes
	Stimulate creation of private mutual guarantees
	Promote foreign direct investment in financial services, supply chain finance (factoring) and leasing
	Facilitate collateral-free loan screening mechanisms
(b) Promote funding for innovation	Provide incentives to attract venture capital investors and business angels
	Encourage equity and risk capital financing modalities
	Provide performance-based loans and incentives for innovation and green growth
	Facilitate use of intellectual property as collateral
(c) Build capacity of financial sector to serve start-ups	Establish national financial charter
	Promote public–private sector access to finance partnerships for specific groups
	Provide capacity-building grants and technical assistance to expand lending activities, such as financial services provision through post offices and other proximity lenders and use of new banking technologies to reach rural areas
(d) Provide financial literacy training to entrepreneurs and encourage responsible borrowing and lending	Set up financial and accounting literacy training
	Undertake appropriate supervision of financial products offered to social entrepreneurs and microenterprises
	Expand private credit bureau and public credit registry coverage
6. Promoting awareness and networking	
(a) Highlight value of entrepreneurship to society and address negative cultural biases	Launch entrepreneurship outreach and awareness campaigns at national, regional and local levels in collaboration with all stakeholders
	Utilize media and spaces for policy dialogues, as well as speeches, addresses and reports to communicate support for entrepreneurship
	Disseminate information about entrepreneurship, including social entrepreneurship, and its impact on the economy
	Publicly celebrate entrepreneurship role models through awards and other initiatives
	Involve entrepreneurs in policy dialogue processes to sensitize government officials
(b) Raise awareness of entrepreneurship opportunities	Advertise business opportunities linked to national sustainable development strategies and related incentive schemes
	Organize information and career fairs, forums and summits on business opportunities, including in specific economic sectors or on specific business models such as microfranchising
(c) Stimulate private sector-led initiatives and strengthen networks between entrepreneurs	Support private sector-led campaigns
	Facilitate business exchange platforms, business portals, fairs, business associations and clubs
	Engage diaspora community in local entrepreneurship networks

Source: UNCTAD, 2012a.

References

Acs ZJ (2008). Foundations of high impact entrepreneurship. *Foundations and Trends in Entrepreneurship*. 4(6):535–620.

Acs ZJ, Desai S and Klapper LF (2008). What does "entrepreneurship" data really show? *Small Business Economics*. 31(3):265–281.

African Centre for Economic Transformation (2014). *2014 Africa Transformation Report: Growth with Depth*. Accra.

African Development Bank (2018). Rwanda Innovation Fund project to receive $30-million loan from African Development Bank. 19 March.

African Development Bank, OECD and United Nations Development Programme, eds. (2017). *African Economic Outlook 2017: Entrepreneurship and Industrialization*. OECD. Paris.

Agarwal R and Audretsch DB (2001). Does entry size matter? The impact of the life cycle and technology on firm survival. *The Journal of Industrial Economics*. 49(1):21–43.

Aghion P and Howitt P (2005). Growth with quality-improving innovations: An integrated framework. In: Aghion P and Durlauf SN, eds. *Handbook of Economic Growth*. Elsevier. Amsterdam: 67–110.

Agriculture for Impact (2014). Small and growing: Entrepreneurship in African agriculture. Montpellier Panel Report.

Ahmad N and Hoffman A (2007). A framework for addressing and measuring entrepreneurship. Entrepreneurship Indicators Steering Group. OECD. Paris.

Ahmad N and Seymour RG (2008). Defining entrepreneurial activity. OECD Statistics Working Papers No. 2008/01. Paris.

Aldrich HE and Fiol CF (1994). Fools rush in? The institutional context of industry creation. *The Academy of Management Review*. 19(4): 645–670.

Alemu AE and Adesina JO (2017). In search of rural entrepreneurship: Non-farm household enterprises as instruments of rural transformation in Ethiopia: In Search of Rural Entrepreneurship. *African Development Review*. 29(2): 259–271.

Amin M and Islam A (2015). Are large informal firms more productive than the small informal firms? Evidence from firm-level surveys in Africa. *World Development*. 74: 374–385.

Amin MN and Sonobe T (2013). The success of the industrial development policy in the pharmaceutical industry in Bangladesh. National Graduate Institute for Policy Studies Discussion Paper No. 13-07. Tokyo.

Andreoni A (2017). Mapping industrial production in [the United Republic of] Tanzania: A disaggregated analysis based on the 2013 mainland census. Inclusive and Sustainable Industrial Development Working Paper Series No. 12/2017. UNIDO. Vienna.

Andreoni A and Chang H-J (2016). Bringing production and employment back into development: Alice Amsden's legacy for a new developmentalist agenda. *Cambridge Journal of Regions, Economy and Society*. 10(1): 173-187.

Angelsberger M, Kraus S, Mas-Tur A and Roig-Tierno N (2017). International opportunity recognition: An overview. *Journal of Small Business Strategy*. 27(1):19–36.

Arcand J-L, Berkes E and Panizza U (2015). Too much finance? *Journal of Economic Growth*. 20(2):105–148.

Ardagna S and Lusardi A (2010). Explaining international differences in entrepreneurship: The role of individual characteristics and regulatory constraints. In: Lerner J and Schoar A, eds. *International Differences in Entrepreneurship*. National Bureau of Economic Research. University of Chicago Press. Cambridge, United States: 17–62.

Asian Development Bank (2013). Agriculture and structural transformation in developing Asia: Review and outlook. Economics Working Paper Series No. 363. Manila.

Atkin D and Jinhange A (2017). Trading up: The benefits of exporting for small firms. Growth Brief Series No. 11. International Growth Centre. London.

Atkinson J. (1958). *Motives in Fantasy, Action and Society: A Method of Assessment and Study*. Van Nostrand. Oxford.

Audretsch DB (1995). *Innovation and Industry Evolution*. The Massachusetts Institute of Technology Press. Cambridge (MA).

Audretsch DB and Fritsch M (2002). Growth regimes over time and space. *Regional Studies*. 36(2):113–124.

Audretsch DB and Keilbach M (2004). Entrepreneurship capital and economic performance. *Regional Studies*. 38(8): 949–959.

Audretsch DB and Keilbach M (2006). Determinants of small firm survival and growth. In: Casson M, Yeung B, Basu A and Wadeson N, eds. *The Oxford Handbook of Entrepreneurship*. Oxford University Press. Oxford: 281–310.

Audretsch DB and Thurik R (2001). Linking Entrepreneurship to Growth. OECD Science, Technology and Industry Working Papers No. 2001/02. Paris.

Auerswald PE (2015). *Enabling Entrepreneurial Ecosystems*. Ewing Marion Kauffman Foundation. Arlington.

Australian Centre for International Agricultural Research (2015). *Planted Teak: Global Production and Markets, with Reference to Solomon Islands*. Australian Centre for International Agricultural Research Technical Report No. 85. Canberra.

Autio E, Kronlund M and Kovalainene A (2007). *High-growth SME Support Initiatives in Nine Countries: Analysis, Categorization and Recommendations*. Ministry of Trade and Industry of Finland. Helsinki.

Ayyagari M, Demirguc-Kunt A and Maksimovic V (2011). Small vs. young firms across the world: Contribution to employment, job creation and growth. Policy Research Working Paper Series No. 5631. World Bank. Washington.

Azmeh S and Nadvi K (2014). Asian firms and the restructuring of global value chains. *International Business Review*. 23(4): 708–717.

Baden S and Barber C (2005). The impact of the second-hand clothing trade on developing countries. Oxfam. Oxford.

Baldwin R (2009). The great trade collapse: What caused it and what does it mean? In: Baldwin R, ed. *The Great Trade Collapse: Causes, Consequences and Prospects*. Centre for Economic Policy Research. London.

Baliamoune-Lutz M (2009). Entrepreneurship and reforms in developing countries. Research Paper No. 2009/04. UNU-WIDER. Helsinki.

Bamber P, Guinn A and Gereffi G (2014). *Burundi in the Energy Global Value Chain: Skills for Private Sector Development*. Centre on Globalization, Governance and Competitiveness. Duke University. Durham (NC).

Bamber P and Staritz C (2016). The Gender Dimensions of Global Value Chains. International Centre for Trade and Sustainable Development (ICTSD). Geneva.

Banga K and te Velde D (2018). Digitalization and the future of manufacturing in Africa. Supporting Economic Transformation Programme. London.

Bannister H (2017). Gastronomic revolution: Peruvian cuisine's journey from cultural entity to commodity. *Undergraduate Research Journal for the Humanities 2 (Spring 2017)*: 135–151.

Barkema HG and Drogendijk R (2007). Internationalizing in small, incremental or larger steps? *Journal of International Business Studies*. 38(7): 1132–1148.

Basnett Y and Bhattacharya D (2015). Exploring spaces for economic transformation in the Sustainable Development Goals. ODI Report. Overseas Development Institute (ODI). London.

Baumol WJ (1990). Entrepreneurship: Productive, unproductive and destructive. *Journal of Political Economy*. 98(5): 893–921.

Baye FM (2013). Household economic well-being: Response to microCredit access in Cameroon. *African Development Review*. 25(4): 447–467.

BBC.com (2018a). Nigerian entrepreneur: We're farming in a shipping container. 2 February. Available at www.bbc.com/news/av/business-42919553/nigerian-entrepreneur-we-re-farming-in-a-shipping-container.

BBC.com (2018b). How Greece is reversing brain drain: Could venture capitalists offer Greece's young talent a way to return home? 6 April. Available at www.bbc.com/capital/story/20180404-one-answer-to-solving-greeces-brain-drain.

BBC News (2018). How the US [United States] and Rwanda have fallen out over second-hand clothes. Available at www.bbc.com/news/world-africa-44252655. 28 May.

Benedictis LD (2005). Three decades of Italian comparative advantages. *The World Economy*. 28(11): 1679–1709.

Beverelli C, Koopman RB, Kummritz V and Neumueller S (2016). Domestic Foundations of Global Value Chains. World Bank. Washington.

Böhme M and Thiele R (2012). Informal–formal linkages and informal enterprise performance in urban West Africa. Working Paper No. 77933. World Bank. Washington.

Brixiova Z (2010). Unlocking productive entrepreneurship in Africa's least developed countries. *African Development Review*. 22(3): 440–451.

Brixiova Z and Kangoye T (2016). Start-up capital and women's entrepreneurship: Evidence from [Eswatini]. Southern Africa Labour and Development Research Unit Working Paper No. 192. University of Cape Town. Cape Town.

Business for Social Responsibility, C and A Foundation, International Centre for Research on Women and Levi Strauss Foundation (2017). Empowering female workers in the apparel industry: Three areas for business action.

van Burg, E, Podoynitsyna KS, Beck L and Lommelen T (2012). Directive deficiencies: How resource constraints direct opportunity identification in SMEs. *The Journal of Product Innovation Management*. 29(6): 1000–1011.

Burkina Faso (2015). *Stratégie nationale de promotion de l'entrepreneuriat féminin 2016–2025*. Ouagadougou.

Bushell B (2008). Women entrepreneurs in Nepal: What prevents them from leading the sector? *Gender and Development*. 16(3): 549–564.

Cacciotti G and Hayton J (2017). National culture and entrepreneurship. In: Ahmetoglu G, Chamorro-Premuzic T, Klinger B and Karucisky T, eds. *The Wiley Handbook of Entrepreneurship*. John Wiley and Sons. Hoboken: 401–422.

Calderon G, Iacovone L and Juarez L (2016). Opportunity versus necessity: Understanding the heterogeneity of female micro-entrepreneurs. Policy Research Working Paper No. 7636. World Bank. Washington.

Campos F, Frese M, Goldstein M, Iacovone L, Johnson H, McKenzie D and Mensmann M (2017). Personality versus practices in the making of an entrepreneur: Experimental evidence from Togo. Draft paper prepared for the Conference of the Centre for the Study of African Economies held in Oxford, 19 March 2017.

Casson M (2003). *The Entrepreneur: An Economic Theory*. Edward Elgar Publishing. Cheltenham, United Kingdom.

Casson M, Yeung B, Basu A and Wadeson N (2006). Introduction. In: Basu A, Casson M, Wadeson N and Yeung B, eds. *The Oxford Handbook of Entrepreneurship*. Oxford University Press. Oxford: 1–30.

Catarino L, Menezes Y and Sardinha R (2015). Cashew cultivation in Guinea-Bissau: Risks and challenges of the success of a cash crop. *Scientia Agricola*. 72(5): 459–467.

CBI (2016). CBI Product Factsheet: Fresh Lychees in Europe. Survey. CBI Market Intelligence. The Hague.

CDC Group (2016). *Development Impact Evaluation: What are the Links Between Power, Economic Growth and Job Creation?* London.

Centre for Research on Multinational Corporations (SOMO) (2015). Fact sheet: Hidden subcontracting in the garment industry – Zooming in on the role of buying companies.

Centre for the Promotion of Imports from Developing Countries (CBI) (2016). CBI Product Fact Sheet: Fresh Lychees in Europe.

Chant S (2014). Exploring the "feminization of poverty" in relation to women's work and home-based enterprise in slums of the global South. *International Journal of Gender and Entrepreneurship*. 6(3): 296–316.

Chhair S and Ung L (2014). Exporting and foreign direct investment spillovers: Cambodia's experience. Working Paper No. 79. UNU-WIDER. Helsinki.

Chiang MH (2016). *Contemporary [Republic of Korea] Economy: Challenges and Prospects*. World Scientific Publishing. Beijing.

Choksy U, Sinkovics N and Sinkovics RR (2017). Exploring the relationship between upgrading and capturing profits from GVC participation for disadvantaged suppliers in developing countries. *Canadian Journal of Administrative Sciences*. 34(4): 356–386.

Chowdhury F, Terjesen S and Audretsch DB (2015). Varieties of entrepreneurship: Institutional drivers across entrepreneurial activity and country. *European Journal of Law and Economics*. 40(1): 121–148.

Christiaensen L and Demery L, eds. (2017). *Agriculture in Africa: Telling Myths from Facts*. World Bank. Washington.

Clement V, Raveane T and Saturnin D (2016). Finland, education and entrepreneurship. Available at http://www.cc.lu/fileadmin/user_upload/cc.lu/Manifestations/20160513_Finland/Entrepreneurship_Education_in_Finland.pdf.

Cooney TM (2012). Entrepreneurship skills for growth-orientated businesses. Prepared for the Workshop on Skills Development for SMEs and Entrepreneurship. Copenhagen. 28 November.

Cornwall A (2007). Of choice, chance and contingency: "Career strategies" and tactics for survival among Yoruba women traders. *Social Anthropology*. 15(1): 27–46.

Costa P. and McCrae R. (1992). Normal personality assessment in clinical practice: The NEO Personality Inventory. *Psychological Assessment*. 4(1): 5–13.

Cressy R (2006). Determinants of small firm survival and growth. In: Casson M, Yeung B, Basu A and Wadeson N, eds. *The Oxford Handbook of Entrepreneurship*. Oxford University Press. Oxford: 161–193.

Criscuolo C and Timmis J (2017). The relationship between global value chains and productivity. *International Productivity Monitor*. 32: 61–83.

CUTS International (2016). Effective participation of developing countries and LDCs in global value chains: A snapshot. Technical note.

Dai L (2013). The Comparative Advantage of Nations: How Global Supply Chains Change Our Understanding of Comparative Advantage. M-RCBG Associate Working Paper Series No. 15. Harvard College. Cambridge (MA).

Das DJ (2000). Problems faced by women entrepreneurs. In: Sasikumar K, ed. *Women Entrepreneurship*. Vikas Publishing House. New Delhi.

Davis B, Di Giuseppe S and Zezza A (2017). Households in rural Africa still rely on agriculture. In: Christiaensen L and Demery L, eds. *Agriculture in Africa: Telling Myths from Facts*. World Bank. Washington: 65–73.

De Backer K and Flaig D (2017). The future of global value chains: business as usual or "a new normal"? OECD Science, Technology and Industry Policy Paper No. 41. Paris.

De Backer K and Miroudot S (2013). Mapping Global Value Chains. OECD Trade Policy Paper No. 159.

De Janvry A and Sadoulet E (2001). Income strategies among rural households in Mexico: The role of off-farm activities. *World Development*. 29(3): 467–480.

De Vita L, Mari M and Poggesi S (2014). Women entrepreneurs in and from developing countries: Evidences from the literature. *European Management Journal*. 32(3): 451–460.

Delanoë-Gueguen S and Fayolle A (2018). Crossing the entrepreneurial Rubicon: A longitudinal investigation. *Journal of Small Business Management*.

Dercon S (2009). Rural poverty: Old challenges in new contexts. *The World Bank Research Observer*. 24(1): 1–28.

Dercon S and Krishnan P (2000). Vulnerability, seasonality and poverty in Ethiopia. *The Journal of Development Studies*. 36(6): 25–53.

Desai S (2011). Measuring entrepreneurship in developing countries. In: Naudé W, ed. *Entrepreneurship and Economic Development*. Palgrave Macmillan. London: 94–107.

Diao X, Kweka J and McMillan MS (2017). Economic transformation in Africa from the bottom up: Evidence from [the United Republic of] Tanzania. Discussion Paper 01603. International Food Policy Research Institute. Washington.

DiCaprio A and Suvannaphakdy S (2017). Are least developed countries sidelined in advanced manufacturing production networks? Asian Development Bank Institute Working Paper No. 711. Manila.

Dihel N, Goswami AG, Hollweg C, Shahid S and Slany A (2017). How does participation in international value chains matter to applicant farmers? In: *Future Fragmentation Processes: Effectively Engaging with the Ascendancy of Global Value Chains*. Commonwealth Secretariat. London.

Djankov S, La Porta R, Lopez-de-Silanes F and Shleifer A (2002). The regulation of entry. *The Quarterly Journal of Economics*. 117(1): 1–37.

Duflo E (2012). Women empowerment and economic development. *Journal of Economic Literature*. 50(4): 1051–1079.

Economic Commission for Africa (2014). *Economic Report on Africa 2014: Dynamic Industrial Policy in Africa* (United Nations publication. Addis Ababa).

Economic Commission for Latin America and the Caribbean (2010). Barbados: Public–private sector partnership. United Nations publication. LC/W 285. Santiago.

Economic Research Institute for ASEAN and East Asia (2014). ASEAN SME Policy Index 2014:Towards competitive and innovative ASEAN SMEs. Research Project Report 2012, No. 8.

Egusa and O'Shee (2016). A look into Chile's innovative start-up government. Tech Crunch. 16 October.

Escobal J (2001). The determinants of non-farm income diversification in rural Peru. *World Development*. 29(3): 497–508.

Esho H (2015). Dynamics of the textiles and apparel industries in Southeast Asia: A preliminary analysis. *Journal of International Economic Studies*. 29(1): 85–106.

Ethiopia (2016). *Micro and Small Enterprise Development Policy and Strategy*.

Ethical Trading Initiative (2009). *ETI [Ethical Trading Initiative] smallholder guidelines: Recommendations for working with smallholders*. London.

European Commission (2016). Managing the refugee crisis: EU [European Union] support to Jordan.

Export.gov (2016). Afghanistan country commercial guide. Afghanistan: Openness and restriction on foreign investment.

Fafchamps M and Shilpi F (2003). The spatial division of labour in Nepal. *The Journal of Development Studies*. 39(6): 23–66.

IZA World of Labour (2016). Do global value chains create jobs? Bonn. Available at https://wol.iza.org/articles/do-global-value-chains-create-jobs/long.

Fatou C and Choi JE (2015). Do firms learn by exporting or learn to export? Evidence from Senegalese manufacturing plant. Working Paper No. 57. UNU-WIDER. Helsinki.

Fiedler Y and Iafrate M (2016). Trends in foreign direct investment in food, beverages and tobacco. FAO Commodity and Trade Policy Research Working Paper No. 51. Rome.

Financial Times (FT) (2018). China scales back investment in Ethiopia East African economy pressured by rising debt and foreign exchange scarcity. 3 June. Available at: https://www.ft.com/content/06b69c2e-63e9-11e8-90c2-9563a0613e56.

Food, Agriculture and Natural Resources Policy Analysis Network (2012). Youth in Agriculture Award Shambani Graduate Enterprise. Available at http://dialogue2012.fanrpan.org/newsroom/youth_in_agriculture_award_shambani_graduate_enterprise.

FAO (2013a). *Enabling Environments for Agribusiness and Agro-Industries Development: Regional and Country Perspectives*. Agribusiness and Food Industries Series. No. 1. Rome.

FAO (2013b). *Trends and Impacts of Foreign Investment in Developing Country Agriculture: Evidence from Case Studies*. Rome.

FAO and International Bank for Reconstruction and Development/World Bank (2018). *Country Economic Memorandum: Rebuilding Resilient and Sustainable Agriculture in Somalia*. Volume 1.

Forbes (2017). The quiet price of entrepreneurship. 18 October. Available at: www.forbes.com/sites/chriscancialosi/2017/10/18/the-quiet-price-of-entrepreneurship/#4af7a9852cb7.

Freund C and Bolaky B (2008). Trade, regulations and income. *Journal of Development Economics*. 87(2): 309–321.

Fu K and Liu K (2013). Policy implications of intellectual property rights and competition policy on entry into entrepreneurship across countries. *Academy of Management Proceedings*. 2013(1).

Gajigo O (2014). Credit constraints and agricultural risk for non-farm enterprises. *African Development Review*. 25(4): 648–662.

Gans J and Persson L (2013). Entrepreneurial commercialization choices and the interaction between intellectual property rights and competition policy. *Industrial and Corporate Change*. 22(1): 131–151.

García-Cabrera A and García-Soto M (2008). Cultural differences and entrepreneurial behaviour: An intra-country cross-cultural analysis in Cape Verde. *Entrepreneurship and Regional Development*. 20(5): 451–483.

Gebreeyesus M (2017). A natural experiment of industrial policy: Floriculture and the metal and engineering industries in Ethiopia. In: Page J and Tarp F, eds. *The Practice of Industrial Policy: Government–Business Coordination in Africa and East Asia*. Oxford University Press. Oxford: 191–210.

GEM (2015). *GEM Uganda 2012 Executive Report*. Kampala.

GEM (2017). *Global Report 2016/17*. Global Entrepreneurship Research Association. London.

GEM (2018). *Global Report 2017/18*. Global Entrepreneurship Research Association. London.

Gennaioli N, La Porta R López-de-Silanes F and Shleifer A(2013). Human capital and regional development. *The Quarterly Journal of Economics*. 128(1): 105–164.

Gereffi G (1999). A commodity chains framework for analysing global industries. Working paper.

Gereffi G (2014). Global value chains in a post-Washington Consensus world. *Review of International Political Economy*. 21(1): 9–37.

Giacomin O, Janssen F, Guyot J and Lohest O (2011). Opportunity and/or necessity entrepreneurship? The impact of the socio-economic characteristics of entrepreneurs. MPRA Paper No. 29506.

Gibb AA (1987). Enterprise culture:Its meaning for education and training. *Journal of European Industrial Training*. 11(2): 2–38.

Gindling TH and Newhouse D (2012). Self-employment in the developing world. Policy Research Working Paper Series No. 6201. World Bank. Washington.

Global Entrepreneurship Summit (2017). Government of India support for innovation and entrepreneurship in India. Available at https://www.ges2017.org/govt-of-india-support-for-entrepreneurs/.

Gollin D (2008). Nobody's business but my own: Self-employment and small enterprise in economic development. *Journal of Monetary Economics*. 55(2): 219–233.

González F, Prem M and Urzúa F (2018). The privatization origins of political corporations. Available at https://papers.ssrn.com/sol3/papers.cfm?abstract_id=3171595.

Government of Malawi, FAO, ILO and United Nations Children's Fund (2018). Local Economy Impacts and Cost–Benefit Analysis of Social Protection and Agricultural Interventions in Malawi.

Greiner LE (1972). Evolution and revolution as organizations grow. *Harvard Business Review*. July–August.

Gries T and Naudé WA (2011). Entrepreneurship and human development: A capability approach. *Journal of Public Economics*. 95(3): 216–224.

Grimm M, Knorringa P and Lay J (2012). Constrained gazelles: High potentials in West Africa's informal economy. *World Development*. 40(7): 1352–1368.

Gurib-Fakim A (2011). Small island developing States of the Indian Ocean Towards an action plan for medicinal plants. *Asian Biotechnology and Development Review*. 13(3): 1–6.

Gust (2016). Global accelerator report 2016. Available at http://gust.com/accelerator_reports/2016/global/.

Hafer R (2017). Female entrepreneurship and IQ. In: Ahmetoglu G, Chamorro-Premuzic T, Klinger B and Karcisky T, eds. *The Wiley Handbook of Entrepreneurship*. John Wiley and Sons. Hoboken, New Jersey, United States: 187–204.

Hagel J, Seely Brown J, Wooll M and de Maar A (2015). Shorten the value chain: Transforming the stages of value delivery. Deloitte University Press.

Hansen MW, Buur L, Therkildsen O and Kjaer M (2014). The political economy of local content in African extractives: lessons from three African countries. Paper presented at the annual meeting of the meeting of the Danish Political Science Association. 23–24 October. Vejle.

Harrison AE, Lin JY and Xu LC (2014). Explaining Africa's (dis)advantage. *World Development*. 63: 59–77.

Hartmann D, Guevara MR, Jara-Figueroa C, Aristarán M and Hidalgo CA (2017). Linking Economic Complexity, Institutions, and Income Inequality. *World Development*. 93: 75–93.

Hastings JS, Madrian BC and Skimmyhorn WL (2013). Financial literacy, financial education and economic outcomes. *Annual Review of Economics*. 5(1): 347–373.

Hartog C, Parker S, van Stel A and Thurik R (2010). The two-way relationship between entrepreneurship and economic performance. EIM Research Report H200822.

Hausmann R and Rodrik D (2003). Economic development as self-discovery. *Journal of Development Economics*. 72(2): 603–633.

Herrington M and Kelley D (2013). *African Entrepreneurship: Sub-Saharan African Regional Report*. University of Cape Town. Cape Town.

Herzberg B and Wright A (2013). The PPD [public–private dialogue] handbook: A toolkit for business environment reformers. Operational guidelines for the charter of good practice in using public–private dialogue for private sector development. Working paper. Department for International Development (United Kingdom), World Bank, International Finance Corporation and OECD Development Centre.

Hessels J and Naudé W (2017). The intersection of the fields of entrepreneurship and development economics: A review towards a new view. Discussion Paper Series No. 11103. Institute of Labour Economics.

Hitt MA, Ireland RD, Camp M and Sexton DL (2001). Strategic entrepreneurship: Entrepreneurial strategies for wealth creation. *Strategic Management Journal*. 22(6–7): 479–491.

Hoffmann A, Larsen M and Oxholm AS (2006). *Quality Assessment of Entrepreneurship Indicators*. Version 2. National Agency for Enterprise and Construction. Copenhagen.

Hofstede G and Bond M (1988). The Confucius connection: From cultural roots to economic growth. *Organizational Dynamics*. 16(1): 5–21.

Hove S (2016). Unlocking infrastructure potential in Africa: The role of sovereign wealth funds. 1 September. Available at www.howwemadeitinafrica.com/unlocking-infrastructure-potential-africa-role-sovereign-wealth-funds/56256/.

Hughes JR (1966). *The Vital Few: American Economic Progress and Its Protagonists*. 1st ed. Houghton Mifflin. New York.

Human Rights Watch (2017). *World Report 2017*. Seven Stories Press. New York.

Humphrey J and Memedovic O (2006). Global value chains in the agrifood sector. Working Papers. UNIDO. Vienna.

Humphrey J and Schmitz H (2002). How does insertion in global value chains affect upgrading in industrial clusters? *Regional Studies*. 36(9): 1017–1027.

Hussain NM (2000). Linkages between SMEs and large industries for increased markets and trade: An African perspective. Economic Research Paper No. 53. African Development Bank. Abidjan.

ICF International (2016). Volume II: Admission of migrant entrepreneurs. Study for an evaluation and an impact assessment on a proposal for a revision of the Council Directive 2009/50/EC ("EU Blue Card Directive").

International Centre for Trade and Sustainable Development (2016). The gender dimensions of global value chains. Issue paper. Geneva.

International Finance Corporation (2014). Stories of Impact: Agribusiness – Opportunities Abound in South Asia.

Intergovernmental Forum on Mining, Minerals, Metals and Sustainable Development (2018). *Guidance for Governments: Local Content Policies*. International Institute for Sustainable Development. Winnipeg.

International Fund for Agricultural Development (2016). *Rural Development Report 2016: Fostering Inclusive Rural Transformation*. Rome.

International Institute for Environment and Development, HIVOS and Mainumby Ñakurutú (2012). *Small Producer Agency in the Globalized Market: Making Choices in a Changing World*. London.

International Institute for Environment and Development and Sustainable Food Lab (2011). Under what conditions are value chains effective tools for pro-poor development?

International Institute for Sustainable Development (2012). *Business Models for Foreign Investment in Agriculture in Laos*. Geneva.

ILO (2011). *Growth, Productive Employment and Decent Work in the Least Developed Countries: Report of ILO for the Fourth United Nations Conference on the Least Developed Countries, 9–13 May*. Geneva.

ILO (2014). *Wages and Working Hours in the Textiles, Clothing, Leather and Footwear Industries*. International Labour Office. Geneva

ILO (2016a). Gender pay gaps persist in Asia's garment and footwear sector. Asia–Pacific Garment and Footwear Sector Research Note. Issue 4. Geneva.

ILO (2016b). Women's entrepreneurship development: Encouraging women entrepreneurs for jobs and development. Fact sheet. 1 March. Geneva.

ILO (2017a). Food and agriculture global value chains: Drivers and constraints for occupational safety and health improvement – Three case studies. Volume Two. Geneva.

ILO (2017b). Recent trade policy developments and possible implications for Cambodia's garment and footwear sector. Cambodian Garment and Footwear Sector Bulletin.Issue 5. Geneva.

ILO (2017c). What explains strong export and weak employment figures in the Cambodian garment sector? Cambodian Garment and Footwear Sector Bulletin. Issue 6. Geneva.

ILO (2018). Entrepreneurship development interventions for women entrepreneurs: An update on what works. Issue Brief No. 7. January. Geneva.

ILO and World Trade Organization (2011). *Making Globalization Socially Sustainable*. World Trade Organization. Geneva.

International Monetary Fund (2015). *Asia and Pacific: Stabilizing and Outperforming Other Regions*. Regional Economic Outlook. Washington.

International Monetary Fund (2018). Shadow economies around the world: What did we learn over the last 20 years? Working Paper No. 18/17. Washington.

International Organization for Migration (2018). *World Migration Report 2018*. Geneva.

International Organization for Migration and Migration Policy Institute (2012). *Developing a Road Map for Engaging Diasporas in Development a Handbook for Policymakers and Practitioners in Home and Host Countries*. Geneva.

International Telecommunication Union (2008). *ICTs, LDCs and the [Sustainable Development Goals]: Achieving Universal and Affordable Internet in the Least Developed Countries*. Geneva.

International Trade Centre (2013). LDCs and global value chains: Using aid for trade to seize new opportunities. Technical paper. Geneva.

International Trade Centre (2015a). *United Republic of Tanzania Cotton-to-clothing Strategy 2016–2020*. Geneva.

International Trade Centre (2015b). *Ethiopia Textile and Clothing Value Chain Road Map 2016–2020*. Geneva.

International Trade Centre (2017). *SME Competitiveness Outlook 2017: The Region : A Door to Global Trade*. Geneva.

Johnson P (2005). Targeting firm births and economic regeneration in a lagging region. *Small Business Economics*. 24(5): 451–464.

Jung T and Kim J (2017). Policy efforts to foster innovative SMEs in [the Republic of] Korea: Lessons for developing countries. In: Williams CC and Gurtoo A, eds. *Routledge Handbook of Entrepreneurship in Developing Economies*. Routledge. London and New York: 511–528.

Kamuganga DN (2012). Does intra-Africa regional trade cooperation enhance export survival? Prepared for the African Economic Conference. Kigali. 30 October–2 November.

Kanbur SM (1979). Of risk taking and the personal distribution of income. *Journal of Political Economy*. 87(4): 769–797.

Kaplinsky R (2005). *Globalization, Poverty and Inequality: Between a Rock and a Hard Place*. Polity. Cambridge.

Karekezi S, McDade S, Boardman B and Kimani J (2012). Energy, poverty and development. In: International Institute for Applied Systems Analysis. *Global Energy Assessment: Towards a Sustainable Future*. Cambridge University Press. Cambridge:151–190.

Keane J (2017). Emerging tiers of suppliers and implications for upgrading in the high-value agriculture supply chains. In: Keane J and Baimbill-Johnson R, eds. *Future Fragmentation Processes: Effectively Engaging with the Ascendancy of Global Value Chains*. Commonwealth Secretariat. London

Keane J and Baimbill-Johnson R, eds. (2017). *Future Fragmentation Processes: Effectively Engaging with the Ascendancy of Global Value Chains*. Commonwealth Secretariat. London.

Keane J and te Velde DW (2008). The role of textile and clothing industries in growth and development strategies and. Overseas Development Institute. London.

Kerr SP, Kerr W, Özden Ç and Parsons C (2016). Global Talent Flows. *Journal of Economic Perspectives*. 30(4): 83–106.

Kibreab G (2009). Forced labour in Eritrea. *The Journal of Modern African Studies*. 47(1): 41–72.

Kirzner IM (1973). *Competition and Entrepreneurship*. University of Chicago Press. Chicago.

Klein PG (2008). Opportunity discovery, entrepreneurial action and economic organization. *Strategic Entrepreneurship Journal*. 2(3): 175–190.

Kowalski P, González JL, Ragoussis A and Ugarte C (2015). Participation of developing countries in global value chains. OECD Trade Policy Papers. No. 179. Paris.

La Porta R and Shleifer A (2008). The Unofficial Economy and Economic Development. Brookings Papers on Economic Activity. 39(2): 275–352.

La Porta R and Shleifer A (2014). Informality and development. *Journal of Economic Perspectives*. 28(3): 109–126.

Lall S (1996). Paradigms of development: The East Asian debate. *Oxford Development Studies*. 24(2): 111–131.

Lall S and Teubal M (1998). "Market-stimulating" technology policies in developing countries: A framework with examples from East Asia. *World Development*. 26(8): 1369–1385.

Landesmann M (1988). Structural change. In: Kurz HD and Salvadori N, eds. *The Elgar Companion to Classical Economics*. Edward Elgar. Cheltenham: 422–428.

Landesmann M, Hagemann H and Scazzieri R (2003). Introduction. In: Landesmann M, Hagemann H and Scazzieri R, eds. *The Economics of Structural Change*. Edward Elgar. Cheltenham: 11–43.

Lanjouw JO and Lanjouw P (2001). The rural non-farm sector: Issues and evidence from developing countries. *Agricultural Economics*. 26(1): 1–23.

Lee N (2012). Assessing the obstacles faced by actual and potential high-growth firms. Big Innovation Centre.

Leibenstein H (1968). Entrepreneurship and development. *American Economic Review*. Papers and Proceedings of the Eightieth Annual Meeting of the American Economic Association. 58(2): 72–83.

Lemma A and Te Velde DW (2017). State–business relations as drivers of economic performance. In: Page J and Tarp F, eds. *The Practice of Industrial*

Policy: Government–Business Coordination in Africa and East Asia. Oxford University Press. Oxford, United Kingdom: 63–79.

Lewis WA (1954). Economic development with unlimited supplies of labour. The Manchester School. 22(2):139–191.

Liedholm C and Kilby P (1989). The role of non-farm activities in the rural economy. In: Panchamukhi VR and Williamson JG, eds. *The Balance between Industry and Agriculture in Economic Development*. Palgrave Macmillan. London:340–366.

Lucas R (1978). On the size distribution of business firms. *Bell Journal of Economics*. 9(2):508–523.

Lundvall B-Å, ed. (1992). *National Systems of Innovation: Towards a Theory of Innovation and Interactive Learning*. Pinter. London.

Makhaya T (2012). The intersection between competition policy and entrepreneurship. 10 February. Available at https://trudimakhaya.co.za/the-intersection-between-competition-policy-and-entrepreneurship.

Malapit HJL (2012). Are women more likely to be credit constrained? Evidence from low-income urban households in the Philippines. *Feminist Economics*. 18(3):81–108.

Maloney WF (2004). Informality revisited. *World Development*. 32(7):1159–1178.

Margolis DN (2014). By choice and by necessity: Entrepreneurship and self-employment in the developing world. *The European Journal of Development Research*. 26(4):419–436.

Mazzucato M (2013). *The Entrepreneurial State: Debunking Public vs. Private Sector Myths*. Anthem Press. London.

Mazzucato M and Pérez C (2014). Innovation as growth policy: The challenge for Europe. Science Policy Research Unite Working Paper 2014-13..

McMillan M, Rodrik D and Sepúlveda C, eds. (2017). *Structural change, Fundamentals and Growth: A Framework and Case Studies*. International Food Policy Research Institute. Washington, D.C.

McMillan M, Rodrik D and Verduzco-Gallo Í (2014). Globalization, structural change and productivity growth, with an update on Africa. *World Development*. 63:11–32.

Mealy P, Farmer JD and Teytelboym A (2018). A new interpretation of the economic complexity index. Institute for New Economic Thinking Oxford Working Paper No. 2018-04.

Medina L and Schneider F (2018). Shadow Economies Around the World: What Did We Learn Over the Last 20 Years? IMF Working Paper No. 18/17. International Monetary Fund (IMF), Washington (DC).

Meet Oluwayimika Angel Adelaja , Nigeria's first female high tech shipping container farmer & hydroponics expert (2017). naijagists.com. See https://naijagists.com/meet-angel-adelaja-nigerias-first-female-high-tech-shipping-container-farmer-hydroponics-expert/.

Mellor J and Lele UJ (1973). Growth linkages of the new food grain technologies. *Indian Journal of Agricultural Economics*. 18(1):35–55.

Metcalfe JS (2006). Entrepreneurship: An evolutionary perspective. In: Basu A, Casson M, Wadeson N and Yeung B, eds. *The Oxford Handbook of Entrepreneurship*. Oxford University Press. Oxford: 59–90.

Minniti M and Naudé W (2010). What do we know about the patterns and determinants of female entrepreneurship across countries? *The European Journal of Development Research*. 22(3):277–293.

Minot N and Ronchi L (2014). Contract farming: Risks and benefits of partnership between farmers and firms. Viewpoint No. 102736. Note No. 344.

Mkandawire T (2001). Thinking about developmental states in Africa. *Cambridge Journal of Economics*. 25(3):279–314.

Mori N (2014). Women's Entrepreneurship Development in [the United Republic of] Tanzania: Insights and Recommendations. ILO. Geneva.

Moyer-Lee J and Prowse M (2012). How traceability is restructuring Malawi's tobacco industry. Working Paper No. 2012.05. Institute of Development Policy and Management. University of Antwerp.

Mudambi R (2008). Location, control and innovation in knowledge-intensive industries. *Journal of Economic Geography*. 8(5):699–725.

Mugabi E (2014). Women's Entrepreneurship Development in Uganda: Insights and Recommendations. ILO. Geneva.

Mulligan G (2017). $12 [million] initiative launched to boost Gambia entrepreneurship, jobs. Disrupt Africa. 13 February.

Murphy KM, Schleifer A and Vishny RW (1991). The allocation of talent: Implications for growth. *Quarterly Journal of Economics*. 106(2):503–530.

Nagler P and Naudé W (2017). Non-farm enterprises in rural Africa: New empirical evidence. Policy Research Working Paper Series No. 7066. World Bank.

NaijaGists.com (2017). Meet Angel Adelaja, Nigeria's first female high-tech shipping container farmer and hydropics expert. 22 August. Available at https://naijagists.com/meet-angel-adelaja-nigerias-first-female-high-tech-shipping-container-farmer-hydroponics-expert/.

Naudé W (2011). Entrepreneurship and economic development: An introduction. In: Naudé W, ed. *Entrepreneurship and Economic Development*. Studies in Development Economics and Policy. Palgrave Macmillan. Basingstoke: 3–17.

Naudé W (2013). Entrepreneurship and economic development: Theory, evidence and policy. Discussion Paper Series No. 7507. Institute of Labour Economics. Bonn.

Negassa A, Baker D, Mugunieri L, Costagli R, Wanyoike F, Abdulle MH and Omore A (2012). *The Somali Chilled Meat Value Chain: Structure, Operation, Profitability and Opportunities to Improve the Competitiveness of Somalia's Chilled Meat Export Trade*. International Livestock Research Institute. Nairobi.

Neill S, Metcalf LE and York JL (2017). Distinguishing entrepreneurial approaches to opportunity perception. *International Journal of Entrepreneurial Behaviour and Research*. 23(2): 296–316.

Nelson RR, ed. (1993). *National Innovation Systems: A Comparative Analysis*. Oxford University Press. New York.

Neumark D and McLennan M (1995). Sex discrimination and women's labor market outcomes. *The Journal of Human Resources*. 30(4): 713–740.

news24 (2017). Guinea-Bissau reaps reward as world goes nuts for cashews. 24 September.

Nightingale P and Coad A (2014). Muppets and gazelles: Political and methodological biases in entrepreneurship research. *Industrial and Corporate Change*. 23(1): 113–143.

Nissanke M (2017). The changing landscape in commodity markets and trade and implications for development. In: Keane J and Baimbill-Johnson R, eds. *Future Fragmentation Processes: Effectively Engaging with the Ascendancy of Global Value Chains*. Commonwealth Secretariat. London.

Nkurunziza JD (2010). The effect of credit on growth and convergence of firm size in Kenyan manufacturing. *The Journal of International Trade and Economic Development*. 19(3): 465–494.

Nolintha V and Jajri I (2015). The Garment Industry in Laos[the Lao People's Democratic Republic]: Technological capabilities, global production chains and competitiveness. Economic Research Institute for the Association of Southeast Asian Nations and East Asia Working Paper No. DP-2015-13.

Nübler I (2011). Industrial policies and capabilities for catching up: Frameworks and paradigms. Employment Working Paper No. 77. International Labour Office. Geneva.

Ocampo JA (2005). The quest for dynamic efficiency: Structural dynamics and economic growth in developing countries. In: Ocampo J A, ed. *Beyond Reforms: Structural Dynamics and Macroeconomic Vulnerability*. Economic Commission for Latin America and the Caribbean, Stanford University Press and World Bank. Washington: 3–44.

Ocampo JA and Vos R (2008). Structural change and economic growth. In: Ocampo JA and Vos R, eds. *Uneven Economic Development*. Zed Books. London: 33–58.

OECD (2005). Corporate governance of State-owned enterprises: A survey of OECD countries. Paris.

OECD (2013a). *An International Benchmarking Analysis of Public Programmes for High-growth Firms*. Final report. OECD Local Economic and Employment Development Programme and Danish Business Authority. OECD Publishing. Paris.

OECD (2013b). Youth entrepreneurship. Background paper. OECD Centre for Entrepreneurship, SMEs and Local Development. Paris.

OECD (2015a). Participation of developing countries in global value chains: Implications for trade and trade-related policies. Summary paper. Paris.

OECD (2015b). *State-owned Enterprises in the Development Process*. OECD. Paris.

OECD (2017a). *Agricultural Policy Monitoring and Evaluation 2017*. Paris.

OECD (2017b). Unlocking the potential of youth entrepreneurship in developing countries: from subsistence to performance. Paris.

OECD (2017c). GVC participation in the agriculture and food sectors January. Available at http://www.oecd.org/officialdocuments/publicdisplaydocumentpdf/?cote=TAD/TC/CA/WP(2016)1/PART2/FINAL&docLanguage=En.

OECD (2018). Enhancing SME access to diversified financing instruments. Discussion paper. Paris.

OECD and European Union (2017). Policy brief on women's entrepreneurship. Paris and Brussels.

OECD and Eurostat (2005). *Oslo Manual: Guidelines for Collecting and Interpreting Innovation Data*. OECD Publishing. Paris.

OECD and FAO (2017). *OECD–FAO Agricultural Outlook 2017–2026*. OECD Publishing. Paris.

OECD and World Bank Group (2015). Inclusive Global Value Chains: Policy options in trade and complementary areas for GVC Integration by small and medium enterprises and low-income developing countries. Paris and Washington.

Origin Africa (2017). Lesotho: Africa's inspired apparel sourcing hotspot. September.

Osondu CK (2014). Determinants of decision for non-farm entrepreneurship by women farmers in Ikwuano Local Government Area, Abia State. *Agrosearch*. 14(2): 154–167.

Owoo NS and Naudé W (2017). Proximity and firm performance: Evidence from non-farm rural enterprises in Ethiopia and Nigeria. *Regional Studies*. 51(5): 688–700.

Oya C, Schaefer F, Skalidou D, McCosker C and Langer L (2017). Effects of certification schemes for agricultural production on socio-economic outcomes in low- and middle-income countries: A systematic review.

Oyson MJ and Whittaker DH (2010). An opportunity-based approach to international entrepreneurship: pursuing opportunities internationally through prospection. Proceedings of The Eighteenth Annual High Technology Small Firms Conference.

Oyson MJ and Whittaker DH (2015). Entrepreneurial cognition and behaviour in the discovery and creation of international opportunities. *Journal of International Entrepreneurship*. 16(3): 303–336.

Page J and Söderbom M (2015). Is small beautiful? Small enterprise, aid and employment in Africa. *African Development Review*. 27(S1): 44–55.

Page J and Tarp F, eds. (2017). *The Practice of Industrial Policy: Government–Business Coordination in Africa and East Asia*. Oxford University Press. Oxford.

Palich LE and Bagby DR (1995). Using cognitive theory to explain entrepreneurial risk-taking: Challenging conventional wisdom. *Journal of Business Venturing*. 10(6): 425–438.

Phillips N (2017). Power and inequality in the global political economy. *International Affairs*. 93(2): 429–444.

Platania M (2014). Trade advantage of Italian industrial districts: Persistence and change. *Regional and Sectoral Economic Studies*. 14(2): 39-52.

van der Pols D (2015). Business opportunity report Ethiopia textile and apparel industry. Nash International.

Ponte S and Sturgeon T (2017). Explaining governance in global value chains: a modular theory-building effort. *Review of International Political Economy*. 21(1): 195–223.

Porter M (1998). Clusters and the new economics of competition. *Harvard Business Review*. 76(6): 77–90.

Poschke M (2013). Who becomes an entrepreneur? Labour market prospects and occupational choice. *Journal of Economic Dynamics and Control*. 37(3): 693–710.

Price Waterhouse Cooper (2015). State-owned enterprises: Catalysts for public value creation?

Pugliese E, Chiarotti GL, Zaccaria A and Pietronero L (2017). Complex economies have a lateral escape from the poverty trap. *PLOS ONE*. 12(1): e0168540.

Purvis M and Grainger A, eds. (2004). *Exploring Sustainable Development: Geographical Perspectives*. Earthscan. London.

Quatraro F and Vivarelli M (2015). Drivers of entrepreneurship and post-entry performance of newborn firms in developing countries. *The World Bank Research Observer*. 30(2): 277–305.

Qureshi MS and te Velde D (2013). State–business relations, investment climate reform and firm productivity in sub-Saharan Africa. *Journal of International Development*. 25(7): 912–935.

Rakhmatullin R and Todeva E (2016). *Industry Global Value Chains, Connectivity and Regional Smart Specialization in Europe an Overview of Theoretical Approaches and Mapping Methodologies*. European Union. Brussels.

Rannikko H and Autio E (2015). The Impact of High-Growth Entrepreneurship Policy in Finland. Science Business Publishing. London.

Rasoanaivo P (2011). Drugs and phytomedicines in Indian Ocean and Madagascar: Issues in research, policy and public health. *Asian Biotechnology and Development Review*. 13(3): 7–25.

Reardon T (1997). Using evidence of household income diversification to inform study of the rural non-farm labour market in Africa. *World Development*. 25(5): 735–747.

Reardon T, Barrett CB, Berdegué JA and Swinnen JFM (2009). Agrifood industry transformation and small farmers in developing countries. *World Development*. 37(11): 1717–1727.

Reardon T, Berdegué JA, Barrett CB and Stamoulis K (2007). Household income diversification into rural non-farm activities. In: Haggblade S, Hazell PBR and Reardon T, eds. *Transforming the Rural Non-farm Economy: Opportunities and Threats in the Developing World*. Johns Hopkins University Press. Baltimore: 115–140.

Rijkers B and Söderbom M (2013). The effects of risk and shocks on non-farm enterprise development in rural Ethiopia. *World Development*. 45: 119–136.

Rijkers B, Söderbom M and Loening JL (2010). A rural–urban comparison of manufacturing enterprise performance in Ethiopia. *World Development*. 38(9): 1278–1296.

Rodrik D (2008). Industrial policy: don't ask why, ask how. *Middle East Development Journal*. (Demo Issue): 1–29.

Rodrik D (2013). The past, present, and future of economic growth. Working Paper 1. Global Citizen Foundation. Geneva.

Romer P (2018). Doing business. 15 January. Available at https://paulromer.net/doing-business/.

Rosenzweig MR (2005). Consequences of migration for developing countries. UN/POP/MIG/2005/08. 30 June.

Rouse J and Jayawarna D (2006). The financing of disadvantaged entrepreneurs. Are enterprise programmes overcoming the finance gap? *International Journal of Entrepreneurial Behaviour and Research*. 12(6): 388–400.

RTI International (2016). Data for Education Programming in Asia and the Middle East (DEP/AME) Lower Mekong Workforce Skills Gap Analysis and Implications for Regional Economic Growth United States Agency for International Development. Washington.

Rwanda, Ministry of Youth and ICT (2015). Smart Rwanda 2020 Master Plan: Towards a knowledge-based society through smart ICT.

Rwanda, Ministry of Trade and Industry (2017). Made in Rwanda Policy. Available at http://www.minicom.gov.rw/fileadmin/minicom_publications/documents/Made_in_Rwanda_Policy_-_Website_Version.pdf.

Sackey S (2013). The venture capital industry in Ghana and the way forward.22 October. Available at www.myjoyonline.com/opinion/2013/October-22nd/the-venture-capital-industry-in-ghana-and-the-way-forward.php.

Santilli J (2015). The recognition of foods and food-related knowledge and practices as an intangible cultural heritage. *DEMETRA: Food, Nutrition and Health*. 10(3): 585–606.

Schumpeter JA (1934). *The Theory of Economic Development: An Inquiry into Profits, Capital, Credit, Interest and the Business Cycle*. Harvard University Press. Cambridge (MA).

Schumpeter JA (1942). *Capitalism, Socialism and Democracy*. Harper and Brothers. 1st ed. New York.

Sharma R (2017). Sovereign wealth funds investment in sustainable development sectors. Background paper prepared for the High-level Conference on Financing for Development and the Means of Implementation of the 2030 Agenda on Sustainable Development, Doha, 18 and 19 November 2017.

Shaver K and Davis A (2017). The psychology of entrepreneurship: a selective review and a path forward. In: Ahmetoglu G, Chamorro-Premuzic T, Klinger B and Karucisky T, eds. *The Wiley Handbook of Entrepreneurship*. John Wiley and Sons. Hoboken: 97–111.

Shaw V and Darroch J (2004). Barriers to internationalization: A study of entrepreneurial new ventures in New Zealand. *Journal of International Entrepreneurship*. 2(4): 327–343.

Shi X, Heerink N and Qu F (2007). Choices between different off-farm employment subcategories: An empirical analysis for Jiangxi Province, China. *China Economic Review*. 18(4): 438–455.

Siba E (2016). Africa in focus:Enabling female entrepreneurs and beyond. Brookings Institute. Washington.

Siba E and Gebreeyesus M (2014). Learning to export and learning by exporting: The case of Ethiopian manufacturing. Working Paper No. 2014/105. UNU-WIDER. Helsinki.

Singh G and Belwal R (2008). Entrepreneurship and SMEs in Ethiopia: Evaluating the role, prospects and problems faced by women in this emergent sector. *Gender in Management: An International Journal*. 23(2): 120–136.

Soete L (2013). Is innovation always good? In: Fagerberg J, Martin B R and Andersen ES, eds. *Innovation Studies*. Oxford University Press: 134–144. Oxford.

Staritz C and Morris M (2013). Local embeddedness, upgrading and skill development: Global value chains and foreign direct investment in Lesotho's apparel industry. Capturing the Gains Working Paper No. 20.

Staritz C, Morris M and Plank L (2016). Clothing global value chains and sub-Saharan Africa: Global exports, regional dynamics and industrial development outcomes. International Trade Working Paper No. 2016/16.

Steel G (2017). Navigating (im)mobility: Female entrepreneurship and social media in Khartoum. *Africa*. 87(2): 233–252.

Storey DJ (1994). *Understanding the Small Business Sector*. Routledge. London.

Strategyzer (nd). Taobao.com: Reinventing (e-)commerce.

Strategyzer (2017). StratChat: Business model design for 21st century companies. Webinar session. Available at https://blog.strategyzer.com/posts/2017/9/26/replay-business-model-design-for-21st-century-companies.

Struthers J (2017). Commodity price volatility: An evolving principal–agent problem. In: Keane J and Baimbill-Johnson R, eds. *Future Fragmentation Processes: Effectively Engaging with the Ascendancy of Global Value Chains*. Commonwealth Secretariat. London.

Struthers J and Nziku D (2018). Rural entrepreneurship and linkages in the least developed countries. Paper prepared for UNCTAD.

Sturgeon TJ and Kawakami M (2010). Global value chains in the electronics industry: Was the crisis a window of opportunity for developing countries? World Bank Policy Research Working Paper No. 5417. Washington.

Sustainable Organic Agriculture Action Network (2013). Best practice guideline for agriculture and value chains.

Syrquin M (1988). Patterns of structural change. In: Chenery H, and In: Srinivasan T N, eds. *Handbook of Development Economics*. Elsevier. Amsterdam: 203–273.

Szirmai A, Naudé WA and Goedhuys M (2011). Entrepreneurship, innovation and economic development: An overview. In: Szirmai A, Naudé W A and Goedhuys M, eds. *Entrepreneurship, Innovation and Economic Development*. UNU-WIDER Studies in Development Economics. Oxford University Press. Oxford: 3–32.

Taglioni D and Winkler D (2017). *Making Global Value Chains Work for Development*. International Bank for Reconstruction and Development/World Bank. Washington.

Tamvada JP (2010). Entrepreneurship and welfare. *Small Business Economics*. 34(1):65–79.

Taube G and Tadesse H (1996). Presumptive taxation in sub-Saharan Africa: Experiences and prospects. International Monetary Fund Working Paper WP/96/5. Washington.

te Velde D. (2010). Effective state-business relations, industrial policy and economic growth: Improving Institutions for Pro-Poor Growth. ODI publication London.

te Velde DW (2013a). Economic transformation: Where are we heading, post-2015? Available at https://www.odi.org/comment/8084-economic-transformation-where-are-we-heading-post-2015.

te Velde DW (2013b). Introduction and overview. In: te Velde DW, ed. *State–Business Relations and Industrial Policy: Current Policy and Research Debates*. Economic and Social Research Council–Department for International Development Growth Research Programme. London.

Teague B and Gartner W. (2017). Toward a theory of entrepreneurial behaviour. In: Ahmetoglu G, Chamorro-Premuzic T, Klinger B and Karucisky T, eds. *The Wiley Handbook of Entrepreneurship*. John Wiley Sons. Hoboken, New Jersey: 71–94.

*The Conversation (*2018). America's petty policy on used clothes for Africa. 17 April.

The Economist (2012a). Comparative advantage: The boomerang effect. 21 April.

The Economist (2012b). The lure of Chilecon Valley. 13 October.

The Economist (2014a). Cooking up a business cluster. 22 February.

The Economist (2014b). Learning to sell online: Cash cow, Taobao. 24 May.

The Economist (2018a). Why there is a worldwide shortage of vanilla: There's a reason why your favourite ice cream may be costing a bit more. 28 March.

The Economist (2018b). The World Bank's "ease of doing business" report faces tricky questions. 20 January.

The Fung Group (2016). In womenswear, price resistance is increasing. Available at http://www.deborahweinswig.com/wp-content/uploads/2016/10/Fung-and-First-Insight-Womenswear-Report-October-26-2016.pdf.

The New York Times (2007). China grabs West's smoke-spewing factories. 21 December.

The Observatory of Economic Complexity (2016). MIT. See https://atlas.media.mit.edu/en/resources/about/.

Thurik R, Wennekers S and Uhlaner L (2002). Entrepreneurship and economic performance: A macro perspective. *International Journal of Entrepreneurship Education.* 1(2): 157–179.

Timm S (2018). GEM looking into questionable data says director. 30 March. Available at http://ventureburn.com/2018/03/gem-looking-questionable-data-says-director/.

Timmer CP (2007). The structural transformation and the changing role of agriculture in economic development: Empirics and implications. Presented at a Wendt Lecture of the American Enterprise Institute. 30 October. Washington.

Timmer CP (2013). Food security in Asia and the Pacific: The Rapidly changing role of rice. *Asia and the Pacific Policy Studies*. 1(1): 73–90.

Tumbewaze P (2013). Rwanda, Korea Telecom sign 4G LTE deal. *The New Times*. 10 June.

Unfairtobacco (2016). Malawi: Tobacco auction started. Available at www.unfairtobacco.org/en/malawi-tobacco-auction-started/.

United Nations (1987). Report of the World Commission on Environment and Development. Annex. A/42/427. New York. 4 August.

United Nations (2005). *TNCs [Transnational Corporations] and the Removal of Textiles and Clothing Quotas* (United Nations publication. Sales No. E.05.II.D.20. New York and Geneva).

United Nations (2011). Programme of Action for the Least Developed Countries for the Decade 2011–2020. A/CONF.219/3/Rev.1. 23 May.

United Nations (2012). General Assembly resolution 66/288. The future we want. A/RES/66/288. New York. 27 July.

United Nations (2015a). General Assembly resolution 70/1. Transforming our world: The 2030 Agenda for Sustainable Development. New York. 25 September.

United Nations (2015b). General Assembly resolution 69/313. Addis Ababa Action Agenda of the Third International Conference on Financing for Development (Addis Ababa Action Agenda). New York. 17 August.

United Nations (2017a). *Expanding Productive Capacity: Lessons Learned from Graduating Least Developed Countries*. Committee for Development Policy. Policy note. (United Nations publication. Sales No. E.18.II.C.3. New York).

United Nations (2017b). *Financing Sustainable Urban Development in the Least Developed Countries*(United Nations publication. New York).

United Nations (2018). International Trade Statistics (Comtrade) database See https://comtrade.un.org/.

UNCTAD (2000). *Tax Incentives and Foreign Direct Investment: A Global Survey*. ASIT Advisory Studies No. 16 (United Nations publication. Sales No. E.01.II.D.5. New York and Geneva).

UNCTAD (2006a). *The Least Developed Countries Report 2006: Developing Productive Capacities* (United Nations publication. Sales No. E.06.II.D.9. New York and Geneva).

UNCTAD (2006b). *A Case Study of the Salmon Industry in Chile* (United Nations publication. New York and Geneva).

UNCTAD (2007). *The Least Developed Countries Report 2007: Knowledge, Technological Learning and Innovation for Development*(United Nations publication. Sales No. E.07.II.D.8. New York and Geneva).

UNCTAD (2009). *The Least Developed Countries Report 2009: The State and Development Governance* (United Nations publication. Sales No. E.09.II.D.9. New York and Geneva).

UNCTAD (2010). *The Least Developed Countries Report 2010: Towards a New International Development Architecture for LDCs* (United Nations publication. Sales No. E.10.II.D.5. New York and Geneva).

UNCTAD (2011a). *Local Production of Pharmaceuticals and Related Technology Transfer in Developing Countries: A Series of Case Studies by the UNCTAD secretariat* (United Nations publication. Sales No. E.11.II.D.18. New York and Geneva).

UNCTAD (2011b). *Technology Innovation Report 2011: Powering Development with Renewable Energy Technologies* (United Nations publication. Sales No. E.11.II.D.20. New York and Geneva).

UNCTAD (2012a). *Entrepreneurship Policy Framework and Implementation Guidance* (United Nations publication. New York and Geneva).

UNCTAD (2012b). FDI data on agriculture. Presentation delivered at FAO Investment Days, 17–18 December 2012, Rome.

UNCTAD (2012c). Bangladesh: Sector-specific investment strategy and action plan – G20 indicators for measuring and maximizing economic value added and job creation from private investment in specific value chains. Pilot study results.

UNCTAD (2012d). *The Least Developed Countries Report 2012: Harnessing Remittances and Diaspora Knowledge to Build Productive Capacities* (United Nations publication. Sales No. E.12.II.D.18. Geneva and New York).

UNCTAD (2013a). *The Least Developed Countries Report 2013: Growth with Employment for Inclusive and Sustainable Development* (United Nations publication. Sales No. E.13.II.D.1. New York and Geneva).

UNCTAD (2013b). *World Investment Report 2013: Global Value Chains – Investment and Trade for Development* (United Nations publication. Sales No. E.13.II.D.5. New York and Geneva).

UNCTAD (2013c). *Trade and Development Report 2013: Adjusting to the Changing Dynamics of the World Economy* (United Nations publication. Sales No. E.13.II.D.3. New York and Geneva).

UNCTAD (2013d). *Strengthening the Creative Industries for Development in the Republic of Korea*. UNCTAD/DITC/TED/2017/4. Web-only.

UNCTAD (2013e). *Economic Development in Africa Report 2013: Intra-African trade – Unlocking Private Sector Dynamism* (United Nations publication. Sales No. E.13.II.D.2. New York and Geneva.

UNCTAD (2014a). *The Least Developed Countries Report 2014: Growth with Structural Transformation – A Post-2015 Development Agenda* (United Nations publication. Sales No. E.14.II.D.7. New York and Geneva).

UNCTAD (2014b). *Transfer of Technology and Knowledge Sharing for Development: Science, Technology and Innovation Issues for Developing Countries*. UNCTAD Current Studies on Science, Technology and Innovation No. 8 (United Nations publication. New York and Geneva).

UNCTAD (2014c). *Empowering Women Entrepreneurs Through Information and Communications Technologies: A Practical Guide* (United Nations publication. New York and Geneva).

UNCTAD (2014d). *Trade and Development Report 2014: Global Governance and Policy Space for Development* (United Nations publication. Sales No. E.14.II.D.4. New York and Geneva).

UNCTAD (2014e). *Economic Development of Africa Report 2014: Catalysing Investment for Transformative Growth in Africa* (United Nations publication. Sales No. E.14.II.D.2. New York and Geneva).

UNCTAD (2014f). How to formalize the informal sector: Make formalization easy and desirable. Unpublished paper. Available at https://businessfacilitation.org/assets/documents/pdf/formalizing-the-informal-sector.pdf.

UNCTAD (2014g), *Looking at Trade through a Gender Lens: Summary of Seven Country Case Studies Conducted by UNCTAD* (United Nations publication. Geneva).

UNCTAD (2015a). *The Least Developed Countries Report 2015: Transforming Rural Economies*

(United Nations publication. Sales No. E.15.II.D.7. New York and Geneva).

UNCTAD (2015b). *Key Statistics and Trends in Trade Policy 2015: Preferential Trade Agreements*. (United Nations publication. New York and Geneva).

UNCTAD (2015c). Why geographical indications for least developed countries?

UNCTAD (2015d). *Information Economy Report 2015: Unlocking the Potential of E-commerce for Developing Countries* (United Nations publication. New York and Geneva).

UNCTAD (2015e). *Technology and Innovation Report 2015: Fostering Innovation Policies for Industrial Development* (United Nations publication. Sales No. E.15.II.D.3. New York and Geneva).

UNCTAD (2016a). *The Least Developed Countries Report 2016: The Path to Graduation and Beyond – Making the Most of the Process* (United Nations publication. Sales No. E.16.II.D.9. New York and Geneva).

UNCTAD (2016b). *Trade and Development Report, 2016: Structural Transformation for Inclusive and Sustained Growth*. (United Nations publication. Sales No. E.16.II.D.5. New York and Geneva).

UNCTAD (2017a). *The Least Developed Countries Report 2017: Transformational Energy Access* (United Nations publication. Sales No. E.17.II.D.6. New York and Geneva).

UNCTAD (2017b). *Trade and Development Report 2017: Beyond Austerity – Towards A Global New Deal* (United Nations publication. Sales No. E.17.II.D.5. New York and Geneva).

UNCTAD (2017c). *Key Statistics and Trends in Trade Policy 2016: G20 Policies and Export Performance of the Least Developed Countries* (United Nations publication. Geneva).

UNCTAD (2017d). *Economic Development in Africa Report 2017: Tourism for Transformative and Inclusive Growth* (United Nations publication. Sales No. E.17.II.D.2. New York and Geneva).

UNCTAD (2017e). *Information Economy Report 2017: Digitalization, Trade and Development* (United Nations publication. Sales No. E.17.II.D.8. New York and Geneva).

UNCTAD (2017f). *The Gambia: Formulating the National Entrepreneurship Policy* (United Nations publication. New York and Geneva).

UNCTAD (2017g). *Science, Technology and Policy Review: Rwanda* (United Nations publication. Geneva).

UNCTAD (2017h). *Rising Product Digitalization and Losing Trade Competitiveness* (United Nations publication. New York and Geneva).

UNCTAD (2017i). *Fishery Exports and the Economic Development of Least Developed Countries:* *Bangladesh, Cambodia, the Comoros, Mozambique, Myanmar and Uganda* (United Nations publication. New York and Geneva).

UNCTAD (2018a). *Achieving the Sustainable Development Goals in the Least Developed Countries: A Compendium of Policy Options* (United Nations publication. New York and Geneva).

UNCTAD (2018b). *World Investment Report 2018: Investment and New Industrial Policies* (United Nations publication. Sales No. E.18.II.D.4. New York and Geneva)

UNCTAD (2018c). *East African Community Regional Integration: Trade and Gender Implications*. Geneva.

UNCTAD (2018d). *Selected Sustainable Development Trends in the Least Developed Countries 2018*. UNCTAD/ALDC/2018/1. Geneva.

UNCTAD (2018e). *Economic Development in Africa Report 2018: Migration for Structural Transformation* (United Nations publication. Sales No. E.18.II.D.2. New York and Geneva).

UNCTAD (2018f). *The Technology and Innovation Report 2018: Harnessing Frontier Technologies for Sustainable Development* (United Nations publication. Sales No. E.18.II.D.3. New York and Geneva).

UNCTAD and UNIDO (2011). *Economic Development in Africa Report 2011: Fostering Industrial Development in Africa in the New Global Environment* (United Nations publication. Sales No. E.11.II.D.14. New York and Geneva).

United Nations Department of Economic and Social Affairs (2006). *World Economic and Social Survey 2006: Diverging Growth and Development*. New York.

United Nations Department of Economic and Social Affairs (2017). Frontier issues: The impact of the technological revolution on labour markets and income distribution. New York.

UNIDO (2013a). *Industrial Development Report 2013: Sustaining Employment Growth: The Role of Manufacturing and Structural Change*. Sales No. E.13.II.B.46. Vienna.

UNIDO (2013b). *The UNIDO Approach to Cluster Development. Key Principles and Project Experiences for Inclusive Growth*. Vienna.

United Nations Research Institute for Social Development (2016). *Policy Innovations for Transformative Change: Implementing the 2030 Agenda for Sustainable Development*. Geneva.

UNU-WIDER, University of Copenhagen and Myanmar Central Statistical Organization (2018). *Descriptive Report: Myanmar Micro, Small and Medium Enterprise Survey 2017*. UNU-WIDER. Helsinki.

World Tourism Organization, International Trade Centre and Enhanced Integrated Framework (2017).

Tourism for Sustainable Development in Least Developed Countries: Leveraging Resources for Sustainable Tourism with the Enhanced Integrated Framework. International Trade Centre. Geneva.

United States Agency for International Development and East Africa Trade Investment Hub (2017). Overview of the used clothing market in East Africa: Analysis of determinants and implications.

Valensisi G and Gauci A (2013). Graduated without passing? The employment dimension and LDCs' prospects under the Istanbul Programme of Action. Available at https://mpra.ub.uni-muenchen.de/86966/.

Valensisi G, Belaid F and Ozsoy T (2018). Firm characteristics and performance in the world's poorest countries. Paper prepared for UNCTAD.

Van der Sluis J, Van Praag M and Vijverberg W (2005). Entrepreneurship selection and performance: A meta-analysis of the impact of education in developing economies. *The World Bank Economic Review*. 19(2): 225–261.

van der Zwan P, Thurik R, Verheul I and Hessels J (2016). Factors influencing the entrepreneurial engagement of opportunity and necessity entrepreneurs. *Eurasian Business Review* 6(3): 273–295.

te Velde DW (2013). Economic transformation: Where are we heading, post-2015? December (accessed 23 January 2014).

Verbeke A, Zargarzadeh MA and Osiyevskyy O (2014). Internalization theory, entrepreneurship and international new ventures. *Multinational Business Review*. 22(3): 246–269.

Verheul I, Wennekers S, Audretsch D and Thurik R (2001). An eclectic theory of entrepreneurship. Tinbergen Institute Discussion Paper.

Vivarelli M (2016). The middle-income trap: A way out based on technological and structural change. *Economic Change and Restructuring*. 49(2–3): 159–193.

de Vries GJ, Timmer MP and de Vries K (2015). Structural transformation in Africa: Static gains, dynamic losses. *Journal of Development Studies*. 51(6): 674–688.

Wagner J (2013). Exports, imports and firm survival: First evidence for manufacturing enterprises in Germany. *Review of World Economics*. 149(1): 113–130.

Wang H and Brown S (2013). The potential of agricultural global value chains for select sub-Saharan African countries: a focus on regulation and trade with Asia. CUTS International. Geneva, Switzerland.

Waste and Resources Action Programme (WRAP) (2016). Textiles Market Situation Report.

Waswa Balunywa et al. (2015). GEM Uganda 2012 Executive Report. Global Entrepreneurship Monitor - GEM. Kampala.

West and Karsten (2015). Start-up Chile: A "start-up for start-ups" in Chilecon Valley. Brookings. 19 August.

Wennekers S, van Stel A, Carree M and Thurik R (2010). The relationship between entrepreneurship and economic development: Is it U-shaped? *Foundations and Trends in Entrepreneurship*. 6(3): 167–237.

Wennekers S and Thurik R (1999). Linking entrepreneurship and economic growth. *Small Business Economics*. 13(1): 27–56.

Wiegratz J (2016). *Neoliberal Moral Economy: Capitalism, Sociocultural Change and Fraud in Uganda*. Rowman and Littlefield. London and New York.

Wiggins S (2016). Agricultural and rural development reconsidered: A guide to issues and debates. Research Series Issue 1. International Fund for Agricultural Development. Rome.

Williams CC and Gurtoo A (2017). Informal entrepreneurship in developing countries: An introductory overview. In: Williams CC and Gurtoo A, eds. *Routledge Handbook of Entrepreneurship in Developing Economies*. Routledge. London: 329–342.

Williams CC, Martinez-Perez A and Kedir AM (2017). Informal entrepreneurship in developing economies: The impacts of starting up unregistered on firm performance. *Entrepreneurship Theory and Practice*. 41(5): 773–799.

Witt P (2004). Entrepreneurs' networks and the success of start-ups. *Entrepreneurship and Regional Development*. 16(5): 391–412.

Women in Informal Employment: Globalizing and Organizing (2013). Informal workers in global horticulture and commodities value chains: A review of literature. Working Paper No. 28.

Wong PK, Ho YP and Autio E (2005). Entrepreneurship, innovation and economic growth: Evidence from GEM data. *Small Business Economics*. 24(3): 335–350.

World Bank (2011). Incentives, exports and international competitiveness in sub-Saharan Africa: Lessons from the apparel industry. No. 70181. Washington.

World Bank (2012). *World Development Report 2013: Jobs*. Washington.

World Bank (2016a). From evidence to policy: Supporting Nepal's trade integration strategy. Policy Note No. 2.

World Bank (2016b). *World Development Report 2016: Digital Dividends*. World Bank.

World Bank (2017). *State of Electricity Access Report*. Washington.

World Bank (2018). *Women, Business and the Law*. Washington.

World Bank Group, Institute of Developing Economies, OECD, Research Centre of Global Value Chains and World Trade Organization (2017). *Global Value Chain Development Report 2017: Measuring and Analysing the Impact of GVCs on Economic Development*. International Bank for Reconstruction and Development/World Bank. Washington.

World Economic Forum (2014). The bold ones: High-impact entrepreneurs who transform industries. Insight Report. Geneva.

World Economic Forum (2016). Competitive cities and their connections to global value chains. White Paper. World Economic Forum Global Agenda Council on Competitiveness. Geneva.

World Economic Forum, World Bank and African Development Bank (2009). *The Africa Competitiveness Report 2009*. World Economic Forum. Geneva.

World Tourism Organization, International Trade Centre and Enhanced Integrated Framework (2017). *Tourism for Sustainable Development in Least Developed Countries: Leveraging Resources for Sustainable Tourism with the Enhanced Integrated Framework*. International Trade Centre. Geneva.

World Trade Organization (2013). Connecting least-developed countries to value chains. www.aid4trade.org.